TExES Core Subjects
211 4-8

Teacher Certification Exam

Sharon Wynne, M.S.

XAMonline, INC.
Boston

XAMonline, Inc.
21 Orient Avenue
Melrose, MA 02176
Toll Free 1-800-301-4647
Email: info@xamonline.com
Web: www.xamonline.com
Fax: 1-617-583-5552

Library of Congress Cataloging-in-Publication Data
Wynne, Sharon A.

TExES Core Subjects 4-8 211 Teacher Certification / Sharon A. Wynne.
   ISBN: 978-1-60787-620-5

1. TExES Core Subjects 4-8   2. Study Guides.   3. TExES
4. Teachers' Certification & Licensure. 5. Careers

Disclaimer:
The opinions expressed in this publication are the sole works of XAMonline and were created independently from the National Education Association (NES), Educational Testing Service (ETS), or any State Department of Education, National Evaluation Systems or other testing affiliates. Between the time of publication and printing, state specific standards as well as testing formats and website information may change that are not included in part or in whole within this product. XAMonline develops sample test questions, and they reflect similar content as on real tests; however, they are not former tests. XAMonline assembles content that aligns with state standards but makes no claims nor guarantees teacher candidates a passing score. Numerical scores are determined by testing companies such as NES or ETS and then are compared with individual state standards. A passing score varies from state to state.

Printed in the United States of America   œ-1
TExES Core Subjects 4-8 211
ISBN: 978-1-60787-620-5

TABLE OF CONTENTS

About XAMonline

Founded in 1996, XAMonline began with a teacher-in-training who was frustrated by the lack of materials available for certification exam preparation. XAMonline has grown from publishing one state-specific guide to offering guides for every state exam in the U.S., as well as the PRAXIS series.

Each study guide offers more than just the competencies and skills required to pass a certification exam. The core text material leads the teacher beyond rote memorization of skills to mastery of the subject matter, a necessary step for effective teaching.

XAMonline's unique publishing model brings currency and innovation to teacher preparation:

- Print-on-demand technology allows for the most up-to-date guides that are first to market when tests change or are updated.
- The highest quality standards are maintained by using seasoned, professional teachers who are experts in their fields to author the guides.
- Each guide includes varied levels of rigor in a comprehensive practice test so that the study experience closely matches the actual in-test experience.
- The content of the guides is relevant and engaging.

At its inception, XAMonline was a forward-thinking company, and we remain committed to bringing new ways of studying and learning to the teaching profession. We choose from a pool of over 1500 certified teachers to review, edit, and write our guides. We partner with technology firms to bring innovation to study habits, offering online test functionality, a personalized flashcard builder, and eBooks that allow teachers-in-training to make personal notes, highlight, and study the material in a variety of ways.

To date, XAMonline has helped nearly 500,000 teachers pass their certification or licensing exams. Our commitment to preparation exceeds the expectation of simply providing the proper material for study; it extends from helping teachers gain mastery of the subject matter and giving them the tools to become the most effective classroom leaders possible to ushering today's students toward a successful future.

What's on the Test?

The TExES Core Subjects 4-8 (211) exam consists of 200 multiple-choice questions. The breakdown of the questions is as follows:

Category	Question Type	Approximate % of the test	Approximate # of Questions
English Language Arts and Reading	Multiple choice	37%	74
Mathematics	Multiple choice	21%	42
Social Studies	Multiple choice	21%	42
Science	Multiple choice	21%	42

Question Types

You're probably thinking, enough already, I want to study! Indulge us a little longer while we explain that there is actually more than one type of multiple-choice question. You can thank us later after you realize how well prepared you are for your exam.

1. **Complete the Statement.** The name says it all. In this question type you'll be asked to choose the correct completion of a given statement. For example: The Dolch Basic Sight Words consist of a relatively short list of words that children should be able to:

   a. Sound out
   b. Know the meaning of
   c. Recognize on sight
   d. Use in a sentence

   The correct answer is C. In order to check your answer, test out the statement by adding the choices to the end of it.

2. **Which of the Following.** One way to test your answer choice for this type of question is to replace the phrase "which of the following" with your selection. Use this example: Which of the following words is one of the twelve most frequently used in children's reading texts:

   a. There
   b. This
   c. The
   d. An

Don't look! Test your answer. _____ is one of the twelve most frequently used in children's reading texts. Did you guess C? Then you guessed correctly.

3. **Roman Numeral Choices.** This question type is used when there is more than one possible correct answer. For example: Which of the following two arguments accurately supports the use of cooperative learning as an effective method of instruction?

 I. Cooperative learning groups facilitate healthy competition between individuals in the group.

 II. Cooperative learning groups allow academic achievers to carry or cover for academic underachievers.

 III. Cooperative learning groups make each student in the group accountable for the success of the group.

 IV. Cooperative learning groups make it possible for students to reward other group members for achieving.

  A. I and II
  B. II and III
  C. I and III
  D. III and IV

Notice that the question states there are **two** possible answers. It's best to read all the possibilities first before looking at the answer choices. In this case, the correct answer is D.

4. **Negative Questions.** This type of question contains words such as "not," "least," and "except." Each correct answer will be the statement that does **not** fit the situation described in the question. Such as: Multicultural education is **not**

  a. An idea or concept
  b. A "tack-on" to the school curriculum
  c. An educational reform movement
  d. A process

Think to yourself that the statement could be anything but the correct answer. This question form is more open to interpretation than other types, so read carefully and don't forget that you're answering a negative statement.

5. **Questions That Include Graphs, Tables, or Reading Passages.** As ever, read the question carefully. It likely asks for a very specific answer and not broad interpretation of the visual. Here is a simple (though not statistically accurate) example of a graph question: In the following graph in how many years did more men take the NYSTCE exam than women?

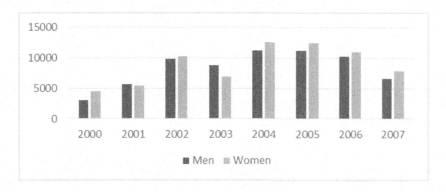

    a. None
    b. One
    c. Two
    d. Three

It may help you to simply circle the two years that answer the question. Make sure you've read the question thoroughly and once you've made your determination, double check your work. The correct answer is C.

Sample Test: Language Arts

1. **If a student has a poor vocabulary the teacher should recommend that**
   (Rigorous) (Skill 1.10)

   A. The student read newspapers, magazines and books on a regular basis.

   B. The student enroll in a Latin class.

   C. The student writes the words repetitively after looking them up in the dictionary.

   D. The student use a thesaurus to locate synonyms and incorporate them into his/her vocabulary.

2. **The arrangement and relationship of words in sentences or sentence structure best describes**
   (Average) (Skill 1.1, 3.13, 7.10)

   A. Style.

   B. Discourse.

   C. Thesis.

   D. Syntax.

3. **Which of the following is a formal reading level assessment?**
   (Easy) (Skill 2.8)

   A. A standardized reading test

   B. A teacher-made reading test

   C. An interview

   D. A reading diary.

4. **The literary device of personification is used in which example below?**
   (Average) (Skill 4.2)

   A. "Beg me no beggary by soul or parents, whining dog!"

   B. "Happiness sped through the halls cajoling as it went."

   C. "O wind thy horn, thou proud fellow."

   D. "And that one talent which is death to hide."

5. **Several students in Mr. Hossfeld's class have not met their grade level expectations in the past. Which teaching method would be most effective for interesting underachievers in his Language Arts class?**
(Rigorous) (Skill 4.11)

A. Assign use of glossary work and extensively footnoted excerpts of great works.

B. Have students take turns reading aloud the anthology selection.

C. Let students choose which readings they'll study and write about.

D. Use a chronologically arranged, traditional text, but assigning group work, panel presentations, and portfolio management.

6. **Which definition below is the best for defining diction?**
(Rigorous) (Skill 5.1)

A. The specific word choices of an author to create a particular mood or feeling in the reader.

B. Writing which explains something thoroughly.

C. The background, or exposition, for a short story or drama.

D. Word choices which help teach a truth or moral.

7. **Which is not a true statement concerning an author's literary tone?**
(Rigorous) (Skill 4.13)

A. Tone is partly revealed through the selection of details.

B. Tone is the expression of the author's attitude toward his/her subject.

C. Tone in literature is usually satiric or angry.

D. Tone in literature corresponds to the tone of voice a speaker uses.

8. **What were two major characteristics of the first American literature?**
(Rigorous) (Skill 5.4 and 5.12)

A. Vengefulness and arrogance

B. Bellicosity and derision

C. Oral delivery and reverence for the land

D. Maudlin and self-pitying geocentricism

9. **Which of the following is a subject of a tall tale?**
(Rigorous) (Skill 5.9)

    A. John Henry.

    B. Paul Bunyan.

    C. George Washington.

    D. Rip Van Winkle.

10. **Which term best describes the form of the following poetic excerpts?**
(Rigorous) (Skill 5.9 and 7.3)

    **And more to lulle him in his slumber soft,
A trickling streame from high rock tumbling downe,
And ever-drizzling raine upon the loft.
Mixt with a murmuring winde, much like a swowne
No other noyse, nor peoples troubles cryes.
As still we wont t'annoy the walle'd towne,
Might there be heard: but careless Quiet lyes,
Wrapt in eternall silence farre from enemyes.**

    A. Ballad

    B. Elegy

    C. Spenserian stanza

    D. Octava rima

11. **Which sonnet form describes the following?**
(Rigorous) (Skill 5.9)

    *My galley, chargèd with forgetfulness,
Thorough sharp seas in winter nights doth pass
'Tween rock and rock; and eke mine en'my, alas,
That is my lord, steereth with cruelness;
And every owre a thought in readiness,
As though that death were light in such a case.
An endless wind doth tear the sail apace
Of forced sighs and trusty fearfulness.
A rain of tears, a cloud of dark disdain,
Hath done the weared cords great hinderance;
Wreathèd with error and eke with ignorance.
The stars be hid that led me to this pain;
Drownèd is Reason that should me comfort,
And I remain despairing of the port.*

    A. Petrarchan or Italian sonnet

    B. Shakespearean or Elizabethan sonnet

    C. Romantic sonnet

    D. Spenserian sonnet

12. **An example of figurative language in which someone or something inhuman is addressed as though present and able to respond describes:**
(Average) (Skill 5.11)

   A. Personification.

   B. Synecdoche.

   C. Metonymy.

   D. Apostrophe.

13. **The quality in a work of literature which evokes feelings of pity or compassion is called**
(Easy) (Skill 5.12)

   A. Colloquy.

   B. Irony.

   C. Pathos.

   D. Paradox.

14. **An extended metaphor which compares two very dissimilar things - one lofty, one lowly, is a definition of a/an**
(Average) (Skill 5.15)

   A. Antithesis.

   B. Aphorism.

   C. Apostrophe.

   D. Conceit.

15. **Which of the following is a complex sentence?**
(Easy) (Skill 6.2)

   A. Anna and Margaret read a total of fifty-four books during summer vacation.

   B. The youngest boy on the team had the best earned run average, which mystifies the coaching staff.

   C. Earl decided to attend Princeton; his twin brother Roy, who aced the ASVAB test, will be going to Annapolis.

   D. "Easy come, easy go," Marcia moaned.

16. **Middle and high school students are more receptive to studying grammar and syntax**
(Rigorous) (Skill 6.2 and 6.6)

   A. Through worksheets and end -of-lesson practices in textbooks.

   B. Through independent, homework assignments.

   C. Through analytical examination of the writings of famous authors.

   D. Though application to their own writing.

17. **A punctuation mark indicating omission, interrupted thought, or an incomplete statement is a/an** *(Rigorous) (Skill 6.2 and 6.6)*

    A. Ellipsis.

    B. Anachronism

    C. Colloquy.

    D. Idiom.

18. **Which of the following contains an error in possessive inflection?** *(Easy) (Skill 6.5 and 6.6)*

    A. Doris's shawl

    B. Mother's-in-law frown

    C. Children's lunches

    D. Ambassador's briefcase

19. **Analyze and correct the information. Wally groaned, "Why do I have to do an oral interpretation of "The Raven."** *(Average) (Skill 6.6)*

    A. Groaned, "Why...of 'The Raven' ?"

    B. Groaned "Why... of "The Raven" ?

    C. Groaned ", Why...of "The Raven?"

    D. Groaned, "Why...of "The Raven."

20. **Analyze and correct the information. Mr. Smith respectfully submitted his resignation and had a new job.** *(Average) (Skill 6.6)*

    A. Respectively submitted his resignation and has

    B. Respectively submitted his resignation before accepting

    C. Respectfully submitted his resignation because of

    D. Respectfully submitted his resignation and has

21. **Analyze and correct the information. There were fewer peices of evidence presented during the second trial.** *(Average) (Skill 6.6)*

    A. Fewer peaces

    B. Less peaces

    C. Less pieces

    D. Fewer pieces

22. **Analyze and correct the information. The teacher <u>implied</u> from our angry words that there was conflict <u>between</u> <u>you and me</u>. (Easy) (Skill 6.6)**

    A. Implied...between you and I

    B. Inferred...between you and I

    C. Inferred...between you and   me

    D. Implied ... between you and me

23. **Which of the following is not one of the four forms of discourse? (Average) (Skill 6.6)**

    A. Exposition

    B. Description

    C. Rhetoric

    D. Persuasion

24. **"Clean as a whistle" or "As Easy as falling off a log" are examples of (Average) (Skill 7.1)**

    A. Semantics

    B. Parody

    C. Irony

    D. Clichés

25. **In the passage below, the dead body of Caesar is addressed as though he were still a living being. What is the figure of speech present in line one below? (Average) (Skill 7.1)**

    "O, pardon me, thou bleeding piece of earth
    That I am meek and gentle with these butchers."
    Marc Antony from Julius *Caesar*

    A. Apostrophe

    B. Allusion

    C. Antithesis

    D. Anachronism

26. **A sixth-grade science teacher has given her class a paper to read on the relationship between food and weight gain. The writing contains signal words such as "because," "consequently," "this is how," and "due to." This paper has which text structure? (Rigorous) (Skill 7.1)**

    A. Cause & effect

    B. Compare & contrast

    C. Description

    D. Sequencing

27. **Mr. Robinson's students are assigned to write one of the following:**
(Average) (Skill 7.1)

- a recipe
- directions for how to play a game
- an interview with a college graduate
- a movie review

By completing this assignment, his students are engaging in which type of writing?

A. Exposition

B. Narration.

C. Persuasion.

D. Description.

28. **The following passage is written from which point of view?**
(Rigorous) (Skill 7.3)

As she mused the pitiful vision of her mother's life laid its spell on the very quick of her being - that life of commonplace sacrifices closing in final craziness. She trembled as she heard again her mother's voice saying constantly with foolish insistence: Derevaun Seraun! Derevaun Seraun!*
* "The end of pleasure is pain!"
(Gaelic)

A. First person, narrator

B. Second person, direct address

C. Third person, omniscient

D. First person, omniscient

29. **Which of the following should not be included in the opening paragraph of an informative essay?**
(Average) (Skill 7.8)

A. Thesis sentence

B. Details and examples supporting the main idea

C. A broad general introduction to the topic

D. A style and tone that grab the reader's attention

30. **Mr. Michaela's students are writing essays using the writing process. Which of the following is not a technique they will use to prewrite?** *(Average) (Skill 7.8)*

A. Clustering

B. Listing

C. Brainstorming

D. Proofreading

31. Which of the following is not an approach to keep students ever conscious of the need to write for audience appeal? *(Rigorous) (Skill 7.3)*

    A. Pairing students during the writing process

    B. Reading all rough drafts before the students write the final copies

    C. Having students compose stories or articles for publication in school literary magazines or newspapers

    D. Writing letters to friends or relatives

32. What does the word "meandered" mean in the sentence below? *(Easy) (Skill 3.13)*

    Michael was taking a long time to return to his seat after sharpening his pencil at the back of the room. After leaving the sharpener, he <u>meandered</u> around the room before eventually making his way back to his own seat.

    A. rolled

    B. roamed

    C. slithered

    D. stomped

33. When reading the book *Stormbreaker* by Anthony Horowitz, the reader feels like they are a part of the action. The author uses so many details to bring the reader into the setting of the story, and this puts the reader right beside Alex Rider, the main character in the story.

    Is this a valid or invalid argument? *(Average) (Skill 5.1)*

    A. Valid

    B. Invalid

34. Let's go see the movie *Alice in Wonderland*. It's a great movie and Johnny Depp is awesome!

    Is this a valid or invalid argument? *(Average) (Skill 5.1)*

    A. Valid

    B. Invalid

35. **DIRECTIONS: Read the following passage and answer the questions that follow.**

Mr. Smith gave instructions for the painting to be hung on the wall. And then it leaped forth before his eyes: the little cottages on the river, the white clouds floating over the valley, and the green of the towering mountain ranges that were seen in the distance. The painting was so vivid that it seemed almost real. Mr. Smith was now absolutely certain that the painting had been worth the money.

Is this passage biased? *(Rigorous) (Skill 4.1)*

A. Yes

B. No

36. **From the last sentence, one can infer that: *(Rigorous) (Skill 4.5)***

A. The painting was expensive.

B. The painting was cheap.

C. Mr. Smith was considering purchasing the painting.

D. Mr. Smith thought the painting was too expensive and decided not to purchase it.

37. **Boys are smarter than girls. Is this sentence fact or opinion? *(Easy) (Skill 11.3)***

A. Fact

B. Opinion

38. **Turkey burgers are better than beef burgers. Is this sentence fact or opinion? *(Easy) (Skill 4.13)***

A. Fact

B. Opinion

39. **What conclusion can be drawn from the passage below? *(Rigorous) (Skill 4.13)***

When she walked into the room she gasped in disbelief as her hands rose to her face and her eyes bulged large. After she picked her jaw up off the floor, a huge smile spread across her face as her best friend came up and wrapped her arms around her and wished her a happy birthday.

A. The girl didn't know anyone in the room

B. The girl saw something shocking

C. The girl was being thrown a surprise party

D. The girl got punched in the face

DIRECTIONS: Read the following passage and answer the questions that follow.

Deciding which animal to get as the family pet can be a very difficult decision, and there are many things to take into consideration. First, you must consider the size of your home and the area that will be dedicated to the pet. If your home is a smaller one, then you probably want to get a small dog or even a cat. If you are lucky enough to have larger home with plenty of room inside and out, then most certainly consider a large or even a more active breed of dog. One other thing to consider is how often and how long you are outside of the home. Cats do not need to be let out to relieve themselves. They are normally trained to use a litter box. On the other hand, dogs require being let out. Dogs also require more exercise than cats and often need to be walked. This can be aggravating to an owner especially on rainy days. Therefore, when deciding which pet is best for your family, it is necessary to consider more than whether or not you want a dog or a cat, but which animal will best fit into your family's lifestyle.

40. **How does the author feel about dogs?**
(Rigorous) (Skill 4.13)

A. The author likes dogs and cats the same

B. The author thinks that dogs are aggravating

C. The author believes they require more care than cats

D. The author feels that dogs are more active than cats

41. **What does the word "interject" mean in the sentence below?**
(Easy) (Skill 3.7)

Nancy was speaking with her best friend Sierra. Nancy's little sister was standing nearby and was eavesdropping on their conversation. Suddenly, she heard something that interested her and had to <u>interject</u> her opinion about the subject the girls were talking about.

A. repeat

B. pierce

C. intersect

D. state

42. **How does the author feel about the size of people's houses?**
(Rigorous) (Skill 4.13)

  A. The author believes that people with larger homes are lucky

  B. The author thinks that if you have a small house you should have a cat

  C. The author feels that only people with large homes should own animals

  D. The author thinks that only those who own homes should own pets

43. **From this passage, one can infer that:**
(Rigorous) (Skill 4.1)

  A. The author owns a cat

  B. More people own dogs than cats

  C. Cats are smarter than dogs

  D. The author owns a dog

44. **From this passage, one can infer that:**
(Rigorous) (Skill 4.1)

  A. Either a dog or cat will be right for every family who wants a pet

  B. Choosing a pet is not solely one family member's job

  C. Only someone who enjoys exercising should get a dog

  D. Big dogs will not survive in a small house

45. **Johnny Depp stars in the movie *Charlie and the Chocolate Factory*. Is this sentence fact or opinion?**
(Easy) (Skill 4.13)

  A. Fact

  B. Opinion

DIRECTIONS: Read the following passage and answer the questions that follow.

According to Factmonster.com, the most popular Internet activity is sending and/or reading email. Approximately 92% of Internet users report using the Internet for this purpose. 89% of Internet users report that they use the Internet to search for information. Two popular search engines are Google and Yahoo! The introduction of the Internet has made it easy to gather and research information quickly. Other reasons that Internet users use the Internet is for social media, to search for driving directions, look into a hobby or interest, or research a product or service before buying, just to name a few. Creative <u>enterprises</u> such as remixing songs or lyrics stood at the bottom of reasons people use the Internet. Surprisingly, only 11% of Internet users said they use the Internet for creative purposes. Perhaps people are using specific software to be creative.

46. **What is the main idea of the passage?**
(Average) (Skill 4.1)

   A. Factmonster has a lot of great facts for people to research

   B. People use the Internet for a variety of reasons

   C. The main reason the Internet is used is to check emails

   D. People aren't as creative as they used to be before the Internet

47. **Why did the author write this article?**
(Average) (Skill 5.12)

   A. To convince the reader to use the Internet

   B. To teach the reader how use the Internet

   C. To encourage the reader to use the Internet

   D. To inform the reader about Internet usage trends

48. **How is the passage organized?**
(Average) (Skill 5.12)

   A. Sequence of events

   B. Cause and effect

   C. Statement support

   D. Compare and contrast

49. **What cause and effect relationship exists in this paragraph?**
(Rigorous) (Skill 5.3)

   A. The U.S. postal service is suffering from the introduction of email

   B. Google and Yahoo! are used most often to search information

   C. The introduction of the Internet has made gathering information easy

   D. People are less creative since they aren't using their computers for this reason

50. **By using the word "surprisingly" in the passage, what is the author implying?**
(Rigorous) (Skill 3.7)

   A. It is thought that the Internet is used more for creative purposes

   B. People are thought to be more creative than they really are

   C. It is thought that fewer than 11% would use the Internet for creative purposes

   D. Software companies are making 11% more creative software

51. **Which transition word could the author have used to connect these two sentences?**
(Average) (Skill 3.7)

Approximately 92% of Internet users report using the Internet for this purpose. 89% of Internet users report that they use the Internet to search for information.

A. Additionally,

B. Therefore,

C. Next,

D. Similarly,

52. **What does the word "enterprises" mean in the passage?**
(Average) (Skill 3.7)

A. people

B. endeavors

C. businesses

D. musicians

DIRECTIONS: Read the following passage and answer the questions that follow.

The poems both use personification to bring the subjects of the poem to life. Both poems were also very entertaining. In "The Subway" the author says that the subway, also known as a dragon, swallows up the people and then spits them out at the next stop. Similarly, in "Steam Shovel," the author says that the steam shovel chews up the dirt that it scoops up and smiles amiably at the people below.

The subjects of the poems are compared to different things. The subway is compared to a dragon with green scales. Dragons breathe fire. The steam shovel is compared to an ancient dinosaur with a long neck and dripping jaws.

53. **How is the passage organized?**
(Average) (Skill 5.18)

A. Compare and contrast

B. Cause and effect

C. Sequence of events

D. Statement support

54. **Which sentence in the passage is irrelevant?**
(Average) (Skill 7.3)

   A. Both poems were also very entertaining.

   B. The subway is also known as a dragon.

   C. The subway swallows people up and spits them out.

   D. The author says that the steam shovel chews up the dirt.

55. **Each of the comparisons mentioned in the paragraph are known as a:**
(Easy) (Skill 7.3)

   A. Metaphor

   B. Hyperbole

   C. Onomatopoeia

   D. None of the above

DIRECTIONS: Read the following passage and answer the questions that follow.

Have you ever wondered what chewing gum is made from? What is it that allows us to chew it for hours without it ever disintegrating? Chicle is a gum, or sap, that comes from the sapodilla tree. The sapodilla tree is an American tropical evergreen that is native to South Florida. Flavorings, corn syrup, and sugar or artificial sweeteners are other ingredients that go into the production of chewing gum. Legend has it that Native Americans chewed spruce resin to quench their thirst. Today, gum is chewed for many reasons by many different groups of people.

56. **What conclusion can be drawn from the passage?**
(Rigorous) (Skill 4.8)

   A. Everyone in South Florida has heard of the sapodilla tree

   B. Many people have wondered what makes gum chewy

   C. Some type of sweetener is used in gum production

   D. Native Americans invented gum

57. What can be inferred from the passage?
(Rigorous) (Skill 4.8)

A. The gum Chiclets took its name from the ingredient chicle used in gum

B. Gum is disgusting after it's been chewed for a few hours

C. Gum is only made in the United States because that's where the sapodilla tree grows

D. When someone is thirsty they should chew gum

DIRECTIONS: Read the following passage and answer the questions that follow.

The word "cycle" comes from the Greek word *kyklos*, which means "circle" or "wheel." There are many different types of cycles. The word "unicycle" comes from the prefix *uni-*, which means "one," combined with the root "cycle." When the prefix and root word cycle are combined, it creates a word that means "one circle or wheel." Unicycles are often used for entertainment rather than exercise.

A prefix *bi-* means "two," which, when combined with the word "cycle," creates the word "bicycle." How many wheels does a bicycle have? Many young children ride a tricycle because it has three wheels and is easy to ride. The prefix *tri-* means "three," and when it is combined with the root word "cycle," the new word is "three wheels." It is even possible to make the word "motorcycle." Once you

know how to use <u>roots</u>, it is easy to figure out the meaning of an unknown word.

58. What is the main idea of the passage? *(Average) (Skill 4.13)*

A. There are many types of cycles

B. The prefix *uni-* means one

C. Words can be defined by their parts

D. Unicycles are often used for entertainment

59. What does the word "roots" mean? *(Easy) (Skill 3.9)*

A. Stable parts of plants

B. Where one originated

C. The base portions of a word

D. A spelling tool

60. Which is an opinion contained in this passage? *(Average) (Skill 4.13)*

A. Once you know how to use roots, it is easy to figure out the meaning of an unknown word

B. Many young children ride a tricycle

C. Unicycles are often used for entertainment rather than exercise

D. The word "cycle" comes from the Greek word *kyklos*

61.   **From this article you can see that the author thinks:**
      (Rigorous) (Skill 4.13)

      A. Riding a bicycle is good exercise

      B. It is important to know about the English language

      C. "Cycle" is a confusing word

      D. It is more important to understand the prefixes and suffixes

      DIRECTIONS: The passage below contains many errors. Read the passage. Then, answer each test item by choosing the option that corrects an error in the underlined portion(s). No more than one underlined error will appear in each item. If no error exists, choose "No change is necessary."

      If you give me ten dollars, I'll give you fifty in return. Does this sound too good to be true? Well, anything that sounds too good to be true probably is. That stands true for herbal supplements. Herbal supplements are main targeted toward improving one type of ailment. There is no cure-all herbal supplement so don't believe what he tells you. Herbal supplement can fix more than one thing.

      Herbal supplements is great and have a lot of positive things to offer its takers and have become very popular with consumers. Many doctors are even suggesting that they try natural herbal remedies before prescribing an over-the-counter medication. Herbal supplements have given

consumers a new power to self-diagnose and consumers can head to the health food store and pick up an herbal supplement rather than heading to the doctor. Herbal supplements take a little long than prescribed medication to clear up any illnesses, but they are a more natural way to go, and some consumers prefer that form of medication.

62.   **Herbal supplements are <u>main</u> targeted <u>toward</u> <u>improving</u> one type of ailment.**
      (Average) (Skill 5.6)

      A. mainly

      B. towards

      C. improve

      D. No change is necessary

63.   **There is <u>no</u> cure-all herbal <u>supplement</u> so don't believe what <u>he tells you</u>.**
      (Easy)(Skill 5.6)

      A. nothing

      B. supplemental

      C. you hear

      D. No change is necessary

64. **Many doctors <u>are</u> even suggesting that <u>they</u> try natural herbal remedies before <u>prescribing</u> an over-the-counter medication.**
(Rigorous) (Skill 5.6)

    A. is

    B. their patients

    C. prescribing,

    D. No change is necessary

65. **Herbal supplements <u>is</u> great and have <u>a lot</u> of positive things to offer <u>its</u> takers and have become very popular with consumers.**
(Easy) (Skill 5.6)

    A. are

    B. alot

    C. it's

    D. No change is necessary

66. **Herbal supplements take a little <u>long</u> <u>than</u> <u>prescribed</u> medications to clear up any illnesses, but they are a more natural way to go, and some consumers prefer that form of medication.**
(Average) (Skill 6.1)

    A. longer

    B. then

    C. perscribed

    D. No changes necessary

67. **Herbal <u>supplements</u> take a little long than prescribed <u>medication</u> to clear up any illnesses, but they are a <u>more natural</u> way to go, and some consumers prefer that form of medication.**
(Rigorous) (Skill 6.1)

    A. supplement

    B. medications

    C. more naturally

    D. No change necessary

68. **Herbal <u>supplement</u> can fix more <u>than</u> one <u>thing</u>.**
(Average) (Skill 6.1)

    A. supplements

    B. then

    C. things

    D. No change is necessary

DIRECTIONS: The passage below contains many errors. Read the passage. Then, answer each test item by choosing the option that corrects an error in the underlined portion(s). No more than one underlined error will appear in each item. If no error exists, choose "No change is necessary."

Bingo has many purposes in the United States. It is used as a learning and entertainment tool for children. Bingo is used as an entertainment tool for parties and picnics to entertain a large number of people easily and quickly. Bingo is also a common game played among elderly and church groups because of its simplistic way of entertaining.

A typical bingo card has the word "bingo" printed across the top with columns of numbers inside boxes underneath. There is a "free" space located directly in the middle. There is usually one person who calls the numbers. For example, a ball or chip may be labeled "B12." Players then look under the "B" column for the number 12 and if it appears on their card, they place a marker on top of it. If there isn't a 12 under the letter "B" on a player's card, then they simply wait for the next number to be called.

69. <u>Players</u> then look under the "B" column for the number 12 and if it appears on <u>his</u> card, <u>they</u> place a marker on top of it.
(*Rigorous*) (*Skill 6.1*)

A. He

B. their

C. him

D. No change is necessary.

70. **Bingo is used as a learning and entertainment tool for children.**

How should this sentence be rewritten? *(Rigorous) (Skill 7.3)*

A. Bingo is used as a learning tool and entertainment for children.

B. Bingo is used for learning and entertainment for children.

C. Bingo is used to both teach and entertain children.

D. No change is necessary

71. **In this step of the writing process, students examine their work and make changes in wording, details, and ideas.** *(Easy) (Skill 7.3)*

A. Drafting

B. Prewriting

C. Revising and Editing

D. Proofreading

DIRECTIONS: Read the following passage and answer the questions.

It is a requirement that all parents volunteer two hours during the course of the season. Or an alternative was to pay $8 so you can have some high school students work a shift for you. Lots of parents liked this idea and will take advantage of the opportunity. Shifts run an hour long, and it is well worth it to pay the money so you don't miss your sons game.

72. **It is a requirement that all parents volunteer two hours during the course of the season.**

    How should the above sentence be rewritten?
    (Average) (Skill 7.3)

    A. It is a requirement of all parents volunteering two hours during the course of the season.

    B. It is required of all parents to volunteer for two hours during the course of the season.

    C. They require all parents to volunteer during the season.

    D. Requiring all parents to volunteer for two hours of the season.

73. **An alternative <u>was</u> to pay $8 so you can have some <u>high school</u> students work a shift for you.**

    Which of the following options corrects an error in one of the underlined portions above?
    (Average) (Skill 6.1)

    A. is

    B. High School

    C. High school

    D. No change is necessary.

74. **Many parents liked this idea and will take advantage of the opportunity.**

    How should the sentence be rewritten?
    (Rigorous) (Skill 7.3)

    A. Many parent's liked this idea and took advantage of the opportunity.

    B. Many parents like this idea and take advantage of the opportunity.

    C. Many parents like this idea and took advantage of the opportunity.

    D. Many parents did like this idea and take advantage of the opportunity.

Sample Test: Mathematics

75. Simplify: $\dfrac{2^{10}}{2^5} =$

(Average) (Skill 10.2)

A. 2^2

B. 2^5

C. 2^{50}

D. $2^{\frac{1}{2}}$

76. Solve: $\left(\dfrac{^-4}{9}\right) + \left(\dfrac{^-7}{10}\right) =$

(Average) (Skill 11.1)

A. $\dfrac{23}{90}$

B. $\dfrac{^-23}{90}$

C. $\dfrac{103}{90}$

D. $\dfrac{^-103}{90}$

77. Find an equivalent expression for 0.74. *(Easy) (Skill 11.1)*

A. $\dfrac{74}{100}$

B. 7.4%

C. $\dfrac{33}{50}$

D. $\dfrac{74}{10}$

78. Multiply: $(5.6) \times (^-0.11) =$
(Average) (Skill 11.1)

A. $^-0.616$

B. 0.616

C. $^-6.110$

D. 6.110

79. Mrs. Kline's classroom store is having a sale. An item that sells for \$3.75 is put on sale for \$1.20. What is the percent of decrease? *(Easy) (Skill 11.1)*

A. 25%

B. 28%

C. 68%

D. 34%

80. **Which of the following denotes an irrational number?**
(Easy) (Skill 11.5)

A. 4.2500000

B. $\sqrt{16}$

C. 0.25252525

D. $\Pi = 3.141592\ldots$

81. **What is the greatest common factor of 16, 28, and 36?**
(Average) (Skill 12.1)

A. 2

B. 4

C. 8

D. 16

82. **Compute the surface area of the prism.**
(Average) (Skill 12.2)

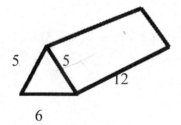

A. 204 units2

B. 216 units2

C. 360 units2

D. 180 units2

83. **What is the area of a square whose side is 13 feet?**
(Easy) (Skill 12.2)

A. 169 feet

B. 169 square feet

C. 52 feet

D. 52 square feet

84. **The owner of a rectangular piece of land 40 yards in length and 30 yards in width wants to divide it into two parts. She plans to join two opposite corners with a fence as shown in the diagram below. The cost of the fencing is approximately $25 per linear foot. What is the estimated cost of the fence needed by the owner?**
(Rigorous) (Skill 12.2)

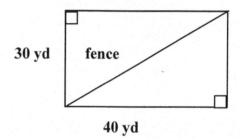

40 yd

A. $1250

B. $62,500

C. $5250

D. $3750

85. **Find the surface area of a box that is 3 feet wide, 5 feet tall, and 4 feet deep.** *(Average) (Skill 12.2)*

    A. 47 square feet

    B. 60 square feet

    C. 94 square feet

    D. 188 square feet

86. **The trunk of a tree has a radius of 2.1 meters. What is its circumference?** *(Average) (Skill 12.2)*

    A. $2.1\,\pi$ square meters

    B. $4.2\,\pi$ meters

    C. $2.1\,\pi$ meters

    D. $4.2\,\pi$ square meters

87. **Sets A, B, C, and U are related as shown in the diagram.**

    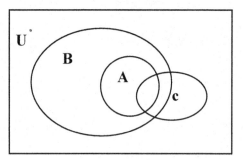

    Which of the following statements is true, assuming none of the six regions is empty? *(Average) (Skill 13.1)*

    A. Any element that is a member of set B is also a member of set A.

    B. No element is a member of all three sets A, B, and C.

    C. Any element that is a member of set U is also a member of set B.

    D. None of the above statements is true.

88. **If $4x - (3 - x) = 7(x - 3) + 10$, then** *(Rigorous) (Skill 13.4)*

    A. x = 8

    B. x = -8

    C. x = 4

    D. x = -4

89. It takes 5 equally skilled people 9 hours to shingle Mr. Joe's roof. Let t be the time required for only 3 of these workers to complete the same job. Select the correct mathematical representation of the given conditions.
(Rigorous) (Skill 14.2)

A. $\dfrac{3}{5} = \dfrac{9}{t}$

B. $\dfrac{9}{5} = \dfrac{3}{t}$

C. $\dfrac{5}{9} = \dfrac{3}{t}$

D. $\dfrac{14}{9} = \dfrac{t}{5}$

90. Find the equation of the line through (5, 6) and (-1, -2) in standard form.
(Rigorous) (Skill 14.3)

A. 3y=4x-2

B. $-2y = \dfrac{4}{3}x - 1$

C. $6y + 5x - 1$

D. $y = 4x - 6$

91. Find the real roots of the equation $3x^2 - 45 + 22x$.
(Rigorous) (Skill 15.1)

A. $\dfrac{^-5}{3}$ and 9

B. $\dfrac{5}{3}$ and $^-9$

C. 5 and 9

D. -5 and -9

92. What is the 40th term in the sequence {1, 4, 7, 10 ...}?
(Rigorous) (Skill 16.1)

A. 43

B. 121

C. 118

D. 120

93. Which term most accurately describes two coplanar lines with no common points?
(Average) (Skill 18.2)

A. Perpendicular

B. Parallel

C. Intersecting

D. Skew

94. Given similar polygons with corresponding sides 6 inches and 8 inches, what is the area of the smaller polygon if the area of the larger is 64 in²?
(Rigorous) (Skill 19.2)

A. 48 in²

B. 36 in²

C. 144 in²

D. 78 in²

95. Study the figures in Options A, B, C, and D. Select the option in which all triangles are similar.
(Easy) (Skill 19.2)

A.

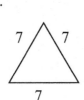

B.

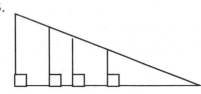

C.

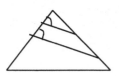

D.

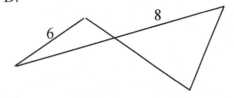

96. Find the midpoint of (2, 5) and (7, -4).
(Rigorous) (Skill 20.5)

A. (9, -1)

B. (5, 9)

C. (9/2, -1/2)

D. (9/2, 1/2)

97. The following chart shows the yearly average number of international tourists visiting Palm Beach for 2010-2014. How many more international tourists visited Palm Beach in 2014 than in 2011?
(Average) (Skill 21.1)

A. 100,000

B. 600,000

C. 1,600,000

D. 8,000,000

98. **What conclusion can be drawn from the graph below?**
(Average) (Skill 21.3)

MLK Elementary

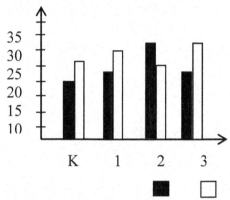

Student Enrollment Girls Boys

A. The number of students in first grade exceeds the number in second grade.

B. There are more boys than girls in the entire school.

C. There are more girls than boys in the first grade.

D. Third grade has the largest number of students.

99. **Mary did comparison shopping on her favorite brand of coffee. Over half of the stores priced the coffee at $1.70. Most of the remaining stores priced the coffee at $1.80, except fora few who charged $1.90. Which of the following statements is true about the distribution of prices?**
(Rigorous) (Skill 21.4)

A. The mean and the mode are the same.

B. The mean is greater than the mode.

C. The mean is less than the mode.

D. The mean is less than the median.

100. **What is the mode of the data in the following sample?**
(Easy) (Skill 21.4)

   9, 10, 11, 9, 10, 11, 9, 13

A. 9

B. 9.5

C. 10

D. 11

101. A coin is tossed and a die is rolled. What is the probability of the coin landing on "heads" and a 3 being rolled on the die?
(Rigorous) (Skill 22.2)

    A. $\dfrac{1}{2}$

    B. $\dfrac{1}{6}$

    C. $\dfrac{1}{12}$

    D. $\dfrac{1}{15}$

102. What is the probability of drawing two consecutive aces from a standard deck of 52 cards if the first card drawn is not replaced?
(Rigorous) (Skill 22.2)

    A. $\dfrac{3}{51}$

    B. $\dfrac{1}{221}$

    C. $\dfrac{2}{104}$

    D. $\dfrac{2}{52}$

103. Which of the following is correct?
(Easy) (Skill 10.5)

    A. $2,365 > 2,340$

    B. $0.75 > 1.25$

    C. $3/4 < 1/16$

    D. $-5 < -6$

104. Simplify: $\dfrac{5^{-2} \times 5^{3}}{5^{5} \times 5^{-7}}$
(Average) (Skill 10.4)

    A. 5^{5}

    B. 125

    C. $\dfrac{1}{125}$

    D. 25

105. Choose the set in which the members are *not* equivalent.
(Average) (Skill 10.2)

    A. $1/2$, 0.5, 50%

    B. $10/5$, 2.0, 200%

    C. $3/8$, 0.385, 38.5%

    D. $7/10$, 0.7, 70%

106. **The digit 8 in the number 975.086 is in the:**
 (Easy) (Skill 10.1)

 A. Tenths place

 B. Ones place

 C. Hundredths place

 D. Hundreds place

107. **The relations given below demonstrate the following addition and multiplication property of real numbers:**
 $a + b = b + a$
 $ab = ba$
 (Easy) (Skill 10.4)

 A. Commutative

 B. Associative

 C. Identity

 D. Inverse

108. **$(3 \times 9)^4 =$**
 (Rigorous) (Skill 10.2)

 A. $(3 \times 9)(3 \times 9)(27 \times 27)$

 B. $(3 \times 9) + (3 \times 9)$

 C. (12×36)

 D. $(3 \times 9) + (3 \times 9) + (3 \times 9) + (3 \times 9)$

109. **Jason can run a distance of 50 yards in 6.5 seconds. At this rate, how many feet can he run in a time of 26 seconds?**
 (Average) (Skill 12.2)

 A. 200

 B. 400

 C. 600

 D. 800

110. **Solve for *x*: $3(5 + 3x) - 8 = 88$**
 (Average) (Skill 10.2)

 A. 30

 B. 9

 C. 4.5

 D. 27

111. You are helping students list the steps needed to solve the word problem:

    "Mr. Jones is 5 times as old as his son. Two years later he will be 4 times as old as his son. How old is Mr. Jones?"

    One of the students makes the following list:

    Assume Mr. Jones' son is x years old. Express Mr. Jones' age in terms of *x*.
    Write how old they will be two years later in terms of *x*.
    Solve the equation for *x*.
    Multiply the answer by 5 to get Mr. Jones' age.

    What step is missing between steps 2 and 3? *(Rigorous) (Skill 10.2)*

    A. Write an equation setting Mr. Jones' age equal to 5 times his son's age

    B. Write an equation setting Mr. Jones' age two years later equal to 5 times his son's age two years later

    C. Write an equation setting Mr. Jones' age equal to 4 times his son's age

    D. Write an equation setting Mr. Jones' age two years later equal to 4 times his son's age two years later

112. Which of the following points does *not* lie on the graph of $|y + 3| < |x - 3|$?
    (Rigorous) (Skill 14.1)

    A. (-5, 4)

    B. (-6, 0)

    C. (-3, -4)

    D. (7, 7)

113. What is the next term in the following sequence?
    (Easy) (Skill 13.1)

    {0.005, 0.03, 0.18, 1.08...}

    A. 1.96

    B. 2.16

    C. 3.32

    D. 6.48

114. A student has taken three tests in his algebra class for which the mean score is 88. He will take one more test and his final grade will be the mean of all four tests. He wants to achieve a final grade of 90. Which one of the following is the correct procedure to determine the score he needs on the fourth test?
(Rigorous) (Skill 13.1)

   A. He needs a score 92 since $(88 + 92) / 2 = 90$.

   B. He needs a score of 89.5 since $(88 + 90 + 90 + 90) / 4 = 89.5$.

   C. He needs a score of 96 since $(88 + 88 + 88 + 96) / 4 = 90$.

   D. He cannot achieve a final grade of 90 since each of his scores on the first three tests is less than 90.

115. Which of the following shapes is *not* a parallelogram?
(Easy) (Skill 18.2)

I

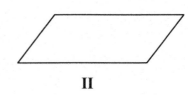

II

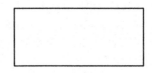

III

   A. I and III

   B. II and III

   C. I only

   D. I, II, and III

116. Given similar polygons with corresponding sides of lengths 9 and 15, find the perimeter of the smaller polygon if the perimeter of the larger polygon is 150 units.
(Average) (Skill 18.2)

   A. 54

   B. 135

   C. 90

   D. 126

Sample Test: Social Studies

117. **The belief that the United States should control all of North America was called:** *(Easy) (Skill 29.1)*

    A. Westward Expansion

    B. Pan Americanism

    C. Manifest Destiny

    D. Nationalism

118. **The area of the United States was effectively double through purchase of the Louisiana Territory under which President?** *(Average) (Skill 29.1)*

    A. John Adams

    B. Thomas Jefferson

    C. James Madison

    D. James Monroe

119. **A major quarrel between colonial Americans and the British concerned a series of British Acts of Parliament dealing with:** *(Easy) (Skill 29.1)*

    A. Taxes

    B. Slavery

    C. Native Americans

    D. Shipbuilding

120. **The international organization established to work for world peace at the end of the Second World War is the:** *(Average) (Skill 29.1)*

    A. League of Nations

    B. United Federation of Nations

    C. United Nations

    D. United World League

121. **Which famous battle fought on Texas soil resulted in Texas independence from Mexico?** *(Rigorous) (Skill 29.2)*

    A. The Battle of the Alamo

    B. The Battle of San Jacinto

    C. The Battle of the Rio Grande

    D. The Battle of Shiloh

122. Why is the system of government in the United States referred to as a federal system?
(Rigorous) (Skill 29.11)

A. There are different levels of government

B. There is one central authority in which all governmental power is vested

C. The national government cannot operate except with the consent of the governed

✓D. Elections are held at stated periodic times, rather than as called by the head of the government

123. The U.S. Constitution, adopted in 1789, provided for:
(Rigorous) (Skill 29.11)

A. Direct election of the President by all citizens

B. Direct election of the President by citizens meeting a standard of wealth

C. Indirect election of the President by electors

D. Indirect election of the President by the U.S. Senate

124. From about 1870 to 1900 the settlement of America's "last frontier," the West, was completed. One attraction for settlers was free land, but it would have been to no avail without:
(Rigorous) (Skill 29.10)

A. Better farming methods and technology

B. Surveying to set boundaries

C. Immigrants and others to seek new land

D. The railroad to get them there

125. Slavery arose in the Southern Colonies partly as a perceived economical way to:
(Average) (Skill 29.13)

A. Increase the owner's wealth through human beings used as a source of exchange

B. Cultivate large plantations of cotton, tobacco, rice, indigo, and other crops

C. Provide Africans with humanitarian aid, such as health care, Christianity, and literacy

D. Keep ships' holds full of cargo on two out of three legs of the "triangular trade" voyage.

126. **The post-Civil War years were a time of low public morality, a time of greed, graft, and dishonesty. Which one of the reasons listed would not be accurate?**
(Rigorous) (Skill 29.15)

A. The war itself, because of the money and materials needed to conduct the War

B. The very rapid growth of industry and big business after the War

C. The personal example set by President Grant

D. Unscrupulous heads of large impersonal corporations

127. **A number of women worked hard in the first half of the 19th century for women's rights, but decisive gains did not come until after 1850. The earliest accomplishments were in:**
(Average) (Skill 29.16)

A. Medicine

B. Education

C. Writing

D. Temperance

128. **Of all the major causes of both World Wars I and II, the most significant one is considered to be:**
(Average) (Skill 29.19)

A. Extreme nationalism

B. Military buildup and aggression

C. Political unrest

D. Agreements and alliances

129. **Meridians, or lines of longitude, not only help in pinpointing locations but are also used for:**
(Rigorous) (Skill 30.1)

A. Measuring distance from the Poles

B. Determining direction of ocean currents

C. Determining the time around the world

D. Measuring distance on the equator

130. **The study of the ways in which different societies around the world deal with the problems of limited resources and unlimited needs and wants is in the area of:**
(Average) (Skill 31.2)

 A. Economics

 B. Sociology

 C. Anthropology

 D. Political Science

131. **Capitalism and communism are alike in that they are both:**
(Easy) (Skill 31.3)

 A. Organic systems

 B. Political systems

 C. Centrally planned systems

 D. Economic systems

132. **The purchase of goods or services on one market for immediate resale on another market is:**
(Average) (Skill 31.13)

 A. Output

 B. Enterprise

 C. Arbitrage

 D. Mercantile

133. **The economic system promoting individual ownership of land, capital, and businesses with minimal governmental regulations is called:**
(Easy) (Skill 31.3)

 A. Macro-economy

 B. Micro-economy

 C. Laissez-faire

 D. Free enterprise

134. **The American labor union movement started gaining new momentum:**
(Rigorous) (Skill 31.5)

 A. During the building of the railroads

 B. After 1865 with the growth of cities

 C. With the rise of industrial giants such as Carnegie and Vanderbilt

 D. During the war years of 1861-1865

135. It can be reasonably stated that the change in the United States from primarily an agricultural country into an industrial power was due to all of the following except:
(Average) (Skill 31.12)

A. Tariffs on foreign imports

B. Millions of hardworking immigrants

C. An increase in technological developments

D. The change from steam to electricity for powering industrial machinery

136. There is no doubt that there was a vast improvement of the US Constitution over the Articles of Confederation. Which one of the four accurate statements below is a unique yet eloquent description of the document?
(Rigorous) (Skill 32.4)

A. The establishment of a strong central government in no way lessened or weakened the individual states.

B. Individual rights were protected and secured.

C. The Constitution is the best representation of the results of the American genius for compromise.

D. Its flexibility and adaptation to change gives it a sense of timelessness.

137. "Marbury vs. Madison (1803)" was an important Supreme Court case which set the precedent for:
(Rigorous) (Skill 32.9)

A. The elastic clause

B. Judicial review

C. The supreme law of the land

D. Popular sovereignty in the territories

138. Which one of the following is not a function or responsibility of the US political parties?
(Rigorous) (Skill 32.10)

A. Conducting elections or the voting process

B. Obtaining funds needed for election campaigns

C. Choosing candidates to run for public office

D. Making voters aware of issues and other public affairs information

139. Which of the following lists elements usually considered to be responsibilities of citizenship under the American system of government? *(Easy) (Skill 32.14)*

   A. Serving in public office, voluntary government service, military duty

   B. Paying taxes, jury duty, upholding the Constitution

   C. Maintaining a job, giving to charity, turning in fugitives

   D. Quartering of soldiers, bearing arms, government service

140. In which of the following disciplines would the study of physical mapping, modern or ancient, and the plotting of points and boundaries be least useful? *(Average) (Skill 34.1)*

   A. Sociology

   B. Geography

   C. Archaeology

   D. History

141. The study of the exercise of power and political behavior in human society today would be conducted by experts in: *(Average) (Skill 34.2)*

   A. History

   B. Sociology

   C. Political Science

   D. Anthropology

142. This writer and scientist was a delegate to the Continental Congress and a signer of the Declaration of Independence. *(Average) (Skill 29.9)*

   A. George Washington

   B. Benjamin Franklin

   C. Orville Wright

   D. Thomas Jefferson

143. This high rugged mountain chain stretches from Alaska into Mexico. *(Average) (Skill 30.1)*

   A. Rocky Mountains

   B. The Pocono Mountains

   C. Yosemite National Mountains

   D. Coast Ranges

144. **Land made from soil left behind in a river as it drains into a larger body of water is known as this:**
(Average) (Skill 30.1)

   A. plain

   B. dam

   C. tributary

   D. delta

145. **Part of an ocean or a lake that extends into land is known as this:**
(Average) (Skill 30.3)

   A. bay

   B. harbor

   C. tributary

   D. oasis

146. **This continent is located in the Southern hemisphere:**
(Easy) (Skill 30.1)

   A. North America

   B. Europe

   C. Asia

   D. Antarctica

147. **The United States has which type of economy?**
(Average) (Skill 31.2)

   A. A market economy

   B. A centrally planned economy

   C. A market socialist economy

   D. None of the above

148. **Which of the following is a primary source document?**
(Average) (Skill 35.9)

   A. A book recounting the events surrounding the 1932 kidnapping of aviator Charles Lindbergh's son

   B. A newspaper story about the Wall Street crash of 1987

   C. The text of Franklin D. Roosevelt's address to Congress of December 8, 1941, requesting a declaration of war against Japan

   D. A movie dramatizing the life of a fictional family living in Poland during the German invasion of 1939

149. **Which of the following is an example of a historical concept?**
(Rigorous)(Skill 29.1)

A. Capitalism

B. Racism

C. Globalization

D. All of the above

150. **What are two factors that can generate and affect landforms?**
(Average) (Skill 30.5)

A. Observing a plateau at various scales

B. Erosion and deposition

C. The presence of oceans, lakes, seas, and canals

D. The dry nature of some plateaus

151. **Denver is called the "mile-high city" because it is:** *(Average)*
(Skill 30.1)

A. Located approximately one mile above the plains of eastern Colorado

B. Located exactly one mile above the base of Cheyenne Mountain

C. Located approximately one mile above sea level

D. The city with the tallest buildings in Colorado

152. **_____ is the southernmost continent in the world.**
(Easy) (Skill 30.1)

A. Australia

B. New Zealand

C. The Arctic

D. Antarctica

153. **Human bones found during construction near an American Civil War battlefield would most likely be delivered to which of the following for study?**
(Average) (Skill 33.9)

A. The Department of Veterans Affairs

B. A state medical examiner

C. A homicide detective

D. An anthropologist

154. **States that are near the Rocky Mountains, such as Montana, have exceptional trout fishing because of which of the following:**
(Average) (Skill 30.5)

   A. Lakes in mountain regions have warm water that trout enjoy

   B. Mountain regions are the only places that have large numbers of the aquatic insects trout like to eat

   C. There are fewer people in these areas, so the fishing pressure is light

   D. Trout thrive in the cold, clean rivers found in mountainous regions

155. **Our present-day alphabet comes from which of the following:**
(Average) (Skill 33.1)

   A. Cuneiform

   B. The Greek alphabet

   C. Hieroglyphic writing

   D. Hebrew Scriptures

156. **The Cold War involved which two countries that both emerged as world powers?**
(Rigorous) (Skill 29.2)

   A. China and Japan

   B. The United States and the Soviet Union

   C. England and Brazil

   D. Afghanistan and the United States

157. **Cultural diffusion is:**
(Rigorous) (Skill 29.4)

   A. The process that individuals and societies go through in changing their behavior and organization to cope with social, economic, and environmental pressures

   B. The complete disappearance of a culture

   C. The exchange or adoption of cultural features when two cultures come into regular direct contact

   D. The movement of cultural ideas or materials between populations independent of the movement of those populations

158. **The Great Plains in the United States are an excellent place to grow corn and wheat for all of the following reasons EXCEPT:** *(Average) (Skill 30.10)*

A. Rainfall is abundant and the soil is rich

B. The land is mostly flat and easy to cultivate

C. The human population is modest in size, so there is plenty of space for large farms

D. The climate is semitropical

Sample Test: Science

159. **When teaching Science rules pertaining to safety, Mrs. Miller explains to her students that chemicals should be stored** *(Easy) (Skill 36.2)*

A. in the principal's office.

B. in a dark room.

C. in an off-site research facility.

D. according to their reactivity with other substances.

160. **Mr. Michalak's lab groups are measuring a liquid using graduated cylinders. Before expecting the students to accurately measure, he must teach them to read each measurement in the floowing way:** *(Average Rigor) (Skill 37.2)*

A. At the highest point of the liquid.

B. At the bottom of the meniscus curve.

C. At the closest mark to the top of the liquid

D. At the top of the plastic safety ring.

161. **When is a hypothesis formed?**
(Easy) (Skill 38.2)

A. Before the data is taken.

B. After the data is taken.

C. After the data is analyzed.

D. Concurrent with graphing the data.

162. **Which of the following is the most accurate definition of a non-renewable resource?**
(Average Rigor) (Skill 39.5)

A. A nonrenewable resource is never replaced once used.

B. A nonrenewable resource is replaced on a timescale that is very long relative to human life-spans.

C. A nonrenewable resource is a resource that can only be manufactured by humans.

D. A nonrenewable resource is a species that has already become extinct.

163. **A middle school science class is reviewing an experiment in which a scientist exposes mice to cigarette smoke, and notes that their lungs develop tumors. Mice that were not exposed to the smoke do not develop as many tumors. Which of the following conclusions may be drawn from these results?**
(Rigorous) (Skill 40.2)

I. Cigarette smoke causes lung tumors.
II. Cigarette smoke exposure has a positive correlation with lung tumors in mice.
III. Some mice are predisposed to develop lung tumors.
IV. Cigarette smoke exposure has a positive correlation with lung tumors in humans.

A. I and II only.

B. II only.

C. I , II, III and IV.

D. II and IV only.

164. Which of the following is a correct explanation for an astronaut's 'weightlessness'? *(Average Rigor) (Skill 41.1)*

A. Astronauts continue to feel the pull of gravity in space, but they are so far from planets that the force is small.

B. Astronauts continue to feel the pull of gravity in space, but spacecraft have such powerful engines that those forces dominate, reducing effective weight.

C. Astronauts do not feel the pull of gravity in space, because space is a vacuum.

D. The cumulative gravitational forces, that the astronaut is experiencing, from all sources in the solar system equal out to a net gravitational force of zero.

165. Physical properties are observable characteristics of a substance in its natural state. Which of the following are considered physical properties. *(Rigorous) (Skill 42.1)*

I. Color
II. Density
III. Specific gravity
IV. Melting Point

A. I only

B. I and II only

C. I, II, and III only

D. III and IV only

166. Intermediate students in Mr. Lang's class are focusing on weather. The students are completing experiments using water in various forms. When the teacher boils water, he explains that the change in phase from liquid to gas is called: *(Rigorous) (Skill 42.2)*

A. Evaporation.

B. Condensation.

C. Vaporization.

D. Boiling.

167. **Which of the following statements is true of all transition elements?**
(Rigorous) (Skill 43.3)

A. They are all hard solids at room temperature.

B. They tend to form salts when reacted with Halogens.

C. They all have a silvery appearance in their pure state.

D. All of the Above

168. **A boulder sitting on the edge of a cliff has which type of energy?**
(Easy) (Skill 44.1)

A. Kinetic energy

B. Latent Energy

C. No energy

D. Potential Energy

169. **A converging lens produces a real image _____.**
(Rigorous) (Skill 44.4)

A. always.

B. never.

C. when the object is within one focal length of the lens.

D. when the object is further than one focal length from the lens.

170. **Which of the following is not a factor in how different materials will conduct seismic waves?**
(Average Rigor) (Skill 44.6)

A. Density

B. Incompressiblity

C. Rigidity

D. Tensile strength

171. **The Law of Conservation of Energy states that _____.**
(Average Rigor) (Skill 45.2)

A. There must be the same number of products and reactants in any chemical equation.

B. Mass and energy can be interchanged.

C. Energy is neither created nor destroyed, but may change form.

D. One form energy must remain intact (or conserved) in all reactions

172. **When you step out of the shower, the floor feels colder on your feet than the bathmat. Which of the following is the correct explanation for this phenomenon?**
(Rigorous) (Skill 45.5)

A. The floor is colder than the bathmat.

B. The bathmat is smaller so that the floor quickly reaches equilibrium with your body temperature.

C. Heat is conducted more easily into the floor.

D. Water is absorbed from your feet into the bathmat. It doesn't evaporate as quickly as it does off the floor, therefore not cooling the bathmat as quickly.

173. **Identify the correct sequence of organization of living things from lower to higher order:**
(Average Rigor) (Skill 46.3)

A. Cell, Organelle, Organ, Tissue, System, Organism.

B. Cell, Tissue, Organ, Organelle, System, Organism.

C. Organelle, Cell, Tissue, Organ, System, Organism.

D. Organelle, Tissue, Cell, Organ, System, Organism.

174. **Catalysts assist reactions by _____ .**
(Easy) (Skill 46.5)

A. lowering required activation energy.

B. maintaining precise pH levels.

C. keeping systems at equilibrium.

D. changing the starting amounts of reactants.

175. **Which process result in a haploid chromosome number?**
(Rigorous) (Skill 47.2)

A. Mitosis.

B. Meiosis I.

C. Meiosis II.

D. Neither mitosis nor meiosis.

176. **A carrier of a genetic disorder is heterozygous for a disorder that is recessive in nature. Hemophilia is a sex-linked disorder. This means that:**
(Easy) (Skill 47.4)

A. Only females can be carriers

B. Only males can be carriers.

C. Both males and females can be carriers.

D. Neither females nor males can be carriers.

177. **During a field trip to the local zoo, a student in Mrs. Meyer's class comments that the giraffe they are observing is as tall as a tree. Using this as a teachable moment, Mrs. Meyers should explain which of the following for scientific biological adaptation?**
(Average Rigor) (Skill 48.2)

A. Giraffes need to reach higher for leaves to eat, so their necks stretch. The giraffe babies are then born with longer necks. Eventually, there are more long-necked giraffes in the population.

B. Giraffes with longer necks are able to reach more leaves, so they eat more and have more babies than other giraffes. Eventually, there are more long-necked giraffes in the population.

C. Giraffes want to reach higher for leaves to eat, so they release enzymes into their bloodstream, which in turn causes fetal development of longer-necked giraffes. Eventually, there are more long-necked giraffes in the population.

D. Giraffes with long necks are more attractive to other giraffes, so they get the best mating partners and have more babies. Eventually, there are more long-necked giraffes in the population.

178. **An animal choosing its mate because of attractive plumage or a strong mating call is an example of:**
(Average Rigor) (Skill 48.4)

A. Sexual Selection.

B. Natural Selection.

C. Mechanical Isolation.

D. Linkage

179. **Many male birds sing long complicated songs that describe thier identity and the area of land that they claim. Which of the answers below is the best decription of this behavior?**
(Rigorous) (Skill 49.1)

A. Innate territorial behavior

B. Learned competitve behavior

C. Innate mating behavior

D. Learned territorial behavior

180. **A wrasse (fish) cleans the teeth of other fish by eating away plaque. This is an example of _____ between the fish.**
(Average Rigor) (Skill 50.2)

A. parasitism.

B. symbiosis (mutualism).

C. competition.

D. predation.

181. **Which of the following causes the Aurora Borealis?**
(Rigorous) (Skill 51.3)

    A. gases escaping from earth

    B. particles from the sun

    C. particles from the moon

    D. electromagnetic discharges from the North Pole.

182. **The transfer of heat from the earth's surface to the atmosphere is called**
(Average Rigor) (Skill 51.6)

    A. Convection

    B. Radiation

    C. Conduction

    D. Advection

183. **Mrs. Miller's class creates models of the water cycle and the students are required to describe each step. What is the most accurate description of the Water Cycle?**
(Rigorous) (Skill 52.2)

    A. Rain comes from clouds, filling the ocean. The water then evaporates and becomes clouds again.

    B. Water circulates from rivers into groundwater and back, while water vapor circulates in the atmosphere.

    C. Water is conserved except for chemical or nuclear reactions, and any drop of water could circulate through clouds, rain, ground-water, and surface-water.

    D. Water flows toward the oceans, where it evaporates and forms clouds, which causes rain, which in turn flow back to the oceans after it falls.

184. **What makes up the largest abiotic portion of the Nitrogen Cycle?**
(Average Rigor) (Skill 52.3)

A. Nitrogen Fixing Bacteria.

B. Nitrates.

C. Decomposers.

D. Atomsphere.

185. **What are the most significant and prevalent elements in the biosphere?**
(Easy) (Skill 52.5)

A. Carbon, Hydrogen, Oxygen, Nitrogen, Phosphorus.

B. Carbon, Hydrogen, Sodium, Iron, Calcium.

C. Carbon, Oxygen, Sulfur, Manganese, Iron.

D. Carbon, Hydrogen, Oxygen, Nickel, Sodium, Nitrogen.

186. **"Neap Tides" are especially weak tides that occur when the Sun and Moon are in a perpendicular arrangement to the Earth, and "Spring Tides" are especially strong tides that occur when the Sun and Moon are in line. At which combination of lunar phases do these tides occur (respectively)?**
(Rigorous) (Skill 53.5)

A. Half Moon, and Full Moon

B. Quarter Moon, and New Moon

C. Gibbous Moon, and Quarter Moon

D. Full Moon and New Moon

187. **The planet with true retrograde rotation is:**
(Rigorous) (Skill 54.1)

A. Pluto

B. Neptune

C. Venus

D. Saturn

188. The phases of the moon are the result of its _____ in relation to the sun.
(Average Rigor) (Skill 54.2)

A. revolution

B. rotation

C. position

D. inclination

189. The end of a geologic era is most often characterized by?
(Average Rigor) (Skill 55.1)

A. A general uplifting of the crust.

B. The extinction of the dominant plants and animals

C. The appearance of new life forms.

D. All of the above.

190. While studying how animals of the past have changed, students in Ms. Kripa's class spend time at their local museum. While there, they learn that the best preserved animal remains have been discovered in:
(Rigorous) (Skill 55.4)

A. Resin

B. Fossil Mold

C. Tar pits

D. Glacial Ice

191. Which type of student activity is most likely to expose a student's misconceptions about science?
(Average Rigor) (Skill 56.4)

A. Multiple-Choice and fill-in-the-blank worksheets.

B. Laboratory activities, where the lab is laid out step by tep with no active thought on the part of the student.

C. Teacher- lead demonstrations.

D. Laboratories in which the student are forced to critically consider the steps taken and the results.

192. As Mrs. Poshing demonstrates the difference between independent and dependent variables in her eighth grade science class, she shows the students a previously conducted medical experiment that involved petri dishes. She then asked them the following: In an experiment measuring the effect of different antibiotic discs on bacteria grown in Petri dishes, what are the independent and dependent variables respectively? *(Rigorous) (Skill 57.6)*

A. Number of bacterial colonies and the antibiotic type.

B. Antibiotic type and the distance between antibiotic and the closest colony.

C. Antibiotic type and the number of bacterial colonies.

D. Presence of bacterial colonies and the antibiotic type.

193. **Which is the correct order of the scientific method? (Easy) (Skill 38.1)**

1. collecting data
2. planning a controlled experiment
3. drawing a conclusion
4. hypothesizing a result
5. re-visiting a hypothesis to answer a question

A. 1,2,3,4,5

B. 4,2,1,3,5

C. 4,5,1,3,2

D. 1,3,4,5,2

194. **For her first project of the year, a student is designing a science experiment to test the effects of light and water on plant growth. You should recommend that she**

_____

(Average Rigor) (Skill 38.1)

A. manipulate the temperature also.

B. manipulate the water pH also.

C. determine the relationship between light and water unrelated to plant growth.

D. omit either water or light as a variable.

195. **When designing a scientific experiment, a student considers all the factors that may influence the results. The process goal is to _____**
    (Average Rigor) (Skill 38.2)

    A. recognize and manipulate independent variables.

    B. recognize and record independent variables.

    C. recognize and manipulate dependent variables.

    D. recognize and record dependent variables.

196. **Which of the following is not an acceptable way for a student to acknowledge sources in a laboratory report?**
    (Rigorous) (Skill 38.8)

    A. The student tells his/her teacher what sources s/he used to write the report.

    B. The student uses footnotes in the text, with sources cited, but not in correct MLA format.

    C. The student uses endnotes in the text, with sources cited, in correct MLA format.

    D. The student attaches a separate bibliography, noting each use of sources.

197. **Factor that is changed in an experiment:**
    (Average) (Skill 38.1)

    A. independent variable

    B. dependent variable

    C. inquiry

    D. control

198. **Which of these is the best example of "negligence"?**
    (Easy) (Skill 38.5)

    A. A teacher fails to give oral instructions to those with reading disabilities.

    B. A teacher fails to exercise ordinary care to ensure safety in the classroom.

    C. A teacher does not supervise a large group of students.

    D. A teacher reasonably anticipates that an event may occur, and plans accordingly.

199. **Formaldehyde should not be used in school laboratories for the following reason:**
    (Average Rigor) (Skill 37.1)

    A. It smells unpleasant.

    B. It is a known carcinogen.

    C. It is expensive to obtain.

    D. It is explosive.

200. **Experiments may be done with any of the following animals except** _____
      (Rigorous) (Skill 38.5)

      A. birds.

      B. invertebrates.

      C. lower order life.

      D. frogs.

ANSWER KEY

1.	A	41.	D	81.	B	121.	B	161.	A
2.	D	42.	A	82.	B	122.	A	162.	B
3.	A	43.	D	83.	B	123.	C	163.	B
4.	C	44.	B	84.	D	124.	D	164.	A
5.	C	45.	A	85.	C	125.	B	165.	C
6.	A	46.	B	86.	B	126.	C	166.	A
7.	C	47.	D	87.	D	127.	B	167.	B
8.	D	48.	C	88.	C	128.	A	168.	D
9.	B	49.	C	89.	C	129.	C	169.	D
10.	D	50.	A	90.	A	130.	A	170.	D
11.	A	51.	A	91.	B	131.	D	171.	C
12.	D	52.	B	92.	C	132.	C	172.	C
13.	C	53.	A	93.	B	133.	D	173.	C
14.	D	54.	A	94.	B	134.	B	174.	A
15.	B	55.	A	95.	B	135.	A	175.	C
16.	D	56.	C	96.	D	136.	C	176.	A
17.	A	57.	A	97.	B	137.	B	177.	B
18.	B	58.	C	98.	B	138.	A	178.	A
19.	A	59.	C	99.	B	139.	B	179.	D
20.	C	60.	A	100.	A	140.	A	180.	B
21.	D	61.	B	101.	C	141.	C	181.	B
22.	C	62.	A	102.	B	142.	B	182.	C
23.	C	63.	C	103.	A	143.	A	183.	C
24.	D	64.	B	104.	B	144.	D	184.	D
25.	B	65.	A	105.	C	145.	A	185.	A
26.	A	66.	A	106.	C	146.	D	186.	B
27.	A	67.	B	107.	A	147.	A	187.	C
28.	C	68.	A	108.	A	148.	C	188.	C
29.	B	69.	B	109.	C	149.	D	189.	D
30.	D	70.	C	110.	B	150.	B	190.	C
31.	B	71.	C	111.	D	151.	C	191.	D
32.	B	72.	B	112.	D	152.	D	192.	B
33.	A	73.	A	113.	D	153.	D	193.	B
34.	B	74.	B	114.	C	154.	D	194.	D
35.	B	75.	B	115.	C	155.	B	195.	A
36.	A	76.	D	116.	C	156.	B	196.	A
37.	B	77.	A	117.	C	157.	D	197.	D
38.	B	78.	A	118.	B	158.	D	198.	B
39.	C	79.	C	119.	A	159.	D	199.	B
40.	C	80.	D	120.	C	160.	B	200.	A

Rationales with Sample Questions: Language Arts

1. **If a student has a poor vocabulary the teacher should recommend that:**
    (Skill 1.10) (Rigorous)

    A. The student read newspapers, magazines and books on a regular basis.

    B. The student enroll in a Latin class.

    C. The student write the words repetitively after looking them up in the dictionary.

    D. The student use a thesaurus to locate synonyms and incorporate them into his/her vocabulary

    Answer A: The student read newspapers, magazines and books on a regular basis.
    It is up to the teacher to help the student choose reading material, but the student must be able to choose where s/he will search for the reading pleasure indispensable for enriching vocabulary.

2. **The arrangement and relationship of words in sentences or sentence structure best describes**
    (Skill 1.10) (Rigorous)

    A. Style.

    B. Discourse.

    C. Thesis.

    D. Syntax.

    Answer D: Syntax
    Syntax is the grammatical structure of sentences.

3.   **Which of the following is a formal reading assessment?**
     (Skill 1.10) (Rigorous)

     A. A standardized reading test

     B. A teacher-made reading test

     C. An interview

     D. A reading diary

     Answer A: A standardized reading test
     If assessment is standardized, it has to be objective, whereas B, C and D are all subjective assessments.

4.   **The literary device of personification is used in which example below?**
     (Skill 4.2) (Average)

     A. "Beg me no beggary by soul or parents, whining dog!"

     B. "Happiness sped through the halls cajoling as it went."

     C. "O wind thy horn, thou proud fellow."

     D. "And that one talent which is death to hide."

     Answer C: "O wind thy horn, thou proud fellow."
     It gives human characteristics to an inanimate object.

5. **Several students in Mr. Hossfeld's class have not met their grade level expectations in the past. Which teaching method would be most effective for interesting underachievers in his Language Arts class?**
    (Skill 4.11) (Rigorous)

    A. Assign use of glossary work and extensively footnoted excerpts of great works.

    B. Have students take turns reading aloud the anthology selection

    C. Let students choose which readings they'll study and write about.

    D. Use a chronologically arranged, traditional text, but assigning group work, panel presentations, and portfolio management

    Answer C: Let students choose which readings they'll study and write about
    It will encourage students to react honestly to literature. Students should take notes on what they're reading so they will be able to discuss the material. They should not only react to literature, but also experience it. Small-group work is a good way to encourage them. The other answers are not fit for junior-high or high school students. They should be encouraged, however, to read critics of works in order to understand criteria work.

6. **Which definition is the best for defining diction?**
    (Skill 5.1) (Rigorous)

    A. The specific word choices of an author to create a particular mood or feeling in the reader.

    B. Writing which explains something thoroughly.

    C. The background, or exposition, for a short story or drama.

    D. Word choices which help teach a truth or moral.

    Answer A: The specific word choices of an author to create a particular mood or feeling in the reader
    Diction refers to an author's choice of words, expressions and style to convey his/her meaning.

7. **Which is <u>not</u> a true statement concerning an author's literary tone?**
    (Skill 4.13) (Rigorous)

    A. Tone is partly revealed through the selection of details.

    B. Tone is the expression of the author's attitude towards his/her subject.

    C. Tone in literature is usually satiric or angry.

    D. Tone in literature corresponds to the tone of voice a speaker uses.

    Answer C: Tone in literature is usually satiric or angry
    Tone in literature conveys a mood and can be as varied as the tone of voice of a speaker (see D), e.g. sad, nostalgic, whimsical, angry, formal, intimate, satirical, sentimental, etc.

8. **What were two major characteristics of the first American literature?**
    (Skill 5.4 and 5.12) (Rigorous)

    A. Vengefulness and arrogance

    B. Bellicosity and derision

    C. Oral delivery and reverence for the land

    D. Maudlin and self-pitying egocentricism

    Answer D: Maudlin and self-pitying egocentricism
    These characteristics can be seen in Captain John Smith's work, as well as William Bradford's, and Michael Wigglesworth's works.

9. **Which of the following is a subject of a tall tale?**
   (Skill 5.9) (Rigorous)

   A. John Henry

   B. Paul Bunyan

   C. George Washington

   D. Rip Van Winkle

Answer B: Paul Bunyan
A tall tale is a Folklore genre, originating on the American frontier, in which the physical attributes, capabilities, and exploits of characters are wildly exaggerated. This is the case of giant logger Paul Bunyan of the American Northwestern forests. James Stevens traced Paul Bunyan to a French Canadian logger named Paul Bunyan. He won a reputation as a great fighter in the Papineau Rebellion against England in 1837 and later became famous as the boss of a logging camp. Paul Bunyan's first appearance in print seems to be in an advertising pamphlet, *Paul Bunyan and His Big Blue Ox*, published by the Red River Company. It immediately became very popular and was reissued many times.

10. **Which term best describes the form of the following poetic excerpt?**
    (Skill 5.9 and 7.3) (Rigorous)

> *And more to lulle him in his*
> *slumber soft,*
> *A trickling streake from high rock*
> *tumbling downe,*
> *And ever-drizzling raine upon*
> *the loft.*
> *Mixt with a murmuring winde,*
> *much like a swowne*
> *No other noyse, nor peoples*
> *troubles cryes.*
> *As still we wont t'annoy the*
> *walle'd towne,*
> *Might there be heard: but*
> *careless Quiet lyes,*
> *Wrapt in eternall silence farre*
> *from enemyes.*

A. Ballad

B. Elegy

C. Spenserian stanza

D. Octava rima

Answer D: Octava rima
The Octava Rima is a specific eight-line stanza whose rhyme scheme is abababcc.

11. **Which sonnet form describes the following?**
    (Skill 5.9) (Rigorous)

My galley, chargèd with forgetfulness,

Thorough sharp seas in winter nights doth pass

'Tween rock and rock; and eke mine en'my, alas,

That is my lord, steereth with cruelness;

And every owre a thought in readiness,

As though that death were light in such a case.

An endless wind doth tear the sail apace

Of forced sighs and trusty fearfulness.

A rain of tears, a cloud of dark disdain,

Hath done the weared cords great hinderance;

Wreathèd with error and eke with ignorance.

The stars be hid that led me to this pain;

Drownèd is Reason that should me comfort,

And I remain despairing of the port.

A. Petrarchan or Italian sonnet

B. Shakespearian or Elizabethan sonnet

C. Romantic sonnet

D. Spenserian sonnet

Answer A: Petrarch or Italian sonnet
The Petrarchan Sonnet, also known as Italian sonnet, is named after the Italian poet Petrarch (1304-74). It is divided into an octave rhyming *abbaabba* and a sestet normally rhyming *cdecde*.

12. **An example of figurative language in which someone or something inhuman is addressed as though present and able to respond describes:**
(Skill 5.11) (Average)

A. Personification.

B. Synecdoche.

C. Metonymy

D. Apostrophe.

Answer D: Apostrophe
Apostrophe gives human reactions and thoughts to animals, things and abstract ideas alike. This figure of speech is often present in allegory: for instance, the Giant Despair in John Bunyan's *Pilgrim's Progress.* Also, fables use personification to make animals able to speak.

13. **The quality in a work of literature which evokes feelings of pity or compassion is called**
(Skill 5.12) (Easy)

A. Colloquy.

B. Irony.

C. Pathos.

D. Paradox

Answer C: Pathos
A very well-known example of pathos is Desdemona's death in Othello, but there are many other examples of pathos.

14. **An extended metaphor which compares two very dissimilar things–one lofty, one lowly, is a definition of a/an**
(Skill 5.15) (Average)

A. Antithesis.

B. Aphorism.

C. Apostrophe.

D. Conceit.

Answer D: Conceit
A conceit is an unusually far-fetched metaphor in which an object, person or situation is presented in a parallel and simpler analogue between two apparently very different things or feelings, one very sophisticated and one very ordinary, usually taken either from nature or a well-known every day concept familiar to both reader and author alike. The conceit was first developed by Petrarch and spread to England in the sixteenth century.

15. **Which of the following is a complex sentence?**
(Skill 6.2) (Easy)

A. Anna and Margaret read a total of fifty-four books during summer vacation.

B. The youngest boy on the team had the best earned run average which mystifies the coaching staff.

C. Earl decided to attend Princeton; his twin brother Roy, who aced the ASVAB test, will be going to Annapolis.

D. "Easy come, easy go," Marcia moaned.

Answer B: The youngest boy on the team had the best earned run average which mystifies the coaching staff.
Here, the use of the relative pronoun "which", whose antecedent is "the best run average, introduces a clause that is dependent on the independent clause "The youngest boy on the team had the best run average". The idea expressed in the subordinate clause is subordinate to the one expressed in the independent clause.

16. **Middle and high school students are more receptive to studying grammar and syntax**
    (Skill 6.2 and 6.6) (Rigorous)

    A. Through worksheets and end of lessons practices in textbooks.

    B. Through independent, homework assignment.

    C. Through analytical examination of the writings of famous authors.

    D. Through application to their own writing.

    Answer D: Through application to their own writing
    At this age, students learn grammatical concepts best through practical application in their own writing.

17. **A punctuation mark indicating omission, interrupted thought, or an incomplete statement is a/an**
    (Skill 6.5 and 6.6) (Easy)

    A. Ellipsis.

    B. Anachronism.

    C. Colloquy.

    D. Idiom.

    Answer A: Ellipsis
    In an ellipsis, a word or words that would clarify the sentence's message are missing, yet it is still possible to understand them from the context.

18. **Which of the following contains an error in possessive inflection?**
(Skill 6.5 and 6.6) (Easy)

A. Doris's shawl

B. mother's-in-law frown

C. children's lunches

D. ambassador's briefcase

Answer B: mother's-in-law frown
Mother-in-Law is a compound common noun and the inflection should be at the end of the word, according to the rule.

19. **Analyze and correct the information. Wally <u>groaned, "Why</u> do I have to do an oral interpretation <u>of "The Raven</u>."**
(Skill 6.6) (Average)

A. Groaned "Why… of 'The Raven'?"

B. Groaned "Why… of "The Raven"?

C. Groaned ", Why… of "The Raven?"

D. Groaned, "Why… of "The Raven."

Answer A: Groaned "Why…of 'The Raven'?"
The question mark in a quotation that is an interrogation should be within the quotation marks. Also, when quoting a work of literature within another quotation, one should use single quotation marks ('…') for the title of this work, and they should close before the final quotation mark.

20. **Analyze and correct the information. Mr. Smith <u>respectfully submitted his resignation and had</u> a new job.**
    (Skill 6.6) (Average)

    A. Respectfully submitted his resignation and has

    B. Respectfully submitted his resignation before accepting

    C. Respectfully submitted his resignation because of

    D. Respectfully submitted his resignation and had

    Answer C: Respectfully submitted his resignation because of
    A eliminates any relationship of causality between submitting the resignation and having the new job. B just changes the sentence and does not indicate the fact that Mr. Smith had a new job before submitting his resignation. D means that Mr. Smith first submitted his resignation, then got a new job.

21. **Analyze and correct the information. There were fewer peices of evidence presented during the second trial.**
    (Skill 6.6) (Average)

    A. Fewer peaces

    B. Less peaces

    C. Less pieces

    D. Fewer pieces

    Answer D: Fewer pieces
    "Less" is impossible is the plural, and "peace" is the opposite of war, not a "piece" of evidence.

22. **Analyze and correct the information. The teacher implied from our angry words that there was conflict between you and me**
    (Skill 6.6) (Easy)

    A. Implied… between you and I

    B. Inferred… between you and I

    C. Inferred… between you and me

    D. Implied… between you and me

Answer C: Inferred…between you and me
The difference between the verb "to imply" and the verb "to infer" is that implying is directing an interpretation toward other people; to infer is to deduce an interpretation from someone else's discourse. Moreover, "between you and I" is grammatically incorrect: after a preposition here "and"), a disjunctive pronoun (me, you, him, her, us, you, them) is needed.

23. **Which of the following is not one of the four forms of discourse?**
    (Skill 6.6) (Average)

    A. Exposition

    B. Description

    C. Rhetoric

    D. Persuasion

Answer C: Rhetoric
Exposition, description and persuasion are styles of writing and ways of influencing a reader or a listener. Rhetoric, on the other hand, is theoretical. It is the theory of expressive and effective speech. Rhetorical figures are ornaments of speech such as anaphora, antithesis, metaphor, etc

24.   **"Clean as a whistle or "As Easy as falling of a log" are examples of**
        (Skill 7.1) (Average)

    A. Semantics

    B. Parody

    C. Irony

    D. Clichés

    Answer D: Clichés
    A cliché is a phrase or expression that has become dull due to overuse.

25.   **In the passage below, the dead body of Caesar is addressed as though he were still a living being. What is the figure of speech present in line one below?**
        (Skill 7.1) (Average)

    O, pardon me, though Bleeding piece of earth
    That I am meek and gentle with
    These butchers.

    -       **Marc Antony from *Julius Caesar***

    A. Apostrophe

    B. Allusion

    C. Antithesis

    D. Anachronism

    Answer B: Allusion
    This rhetorical figure addresses personified things, absent people or gods. An antithesis is a contrast between two opposing viewpoints, ideas, or presentation of characters. An anachronism is the placing of an object or person out of its time with the time of the text. The best known example is the clock in Shakespeare's *Julius Caesar*

26. **A sixth-grade science teacher has given her class a paper to read on the relationship between food and weight gain. The writing contains signal words such as "because," "consequently," "this is how," and "due to." This paper has which text structure?**
(Skill 7.1) (Rigorous)

A. Cause & effect

B. Compare & contrast

C. Description

D. Sequencing

Answer A: Cause & effect
Cause and effect is the relationship between two things when one thing makes something else happen. Writers use this text structure to show order, inform, speculate, and change behavior. This text structure uses the process of identifying potential causes of a problem or issue in an orderly way. It is often used to teach social studies and science concepts. It is characterized by signal words such as because, so, so that, if... then, consequently, thus, since, for, for this reason, as a result of, therefore, due to, this is how, nevertheless, and accordingly.

27. **Mr. Robinson's students are assigned to write one of the following:**
(Skill 7.1) (Average)

- **a recipe**
- **directions for how to play a game**
- **an interview with a college graduate**
- **a movie review**

By completing this assignment, his students are engaging in which type of writing?

A. Exposition.

B. Narration.

C. Persuasion.

D. Description.

Answer A: Exposition
Exposition sets forth a systematic explanation of any subject. It can also introduce the characters of a literary work and their situations in the story.

28. **The following passage is written from which point of view?**
    (Skill 7.3) (Rigorous)

    As she mused the pitiful vision of her mother's life laid its spell on the very quick of her being – that life of commonplace sacrifices closing in final craziness. She trembled as she heard again her mother's voice saying constantly with foolish insistence: Dearevaun Seraun! Dearevaun Seraun!* * "The end of pleasure is pain!" (Gaelic)

    A. First person, narrator

    B. Second person, direct address

    C. Third person, omniscient

    D. First person, omniscient

    Answer C: Third person, omniscient
    The passage is in the third person (the subject is "she"), and it is omniscient since it gives the characters' inner thoughts.

29. **Which of the following should not be included in the opening paragraph of an informative essay?**
    (Skill 7.8) (Average)

    A. Thesis sentence

    B. Details and examples supporting the main idea

    C. Broad general introduction to the topic

    D. A style and tone that grabs the reader's attention

    Answer B: Details and examples supporting the main idea
    The introductory paragraph should introduce the topic, capture the reader's interest, state the thesis and prepare the reader for the main points in the essay. Details and examples, however, should be given in the second part of the essay, so as to help develop the thesis presented at the end of the introductory paragraph, following the inverted triangle method consisting of a broad general statement followed by some information, and then the thesis at the end of the paragraph.

30. **Mr. Michaela's students are writing essays using the writing process. Which of the following is not a technique they will use to prewrite?**
(Skill 7.8) (Average)

   A. Clustering

   B. Listing

   C. Brainstorming

   D. Proofreading

   Answer D: Proofreading
   Proofreading should be reserved for the final draft.

31. **Which of the following is not an approach to keep students ever conscious of the need to write for audience appeal?**
(Skill 7.10 and 7.11) (Rigorous)

   A. Pairing students during the writing process

   B. Reading all rough drafts before the students write the final copies

   C. Having students compose stories or articles for publication in school literary magazines or newspaper

   D. Writing letters to friends or relatives

   Answer B: Reading all rough drafts before the students write the final copies
   Reading all rough drafts will not encourage the students to take control of their text and might even inhibit their creativity. On the contrary, pairing students will foster their sense of responsibility, and having them compose stories for literary magazines will boost their self-esteem as well as their organization skills. As far as writing letters is concerned, the work of authors such as Madame de Sevigne in the seventeenth century is a good example of epistolary literary work.

32. **What does the word "meandered" mean in the sentence below?**
     (Easy) (Skill 3.13)

     Michael was taking a long time to return to his seat after sharpening his pencil at the back of the room. After leaving the sharpener, he <u>meandered</u> around the room before eventually making his way back to his own seat.

     A. rolled

     B. roamed

     C. slithered

     D. stomped

     Answer: B. roamed
     The student *roamed* around the room before returning to his seat.

33. **When reading the book *Stormbreaker* by Anthony Horowitz, the reader feels like they are a part of the action. The author uses so many details to bring the reader into the setting of the story, and this puts the reader right beside Alex Rider, the main character in the story.**

     Is this a valid or invalid argument?
     (Average) (Skill 5.1)

     A. Valid

     B. Invalid

     Answer: A. Valid
     The argument is valid because there is support that backs up the argument that while reading *Stormbreaker*, the reader feels as if they are a part of the action.

34. **Let's go see the movie *Alice in Wonderland*. It's a great movie and Johnny Depp is awesome!**

    Is this a valid or invalid argument?
    (Average) (Skill 5.1)

    A. Valid

    B. Invalid

    Answer: B. Invalid
    The speaker does not offer any support for why they should go and see the movie *Alice in Wonderland* other than the fact that it's a great movie and Johnny Depp is awesome in it.

    DIRECTIONS: Read the following passage and answer the questions that follow.

    Mr. Smith gave instructions for the painting to be hung on the wall. And then it leaped forth before his eyes: the little cottages on the river, the white clouds floating over the valley, and the green of the towering mountain ranges that were seen in the distance. The painting was so vivid that it seemed almost real. Mr. Smith was now absolutely certain that the painting had been worth the money.

35. **Is this passage biased?**
    (Rigorous) (Skill 4.1)

    A. Yes

    B. No

    Answer: B. No
    The author appears to be simply relating what happened when Mr. Smith had his new painting hung on the wall.

36.   **From the last sentence, one can infer that:**
        (Rigorous) (Skill 4.5)

        A. The painting was expensive.

        B. The painting was cheap.

        C. Mr. Smith was considering purchasing the painting.

        D. Mr. Smith thought the painting was too expensive and decided not to purchase it.

        Answer: A. The painting was expensive
        The correct answer is A. Option B is incorrect because, had the painting been cheap, chances are that Mr. Smith would not have considered his purchase. Options C and D are ruled out by the fact that the painting had already been purchased, as is clear in the phrase "...the painting had been worth the money."

37.   **Boys are smarter than girls. Is this sentence fact or opinion?**
        (Easy) (Skill 11.3)

        A. Fact

        B. Opinion

        Answer: B. Opinion
        There isn't any scientific evidence to back up this idea.

38.   **Turkey burgers are better than beef burgers. Is this sentence fact or opinion?**
        (Easy) (Skill 4.13)

        A. Fact

        B. Opinion

        Answer: B. Opinion
        Those who believe that turkey burgers are better than beef burgers might think this statement is a fact. However, it is not able to be proven and can in fact be argued so therefore, it is an opinion.

39. **What conclusion can be drawn from the passage below?**
(Rigorous) (Skill 4.13)

When she walked into the room she gasped in disbelief as her hands rose to her face and her eyes bulged large. After she picked her jaw up off the floor, a huge smile spread across her face as her best friend came up and wrapped her arms around her and wished her a happy birthday.

A. The girl didn't know anyone in the room

B. The girl saw something shocking

C. The girl was being thrown a surprise party

D. The girl got punched in the face

Answer: C. The girl was being thrown a surprise party
The last sentence of the paragraph solidifies the idea that the girl is being thrown a surprise party for her birthday.

DIRECTIONS: Read the following passage and answer the questions that follow.

Deciding which animal to get as the family pet can be a very difficult decision, and there are many things to take into consideration. First, you must consider the size of your home and the area that will be dedicated to the pet. If your home is a smaller one, then you probably want to get a small dog or even a cat. If you are lucky enough to have larger home with plenty of room inside and out, then most certainly consider a large or even a more active breed of dog. One other thing to consider is how often and how long you are outside of the home. Cats do not need to be let out to relieve themselves. They are normally trained to use a litter box. On the other hand, dogs require being let out. Dogs also require more exercise than cats and often need to be walked. This can be aggravating to an owner especially on rainy days. Therefore, when deciding which pet is best for your family, it is necessary to consider more than whether or not you want a dog or a cat, but which animal will best fit into your family's lifestyle.

40. **How does the author feel about dogs?**
(Rigorous) (Skill 4.13)

A. The author likes dogs and cats the same

B. The author thinks that dogs are aggravating

C. The author believes they require more care than cats

D. The author feels that dogs are more active than cats

Answer: C. The author believes they require more care than cats
The author gives two examples of things dogs need more than cats. It is stated that dogs require being let out and that they require more exercise.

41. **What does the word "interject" mean in the sentence below?**
    (Easy) (Skill 3.7)

    Nancy was speaking with her best friend Sierra. Nancy's little sister was standing nearby and was eavesdropping on their conversation. Suddenly, she heard something that interested her and had to <u>interject</u> her opinion about the subject the girls were talking about.

    A. repeat

    B. pierce

    C. intersect

    D. state

    Answer: D. state
    By *interjecting* her opinion, Nancy's little sister had to "state" her opinion, or make her idea known.

42. **How does the author feel about the size of people's houses?**
    (Rigorous) (Skill 4.13)

    A. The author believes that people with larger homes are lucky

    B. The author thinks that if you have a small house you should have a cat

    C. The author feels that only people with large homes should own animals

    D. The author thinks that only those who own homes should own pets

    Answer: A. The author believes that people with larger homes are lucky
    Within the passage the author says, "If you are lucky enough to own a large house."

43. **From this passage, one can infer that:**
(Rigorous) (Skill 4.1)

A. The author owns a cat

B. More people own dogs than cats

C. Cats are smarter than dogs

D. The author owns a dog

Answer: D. The author owns a dog
One sentence in particular gives the reader the idea that the author owns a dog because she says, "This [walking the dog or letting it out] can be aggravating to an owner especially on rainy days."

44. **From this passage, one can infer that:**
(Rigorous) (Skill 4.1)

A. Either a dog or cat will be right for every family who wants a pet

B. Choosing a pet is not solely one family member's job

C. Only someone who enjoys exercising should get a dog

D. Big dogs will not survive in a small house

Answer: B. Choosing a pet is not solely one family member's job
The word "family" is used several times in the article, and therefore, the reader knows that choosing a pet is a family's responsibility—not just one member's.

45. **Johnny Depp stars in the movie *Charlie and the Chocolate Factory*. Is this sentence fact or opinion?**
(Easy) (Skill 4.13)

A. Fact

B. Opinion

Answer: A. Fact
It can be proven that Johnny Depp is the actor who stars in a leading role in *Charlie and the Chocolate Factory.*

DIRECTIONS: Read the following passage and answer the questions that follow.

According to Factmonster.com, the most popular Internet activity is sending and/or reading email. Approximately 92% of Internet users report using the Internet for this purpose. 89% of Internet users report that they use the Internet to search for information. Two popular search engines are Google and Yahoo! The introduction of the Internet has made it easy to gather and research information quickly. Other reasons that Internet users use the Internet is for social media, to search for driving directions, look into a hobby or interest, or research a product or service before buying, just to name a few. Creative <u>enterprises</u> such as remixing songs or lyrics stood at the bottom of reasons people use the Internet. Surprisingly, only 11% of Internet users said they use the Internet for creative purposes. Perhaps people are using specific software to be creative.

46. **What is the main idea of the passage?**
(Average) (Skill 4.1)

A. Factmonster has a lot of great facts for people to research

B. People use the Internet for a variety of reasons

C. The main reason the Internet is used is to check emails

D. People aren't as creative as they used to be before the Internet

Answer: B. People use the Internet for a variety of reasons
The passage lists the top reasons why people use the Internet. Therefore, the best choice is B.

47.   **Why did the author write this article?**
       (Average) (Skill 5.12)

       A. To convince the reader to use the Internet

       B. To teach the reader how use the Internet

       C. To encourage the reader to use the Internet

       D. To inform the reader about Internet usage trends

       Answer: D. To inform the reader about Internet usage trends

       The author wants to let the reader know what the Internet is mostly being used for. The statistics offered are synonymous of Internet usage trends.

48.   **How is the passage organized?**
       (Average) (Skill 5.12)

       A. Sequence of events

       B. Cause and effect

       C. Statement support

       D. Compare and contrast

       Answer: C. Statement support
       The passage makes a statement at the beginning and then supports it with details in the rest of the passage.

49. **What cause and effect relationship exists in this paragraph?**
   (Rigorous) (Skill 5.3)

   A. The U.S. postal service is suffering from the introduction of email

   B. Google and Yahoo! are used most often to search information

   C. The introduction of the Internet has made gathering information easy

   D. People are less creative since they aren't using their computers for this reason

   Answer: C. The introduction of the Internet has made gathering information easy
   Because the Internet was introduced, people are able to search for information easier than they used to be able to. This is a cause and effect relationship.

50. **By using the word "surprisingly" in the passage, what is the author implying?**
   (Rigorous) (Skill 3.7)

   A. It is thought that the Internet is used more for creative purposes

   B. People are thought to be more creative than they really are

   C. It is thought that fewer than 11% would use the Internet for creative purposes

   D. Software companies are making 11% more creative software

   Answer: A. It is thought that the Internet is used more for creative purposes
   By using the word "surprisingly," the author is saying that she is surprised that only 11% of Internet users use the Internet for creative purposes. The author would expect that number to be higher.

51. **Which transition word could the author have used to connect these two sentences?**
(Average) (Skill 3.7)

Approximately 92% of Internet users report using the Internet for this purpose. 89% of Internet users report that they use the Internet to search for information.

A. Additionally,

B. Therefore,

C. Next,

D. Similarly,

Answer: A. Additionally,
The author wants to add more information about Internet usage, so "additionally" is the best choice for a transition word.

52. **What does the word "enterprises" mean in the passage?**
(Average) (Skill 3.7)

A. people

B. endeavors

C. businesses

D. musicians

Answer: B. endeavors
The words "endeavors" and "enterprises" are synonymous, and either word could be used in the passage.

DIRECTIONS: Read the following passage and answer the questions that follow.

The poems both use personification to bring the subjects of the poem to life. Both poems were also very entertaining. In "The Subway" the author says that the subway, also known as a dragon, swallows up the people and then spits them out at the next stop. Similarly, in "Steam Shovel," the author says that the steam shovel chews up the dirt that it scoops up and smiles amiably at the people below.

    The subjects of the poems are compared to different things. The subway is compared to a dragon with green scales. Dragons breathe fire. The steam shovel is compared to an ancient dinosaur with a long neck and dripping jaws.

53.   **How is the passage organized?**
(Average) (Skill 5.18)

    A. Compare and contrast

    B. Cause and effect

    C. Sequence of events

    D. Statement support

Answer: A. Compare and contrast
This passage compares (gives similarities) and contrasts (shows differences) between two poems.

54.   **Which sentence in the passage is irrelevant?**
(Average) (Skill 7.3)

    A. Both poems were also very entertaining.

    B. The subway is also known as a dragon.

    C. The subway swallows people up and spits them out.

    D. The author says that the steam shovel chews up the dirt.

Answer: A. Both poems were also very entertaining.
Although this may be a similarity between the two poems, it is an opinion that is not necessary to include within the passage, since the focus of the first paragraph is personification.

55. **Each of the comparisons mentioned in the paragraph are known as a:**
(Easy) (Skill 7.3)

A. Metaphor

B. Hyperbole

C. Onomatopoeia

D. None of the above

Answer: A. Metaphor
Metaphors compare two or more things to one another. The examples listed above are considered metaphors.

DIRECTIONS: Read the following passage and answer the questions that follow.

Have you ever wondered what chewing gum is made from? What is it that allows us to chew it for hours without it ever disintegrating? Chicle is a gum, or sap, that comes from the sapodilla tree. The sapodilla tree is an American tropical evergreen that is native to South Florida. Flavorings, corn syrup, and sugar or artificial sweeteners are other ingredients that go into the production of chewing gum. Legend has it that Native Americans chewed spruce resin to quench their thirst. Today, gum is chewed for many reasons by many different groups of people.

56. **What conclusion can be drawn from the passage?**
(Rigorous) (Skill 4.8)

A. Everyone in South Florida has heard of the sapodilla tree

B. Many people have wondered what makes gum chewy

C. Some type of sweetener is used in gum production

D. Native Americans invented gum

Answer: C. Some type of sweetener is used in gum production
It is defined in the passage that sugar or artificial sweeteners are used in gum production.

57. **What can be inferred from the passage?**
(Rigorous) (Skill 4.8)

A. The gum Chiclets took its name from the ingredient chicle used in gum

B. Gum is disgusting after it's been chewed for a few hours

C. Gum is only made in the United States because that's where the sapodilla tree grows

D. When someone is thirsty they should chew gum

Answer: A. The gum Chiclets took its name from the ingredient chicle used in gum
It can be inferred from the passage that the brand of gum called Chiclets most likely took its name from the ingredient chicle, or sap, that is found in gum.

DIRECTIONS: Read the following passage and answer the questions that follow.

The word "cycle" comes from the Greek word *kyklos*, which means "circle" or "wheel." There are many different types of cycles. The word "unicycle" comes from the prefix *uni-*, which means "one," combined with the root "cycle." When the prefix and root word cycle are combined, it creates a word that means "one circle or wheel." Unicycles are often used for entertainment rather than exercise.

    A prefix *bi-* means "two," which, when combined with the word "cycle," creates the word "bicycle." How many wheels does a bicycle have? Many young children ride a tricycle because it has three wheels and is easy to ride. The prefix *tri-* means "three," and when it is combined with the root word "cycle," the new word is "three wheels." It is even possible to make the word "motorcycle." Once you know how to use <u>roots,</u> it is easy to figure out the meaning of an unknown word.

58.   **What is the main idea of the passage?**
        (Average) (Skill 4.13)

        A. There are many types of cycles

        B. The prefix *uni-* means one

        C. Words can be defined by their parts

        D. Unicycles are often used for entertainment

        Answer: C. Words can be defined by their parts
        Only Option C covers the whole passage and not just one small detail contained within it.

59. **What does the word "roots" mean?**
(Easy) (Skill 3.9)

A. Stable parts of plants

B. Where one originated

C. The base portions of a word

D. A spelling tool

Answer: C. The base portions of a word
"Roots" is a multiple-meaning word, but in the context of the passage, it means the base portions of a word.

60. **Which is an opinion contained in this passage?**
(Average) (Skill 4.13)

A. Once you know how to use roots, it is easy to figure out the meaning of an unknown word

B. Many young children ride a tricycle

C. Unicycles are often used for entertainment rather than exercise

D. The word "cycle" comes from the Greek word *kyklos*

Answer: A. Once you know how to use roots, it is easy to figure out the meaning of an unknown word
Options B and C could be opinions, but they both have clarifying words like "many" and "often," which makes them facts.

61. **From this article you can see that the author thinks:**
     (Rigorous) (Skill 4.13)

     A. Riding a bicycle is good exercise

     B. It is important to know about the English language

     C. "Cycle" is a confusing word

     D. It is more important to understand the prefixes and suffixes

Answer: B. It is important to know about the English language

The author wrote this passage to teach readers about the English language. Therefore, we know that the author thinks it is important to understand the English language.

DIRECTIONS: The passage below contains many errors. Read the passage. Then, answer each test item by choosing the option that corrects an error in the underlined portion(s). No more than one underlined error will appear in each item. If no error exists, choose "No change is necessary."

If you give me ten dollars, I'll give you fifty in return. Does this sound too good to be true? Well, anything that sounds too good to be true probably is. That stands true for herbal supplements. Herbal supplements are main targeted toward improving one type of ailment. There is no cure-all herbal supplement so don't believe what he tells you. Herbal supplement can fix more than one thing.

Herbal supplements is great and have a lot of positive things to offer its takers and have become very popular with consumers. Many doctors are even suggesting that they try natural herbal remedies before prescribing an over-the-counter medication. Herbal supplements have given consumers a new power to self-diagnose and consumers can head to the health food store and pick up an herbal supplement rather than heading to the doctor. Herbal supplements take a little long than prescribed medication to clear up any illnesses, but they are a more natural way to go, and some consumers prefer that form of medication.

62. **Herbal supplements are <u>main</u> targeted <u>toward</u> <u>improving</u> one type of ailment.**
     (Average) (Skill 5.6)

     A. mainly

     B. towards

     C. improve

     D. No change is necessary

     Answer: A. mainly
     Option B doesn't work because the correct form of the word is indeed "toward." The gerund "improving" is necessary in the sentence. Therefore, Option A, "mainly," is the correct adverb needed.

63. There is <u>no</u> cure-all herbal <u>supplement</u> so don't believe what <u>he tells you</u>.
     (Easy) (Skill 5.6)

     A. nothing

     B. supplemental

     C. you hear

     D. No change is necessary

     Answer: C. you hear
     As the sentence reads now, "he" is a pronoun that doesn't refer to anyone.
     Therefore, it shouldn't be used at all.

64. Many doctors <u>are</u> even suggesting that <u>they</u> try natural herbal remedies
     before <u>prescribing</u> an over-the-counter medication.
     (Rigorous) (Skill 5.6)

     A. is

     B. their patients

     C. prescribing,

     D. No change is necessary

     Answer: B. their patients
     The pronoun "they" is used incorrectly because it implies that the doctors should
     try natural herbal remedies. However, "they" is being used to take the place of
     their patients but has not been introduced prior to this point in the passage.

65. **Herbal supplements <u>is</u> great and have <u>a lot</u> of positive things to offer <u>its</u> takers and have become very popular with consumers.**
   (Easy) (Skill 5.6)

   A. are

   B. alot

   C. it's

   D. No change is necessary

   Answer: A. are
   The linking verb must agree with the word supplements which is plural. Therefore, the correct verb must be "are," not "is."

66. **Herbal supplements take a little <u>long</u> <u>than</u> <u>prescribed</u> medications to clear up any illnesses, but they are a more natural way to go, and some consumers prefer that form of medication.**
   (Average) (Skill 6.1)

   A. longer

   B. then

   C. perscribed

   D. No changes necessary

   Answer: A. longer
   The sentence is comparing two things—herbal supplements to prescribed medications. The comparative form of the adjective "long" needs to be used and should be "longer."

67. **Herbal <u>supplements</u> take a little long than prescribed <u>medication</u> to clear up any illnesses, but they are a <u>more natural</u> way to go, and some consumers prefer that form of medication.**
(Rigorous) (Skill 6.1)

   A. supplement

   B. medications

   C. more naturally

   D. No change necessary

Answer: B. medications
Since the sentence begins talking about herbal supplements—plural—the comparison, prescribe medications, must be the same and be a plural too.

68. **Herbal <u>supplement</u> can fix more <u>than</u> one <u>thing</u>.**
(Average) (Skill 6.1)

   A. supplements

   B. then

   C. things

   D. No change is necessary

Answer: A. supplements
The article talks about herbal supplements and therefore must agree at all times throughout the article. Option B is incorrect because then indicates that something happens next. "Than" is the correct word used in comparisons.

DIRECTIONS: The passage below contains many errors. Read the passage. Then, answer each test item by choosing the option that corrects an error in the underlined portion(s). No more than one underlined error will appear in each item. If no error exists, choose "No change is necessary."

Bingo has many purposes in the United States. It is used as a learning and entertainment tool for children. Bingo is used as an entertainment tool for parties and picnics to entertain a large number of people easily and quickly. Bingo is also a common game played among elderly and church groups because of its simplistic way of entertaining.

A typical bingo card has the word "bingo" printed across the top with columns of numbers inside boxes underneath. There is a "free" space located directly in the middle. There is usually one person who calls the numbers. For example, a ball or chip may be labeled "B12." Players then look under the "B" column for the number 12 and if it appears on their card, they place a marker on top of it. If there isn't a 12 under the letter "B" on a player's card, then they simply wait for the next number to be called.

69. **Players then look under the "B" column for the number 12 and if it appears on his card, they place a marker on top of it.**
   (Rigorous) (Skill 6.1)

   A. He

   B. their

   C. him

   D. No change is necessary.

   Answer: B. their
   The sentence begins with the plural word "player" and is followed by the plural word "they." Therefore, the possessive word "their" is needed rather than the singular word "he" or "him."

70. **Bingo is used as a learning and entertainment tool for children.**

    How should this sentence be rewritten?
    (Rigorous) (Skill 7.3)

    A. Bingo is used as a learning tool and entertainment for children.

    B. Bingo is used for learning and entertainment for children.

    C. Bingo is used to both teach and entertain children.

    D. No change is necessary

    Answer: C. Bingo is used to both teach and entertain children.
    The best answer is Option C because the correlative conjunction "both" is used, and there is a similar sentence structure on both sides of the word. In both options A and B, the words being compared do not have the same structure.

71. **In this step of the writing process, students examine their work and make changes in wording, details, and ideas.**
    (Easy) (Skill 7.3)

    A. Drafting

    B. Prewriting

    C. Revising and Editing

    D. Proofreading

    Answer: C. Revising and Editing
    Revision is probably the most important step in the writing process. In this step, students examine their work and make changes in wording, details, and ideas.

DIRECTIONS: Read the following passage and answer the questions.

It is a requirement that all parents volunteer two hours during the course of the season. Or an alternative was to pay $8 so you can have some high school students work a shift for you. Lots of parents liked this idea and will take advantage of the opportunity. Shifts run an hour long, and it is well worth it to pay the money so you don't miss your sons game.

72.   **It is a requirement that all parents volunteer two hours during the course of the season.**

        How should the above sentence be rewritten?
        (Average) (Skill 7.3)

        A. It is a requirement of all parents volunteering two hours during the course of the season.

        B. It is required of all parents to volunteer for two hours during the course of the season.

        C. They require all parents to volunteer during the season.

        D. Requiring all parents to volunteer for two hours of the season.

        Answer: B. It is required of all parents to volunteer for two hours during the course of the season.
        This is the only choice that works. Option C makes sense, but the pronoun "they" is not established and cannot be used in the first sentence of the paragraph.

73. An alternative <u>was</u> to pay $8 so you can have some <u>high school</u> students work a shift for you.

    Which of the following options corrects an error in one of the underlined portions above?
    (Average) (Skill 6.1)

    A. is

    B. High School

    C. High school

    D. No change is necessary.

    Answer: A. is
    The first sentence puts this passage in the present tense. Therefore, the verb tense must remain the same throughout the passage and "was" is a past tense verb.

74. **Many parents liked this idea and will take advantage of the opportunity.**

    How should the sentence be rewritten?
    (Rigorous) (Skill 7.3)

    A. Many parent's liked this idea and took advantage of the opportunity.

    B. Many parents like this idea and take advantage of the opportunity.

    C. Many parents like this idea and took advantage of the opportunity.

    D. Many parents did like this idea and take advantage of the opportunity.

    Answer: B. Many parents like this idea and take advantage of the opportunity.
    The verb tense between "like" and "take" must remain consistent in the sentence and consistent with the verb tense of the paragraph.

Answers with Rationales: Mathematics

75. Simplify: $\dfrac{2^{10}}{2^5} =$

(Average) (Skill 10.2)

A. 2^2

B. 2^5

C. 2^{50}

D. $2^{\frac{1}{2}}$

Answer: B. 2^5

The quotient rule of exponents states that $\dfrac{a^m}{a^n} = a^{(m-n)}$, so $\dfrac{2^{10}}{2^5} = 2^{(10-5)} = 2^5$.

76. Solve: $\left(\dfrac{^-4}{9}\right) + \left(\dfrac{^-7}{10}\right) =$

(Average) (Skill 11.1)

A. $\dfrac{23}{90}$

B. $\dfrac{^-23}{90}$

C. $\dfrac{103}{90}$

D. $\dfrac{^-103}{90}$

Answer: D. $\dfrac{^-103}{90}$

Find the LCD of $\dfrac{^-4}{9}$ and $\dfrac{^-7}{10}$. The LCD is 90. Writing the fractions in terms of

a common denominator, we get $\quad \dfrac{^-40}{90} + \dfrac{^-63}{90} = \dfrac{^-103}{90}$.

77. **Find an equivalent expression for 0.74.**
    (Easy) (Skill 11.1)

    A. $\dfrac{74}{100}$

    B. 7.4%

    C. $\dfrac{33}{50}$

    D. $\dfrac{74}{10}$

    Answer: A. $\dfrac{74}{100}$

    In the decimal number 0.74, the 4 is in the hundredths place. Therefore, the answer is $\dfrac{74}{100}$.

78. **Multiply:** $(5.6) \times (^{-}0.11) =$
    (Average) (Skill 11.1)

    A. $^{-}0.616$

    B. 0.616

    C. $^{-}6.110$

    D. 6.110

    Answer: A. $^{-}0.616$

    This is a straightforward multiplication problem. The answer is negative because a positive number times a negative number gives a negative number.

79. **Mrs. Kline's classroom store is having a sale. An item that sells for $3.75 is put on sale for $1.20. What is the percent of decrease?**
(Easy) (Skill 11.1)

A. 25%

B. 28%

C. 68%

D. 34%

Answer: C. 68%
Set up the equation $3.75(1 - x) = 1.20$, where $(1 - x)$ is the discount. We can eliminate the decimals by multiplying both sides of the equation by 100 to get $375(1 - x) = 120$. Then:

$$375(1 - x) = 120 \rightarrow 375 - 375x = 120 \rightarrow -375x = -255 \rightarrow x = 0.68 = 68\%$$

80. **Which of the following denotes an irrational number?**
(Easy) (Skill 11.5)

A. 4.2500000

B. $\sqrt{16}$

C. 0.25252525

D. $\Pi = 3.141592...$

Answer: D. $\Pi = 3.141592...$
An irrational number is neither terminating nor repeating. Rational numbers are either terminal or repeating. Only the value of pi is an irrational number.

81. **What is the greatest common factor of 16, 28, and 36?**
(Average) (Skill 12.1)

A. 2

B. 4

C. 8

D. 16

Answer: B. 4
The smallest number in this set is 16; its factors are 1, 2, 4, 8, and 16. 16 is the largest factor, but it does not divide evenly into 28 or 36. The factor 8 also does not divide evenly into 28 or 36. The factor 4 divides evenly into both 28 and 36; therefore, the correct answer is B.

82. **Compute the surface area of the prism.**
(Average) (Skill 12.2)

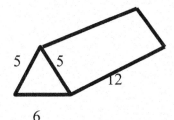

A. 204 units^2

B. 216 units^2

C. 360 units^2

D. 180 units^2

Answer: B. 216 units^2
There are five surfaces that make up the prism. The bottom rectangle has area 6 × 12 = 72. The sloping sides are both rectangles with an area of 5 × 12 = 60. Using the Pythagorean theorem, the height of the prism (and the triangular bases) is determined to be 4. Therefore, each triangle has area $(1/2)bh = (1/2)(6)(4) = 12$. Thus, the surface area is 72 + 60 + 60 + 12 + 12 = 216.

83. **What is the area of a square whose side is 13 feet?**
    (Easy) (Skill 12.2)

    A. 169 feet

    B. 169 square feet

    C. 52 feet

    D. 52 square feet

    Answer: B. 169 square feet
    Area = length times width
    Length = 13 feet
    Width = 13 feet (The figure is a square, so its length and width are the same.)
    Area = $13 \times 13 = 169$ square feet. (Area is measured in square units.)

84. The owner of a rectangular piece of land 40 yards in length and 30 yards in width wants to divide it into two parts. She plans to join two opposite corners with a fence as shown in the diagram below. The cost of the fencing is approximately $25 per linear foot. What is the estimated cost of the fence needed by the owner?
(Rigorous) (Skill 12.2)

30 yd   fence

40 yd

A. $1,250

B. $62,500

C. $5,250

D. $3,750

Answer: D. $3,750
Let x be the length of the diagonal. Use the Pythagorean theorem to find the length.

$$30^2 + 40^2 = x^2 \rightarrow 900 + 1600 = x^2$$
$$2500 = x^2 \rightarrow \sqrt{2500} = \sqrt{x^2}$$
$$x = 50 \text{ yards}$$

Convert to feet. $\dfrac{50 \text{ yards}}{x \text{ feet}} = \dfrac{1 \text{ yard}}{3 \text{ feet}} \rightarrow 150 \text{ feet}$

The fencing costs $25.00 per linear foot, so the total cost is (150 ft.) ($25/ft.) = $3,750.

85.	**Find the surface area of a box that is 3 feet wide, 5 feet tall, and 4 feet deep.** *(Average) (Skill 12.2)*

A. 47 square feet

B. 60 square feet

C. 94 square feet

D. 188 square feet

Answer: C. 94 square feet
Let's assume that the base of the rectangular solid (box) is 3 by 4, and the height is 5. Then the surface area of the top and bottom together is 2(12) = 24. The sum of the areas of the front and back is 15 + 15 = 30, while the sum of the areas of the sides is 20 + 20 = 40. The total surface area is therefore 24 + 30 + 40 = 94 square feet.

86.	**The trunk of a tree has a radius of 2.1 meters. What is its circumference?** *(Average) (Skill 12.2)*

A. 2.1π square meters

B. 4.2π meters

C. 2.1π meters

D. 4.2π square meters

Answer: B. 4.2^{π} meters
The circumference of a circle is given by $C = 2\pi r$, where r is the radius. The circumference is $(2)\pi(2.1) = 4.2\pi$ meters (not square meters because we are not measuring area).

87.   Sets *A*, *B*, *C*, and *U* are related as shown in the diagram.

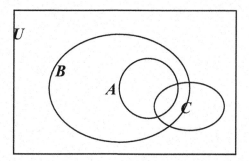

Which of the following statements is true, assuming none of the six regions is empty? *(Average) (Skill 13.1)*

A. Any element that is a member of set *B* is also a member of set *A*.

B. No element is a member of all three sets *A*, *B*, and *C*.

C. Any element that is a member of set *U* is also a member of set *B*.

D. None of the above statements is true.

Answer: D. None of the above statements is true.
Option A is incorrect because not all members of set *B* are also in set *A*. Option B is incorrect because there are elements that are members of all three sets *A*, *B*, and *C*. Option C is incorrect because not all members of set *U* are members of set *B*. This leaves Option D, which states that none of the options are true.

88. If $4x - (3 - x) = 7(x - 3) + 10$, then:
    (Rigorous) (Skill 13.4)

    A. $x = 8$

    B. $x = -8$

    C. $x = 4$

    D. $x = -4$

    Answer: C. $x = 4$
    Solve for x.
    $$4x - (3 - x) = 7(x - 3) + 10$$
    $$4x - 3 + x = 7x - 21 + 10$$
    $$5x - 3 = 7x - 11$$
    $$5x = 7x - 11 + 3$$
    $$5x - 7x = {}^- 8$$
    $${}^- 2x = {}^- 8$$
    $$x = 4$$

89. **It takes 5 equally skilled people 9 hours to shingle Mr. Joe's roof. Let *t* be the time required for only 3 of these workers to complete the same job. Select the correct mathematical representation of the given conditions.**
    (Rigorous) (Skill 14.2)

    A. $\dfrac{3}{5} = \dfrac{9}{t}$

    B. $\dfrac{9}{5} = \dfrac{3}{t}$

    C. $\dfrac{5}{9} = \dfrac{3}{t}$

    D. $\dfrac{14}{9} = \dfrac{t}{5}$

    Answer: C. $\dfrac{5}{9} = \dfrac{3}{t}$

    $$\dfrac{5 \text{ people}}{9 \text{ hours}} = \dfrac{3 \text{ people}}{t \text{ hours}}$$

90. **Find the equation of the line through (5, 6) and (-1, -2) in standard form.**
(Rigorous) (Skill 14.3)

A. $-4x + 3y = -2$

B. $-2y = \dfrac{4}{3}x - 1$

C. $6y + 5x - 1$

D. $y = 4x - 6$

Answer: A. $-4x + 3y = -2$

$$\text{slope} = \frac{y_2 - y_1}{x_2 - x_1} = \frac{-2 - 6}{-1 - 5} = \frac{-8}{-6} = \frac{4}{3}$$

$$y - y_a = m(x - x_a) \rightarrow y + 2 = \frac{4}{3}(x + 1) \rightarrow$$

$$y + 2 = \frac{4}{3}x + \frac{4}{3}$$

$$y = \frac{4}{3}x - \frac{2}{3} \qquad \text{This is the slope-intercept form}$$

Multiply by 3 to eliminate fractions and rearrange terms:

$$3y = 4x - 2$$

$$-4x + 3y = -2 \qquad \text{This is the standard form}$$

91. **Find the real roots of the equation** $3x^2 - 45 + 22x = 0$.
     (Rigorous) (Skill 15.1)

    A. $\dfrac{^-5}{3}$ and 9

    B. $\dfrac{5}{3}$ and $^-9$

    C. 5 and 9

    D. -5 and -9

Answer: B. $\dfrac{5}{3}$ **and** $^-9$

Factor the left-hand side of the equation:
$(3x - 5)(x + 9) = 0$

Set each part equal to 0 and solve for *x*.

$3x - 5 = 0$

$3x = 5$

$x = \dfrac{5}{3}$

$x + 9 = 0$

$x = ^-9$

92. **What is the 40th term in the sequence** $\{1, 4, 7, 10, \ldots\}$**?**
     (Rigorous) (Skill 16.1)

    A. 43

    B. 121

    C. 118

    D. 120

Answer: C. 118
The 40th term in the sequence is 118. The sequence adds 3 to each consecutive number and the 40th number is 118. There are four numbers displayed in the sequence and 36 numbers to go in the series to get to the 40th number in the sequence. 3 x 36 = 108 + 10 = 118.

93. **Which term most accurately describes two coplanar lines with no common points?**
(Average) (Skill 18.2)

A. Perpendicular

B. Parallel

C. Intersecting

D. Skew

Answer: B. Parallel
By definition, parallel lines are coplanar lines with no common points.

94. **Given similar polygons with corresponding sides measuring 6 inches and 8 inches, what is the area of the smaller polygon if the area of the larger is 64 in^2?**
(Rigorous) (Skill 19.2)

A. 48 in^2

B. 36 in^2

C. 144 in^2

D. 78 in^2

Answer: B. 36 in^2
For similar polygons, the areas are proportional to the squares of the sides. We can set up the proportion $6^2/8^2 = 36/64 = x/64$. Therefore, $x = 36$.

95. **Study the figures in Options A, B, C, and D. Select the option in which all triangles are similar.**
(Easy) (Skill 19.2)

A.

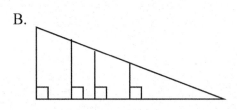

B.

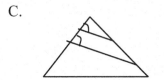

C.

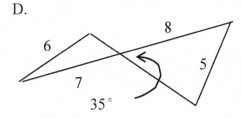

D.

Answer: B
Option A is not correct because one triangle is equilateral and the other is isosceles. Option C is not correct because the two smaller triangles are similar, but the large triangle is not similar to the smaller triangles. Option D is not correct because the lengths and angles are not proportional to each other. The correct answer is B because all the triangles in the figure have the same angles.

96.   **Find the midpoint of the line segment joining (2, 5) and (7, -4).**
        (Rigorous) (Skill 20.5)

        A. (9, -1)

        B. (5, 9)

        C. (9/2, -1/2)

        D. (9/2, 1/2)

        Answer: D. (9/2, 1/2)
        Using the midpoint formula. $x = (2 + 7)/2; y = (5 + (-4))/2$

97.   **The following chart shows the average annual number of international tourists visiting Palm Beach from 2010 to 2014. How many more international tourists visited Palm Beach in 2014 than in 2011?**
        (Average) (Skill 21.1)

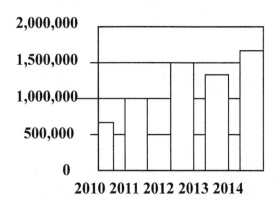

        A. 100,000

        B. 600,000

        C. 1,600,000

        D. 8,000,000

        Answer: B. 600,000
        The number of tourists in 2011 was 1,000,000, and the number in 2014 was 1,600,000. Subtract to get a difference of 600,000.

98. **What conclusion can be drawn from the graph below?**
(Average) (Skill 21.3)

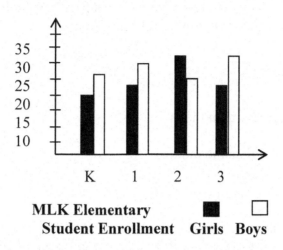

MLK Elementary
Student Enrollment   Girls   Boys

A. The number of students in first grade exceeds the number in second grade.

B. There are more boys than girls in the entire school.

C. There are more girls than boys in the first grade.

D. Third grade has the largest number of students.

Answer: B. There are more boys than girls in the entire school.
In kindergarten, first grade, and third grade, there are more boys than girls. The number of extra girls in grade 2 is more than made up for by the extra boys in all the other grades put together.

99. **Mary did comparison shopping on her favorite brand of coffee. Over half of the stores priced the coffee at $1.70. Most of the remaining stores priced the coffee at $1.80, except fora few who charged $1.90. Which of the following statements is true about the distribution of prices?**
(Rigorous) (Skill 21.4)

A. The mean and the mode are the same.

B. The mean is greater than the mode.

C. The mean is less than the mode.

D. The mean is less than the median.

Answer: B. The mean is greater than the mode.
Over half the stores priced the coffee at $1.70 per pound, which means that this price is the mode. The mean would be slightly over $1.70 because other stores priced the coffee at over $1.70 per pound.

100. **What is the mode of the data in the following sample?**
(Easy) (Skill 21.4)

$$9, 10, 11, 9, 10, 11, 9, 13$$

A. 9

B. 9.5

C. 10

D. 11

Answer: A. 9
The mode is the number that appears most frequently. The number 9 appears three times, which is more often than any of the other numbers.

101. **A coin is tossed and a die is rolled. What is the probability of the coin landing on "heads" and a 3 being rolled on the die?**
(Rigorous) (Skill 22.2)

A. $\dfrac{1}{2}$

B. $\dfrac{1}{6}$

C. $\dfrac{1}{12}$

D. $\dfrac{1}{15}$

Answer: C $\dfrac{1}{12}$

$P(\text{head}) = \dfrac{1}{2}; \quad P(3) = \dfrac{1}{6}$

$P(\text{head and } 3) = P(\text{head}) \times P(3)$
$$= \dfrac{1}{2} \times \dfrac{1}{6} = \dfrac{1}{12}$$

102.   **What is the probability of drawing two consecutive aces from a standard deck of 52 cards if the first card drawn is not replaced?**
(Rigorous) (Skill 22.2)

A. $\dfrac{3}{51}$

B. $\dfrac{1}{221}$

C. $\dfrac{2}{104}$

D. $\dfrac{2}{52}$

Answer: B $\dfrac{1}{221}$

There are four aces in the 52-card deck. $P(\text{ace on first draw}) = \dfrac{4}{52}$; $P(\text{ace on second draw given ace on first draw}) = \dfrac{3}{51}$.

$P(\text{two consecutive aces}) = P(\text{ace on first draw}) \times P(\text{ace on second draw given ace on first draw}) = \dfrac{4}{52} \times \dfrac{3}{51} = \dfrac{1}{221}$

103.   **Which of the following is correct?**
(Easy) (Skill 10.5)

A. $2{,}365 > 2{,}340$

B. $0.75 > 1.25$

C. $3/4 < 1/16$

D. $-5 < -6$

Answer: A. 2,365 > 2,340
2,365 is greater than 2,340. None of the other comparisons are correct.

104. **Simplify:**

$$\frac{5^{-2} \times 5^3}{5^5 \times 5^{-7}}$$

(Average) (Skill 10.4)

A. 5^5

B. 125

C. $\dfrac{1}{125}$

D. 25

Answer: B. 125

$$\frac{5^{-2} \times 5^3}{5^5 \times 5^{-7}} = \frac{5^{-2+3}}{5^{5-7}} = \frac{5}{5^{-2}} = 5^{1+2} = 5^3 = 125.$$

105. **Choose the set in which the members are *not* equivalent.**
(Average) (Skill 10.2)

A. 1/2, 0.5, 50%

B. 10/5, 2.0, 200%

C. 3/8, 0.385, 38.5%

D. 7/10, 0.7, 70%

Answer: C. 3/8, 0.385, 38.5%
3/8 is equivalent to .375 and 37.5%.

106. **The digit 8 in the number 975.086 is in the:**
     (Easy) (Skill 10.1)

     A. Tenths place

     B. Ones place

     C. Hundredths place

     D. Hundreds place

     Answer: C. Hundredths place
     The digit 8 is in the hundredths place; the digit 0 is in the tenths place.

107. **The relations given below demonstrate the following addition and multiplication property of real numbers: (Easy) (Skill 10.4)**

     $a + b = b + a$
     $ab = ba$

     A. Commutative

     B. Associative

     C. Identity

     D. Inverse

     Answer: A. Commutative
     Both addition and multiplication of real numbers satisfy the commutative property according to which changing the order of the operands does not change the result of the operation.

108. **$(3 \times 9)^4 =$**
(Rigorous) (Skill 10.2)

   A. $(3 \times 9)(3 \times 9)(27 \times 27)$

   B. $(3 \times 9) + (3 \times 9)$

   C. (12×36)

   D. $(3 \times 9) + (3 \times 9) + (3 \times 9) + (3 \times 9)$

   Answer: A. $(3 \times 9)(3 \times 9)(27 \times 27)$
   $(3 \times 9)^4 = (3 \times 9)(3 \times 9)(3 \times 9)(3 \times 9)$, which, when solving two of the parentheses, is $(3 \times 9)(3 \times 9)(27 \times 27)$.

109. **Jason can run a distance of 50 yards in 6.5 seconds. At this rate, how many feet can he run in a time of 26 seconds?**
(Average) (Skill 12.2)

   A. 200

   B. 400

   C. 600

   D. 800

   Answer: C. 600
   $26/6.5 = 4$, so Jason can run a distance of $(4)(50) = 200$ yards in 26 seconds. Since 1 yard is equivalent to 3 feet, 200 yards is equivalent to $(200)(3) = 600$ feet.

110. **Solve for x: $3(5 + 3x) - 8 = 88$**
(Average) (Skill 10.2)

   A. 30

   B. 9

   C. 4.5

   D. 27

   Answer: B. 9
   $3(5 + 3x) - 8 = 88$; $15 + 9x - 8 = 88$; $7 + 9x = 88$; $9x = 81$; $x = 9$.

111. **You are helping students list the steps needed to solve the word problem:**

"Mr. Jones is 5 times as old as his son. Two years later he will be 4 times as old as his son. How old is Mr. Jones?"

One of the students makes the following list:

Assume Mr. Jones' son is x years old. Express Mr. Jones' age in terms of *x*.
Write how old they will be two years later in terms of *x*.
Solve the equation for *x*.
Multiply the answer by 5 to get Mr. Jones' age.

What step is missing between steps 2 and 3?
(Rigorous) (Skill 10.2)

A. Write an equation setting Mr. Jones' age equal to 5 times his son's age

B. Write an equation setting Mr. Jones' age two years later equal to 5 times his son's age two years later

C. Write an equation setting Mr. Jones' age equal to 4 times his son's age

D. Write an equation setting Mr. Jones' age two years later equal to 4 times his son's age two years later

Answer: D. Write an equation setting Mr. Jones' age two years later equal to 4 times his son's age two years later
For step 2, we can represent Mr. Jones' age in two years as $5x + 2$ and his son's age in two years as $x + 2$. But before we can solve an equation for *x,* we need to state that Mr. Jones' age in two years will be 4 times his son's age in two years. This will show the relationship between father and son in two years. The actual equation becomes $5x + 2 = 4(x + 2)$, which will lead to x = 6 (the son's current age). Note that Mr. Jones' current age must be $(5)(6) = 30$. As a check, we observe that in two years the son will be 8 years old and Mr. Jones will be 32 years old.

112. **Which of the following points does *not* lie on the graph of**
$|y + 3| < |x - 3|$?
(Rigorous) (Skill 14.1)

A. (-5, 4)

B. (-6, 0)

C. (-3, -4)

D. (7, 7)

Answer: D. (7, 7)
By substitution, we get $|7 + 3| < |7 + 3|$ → $|10| < |4|$ → $10 < 4$, which is false. Thus, (7, 7) does not lie on the graph of $|y + 3| < |x - 3|$. Note that by substituting the three points listed in the other answer choices, the inequality is correct. For Option A, we get $|7| < |-8|$, which is true. For Option B, we get $|3| < |-9|$, which is true. For Option C, we get $|-1| < |-6|$, which is true.

113. **What is the next term in the following sequence?**
(Easy) (Skill 13.1)

{0.005, 0.03, 0.18, 1.08...}

A. 1.96

B. 2.16

C. 3.32

D. 6.48

Answer: D. 6.48
This is a geometric sequence where each term is obtained by multiplying the preceding term by the common ratio 6. Thus, the next term in the sequence is 1.08 x 6 = 6.48.

114. **A student has taken three tests in his algebra class for which the mean score is 88. He will take one more test and his final grade will be the mean of all four tests. He wants to achieve a final grade of 90. Which one of the following is the correct procedure to determine the score he needs on the fourth test?** *(Rigorous) (Skill 13.1)*

A. He needs a score 92 since $(88 + 92) / 2 = 90$.

B. He needs a score of 89.5 since $(88 + 90 + 90 + 90) / 4 = 89.5$.

C. He needs a score of 96 since $(88 + 88 + 88 + 96) / 4 = 90$.

D. He cannot achieve a final grade of 90 since each of his scores on the first three tests is less than 90.

Answer: C. He needs a score of 96 since $(88 + 88 + 88 + 96) / 4 = 90$.
The sum of all four tests must be $(90)(4) = 360$ in order to achieve a mean score of 90. Since he has averaged 88 on his first three tests, the sum of his scores thus far is $(88)(3) = 264$. Therefore he needs a score of $360 - 264 = 96$ on his fourth test.

115. **Which of the following shapes is *not* a parallelogram?**
     (Easy) (Skill 18.2)

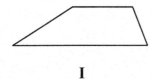  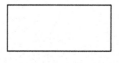

I   II   III

A. I and III

B. II and III

C. I only

D. I, II, and III

Answer: C. I only
A parallelogram is a quadrilateral with two pairs of parallel sides.

116. **Given similar polygons with corresponding sides of lengths 9 and 15, find the perimeter of the smaller polygon if the perimeter of the larger polygon is 150 units.**
     (Average) (Skill 18.2)

A. 54

B. 135

C. 90

D. 126

Answer: C. 90
The perimeters of similar polygons are directly proportional to the lengths of their sides, therefore $9/15 = x/150$. Cross-multiply to obtain $1350 = 15x$, then divide by 15 to obtain the perimeter of the smaller polygon.

Rationales with Sample Questions: Social Studies

117. **The belief that the United States should control all of North America was called:**
(Skill 29.1) (Easy)

A. Westward Expansion

B. Pan Americanism

C. Manifest Destiny

D. Nationalism

Answer: C. Manifest Destiny
The belief that the United States should control all of North America was called (C) Manifest Destiny. This idea fueled much of the violence and aggression towards those already occupying the lands such as the Native Americans. Manifest Destiny was certainly driven by sentiments of (D) nationalism, and gave rise to (A) westward expansion.

118. **The area of the United States was effectively double through purchase of the Louisiana Territory under which President?**
(Skill 29.1) (Average)

A. John Adams

B. Thomas Jefferson

C. James Madison

D. James Monroe

Answer: B. Thomas Jefferson
The Louisiana Purchase, an acquisition of territory from France in 1803, occurred during the presidency of Thomas Jefferson. (A) John Adams (1735-1826) was president from 1797–1801, before the purchase. (C) James Madison (1751-1836) after the purchase (1809-1817). (D) James Monroe (1758-1831) was actually a signatory on the Purchase, but did not become President until 1817.

119. **A major quarrel between colonial Americans and the British concerned a series of British Acts of Parliament dealing with:**
(Skill 29.1) (Easy)

A. Taxes

B. Slavery

C. Native Americans

D. Shipbuilding

Answer: A. Taxes
Acts of Parliament imposing taxes on the colonists always provoked resentment. Because the colonies had no direct representation in Parliament, they felt it unjust that that body should impose taxes on them, with so little knowledge of their very different situation in America and no real concern for the consequences of such taxes. (B) While slavery continued to exist in the colonies long after it had been completely abolished in Britain, it never was a source of serious debate between Britain and the colonies. By the time Britain outlawed slavery in its colonies in 1833, the American Revolution had already occurred and the United States was free of British control. (C) There was no series of British Acts of Parliament passed concerning Native Americans. (D) Colonial shipbuilding was an industry, which received little interference from the British.

120. **The international organization established to work for world peace at the end of the Second World War is the:**
(Skill 29.1) (Average)

A. League of Nations

B. United Federation of Nations

C. United Nations

D. United World League

Answer: C. United Nations
The international organization established to work for world peace at the end of the Second World War was the United Nations. From the ashes of the failed League of Nations, established following World War I, the United Nations continues to be a major player in world affairs today.

121. **Which famous battle fought on Texas soil resulted in Texas independence from Mexico?**
(Skill 29.2) (Rigorous)

A. The Battle of the Alamo

B. The Battle of San Jacinto

C. The Battle of the Rio Grande

D. The Battle of Shiloh

Answer: B. The Battle of San Jacinto
It was the battle of San Jacinto in which Sam Houston and the Texicans defeated the Mexican army and captured Mexican General and Commander Santa Anna. The result was the independence of the Republic of Texas from Mexican control. (B) The Battle of the Alamo, despite the defeat of the Texans by Santa Anna's troops was a critical event which enabled Houston to gather troops and prepare for the Battle of San Jacinto. (D) The Battle of Shiloh occurred during the Civil War, and it was not in Texas. (C) There was no major battle called the Battle of the Rio Grande.

122. **Why is the system of government in the United States referred to as a federal system?**
(Skill 29.11) (Rigorous)

A. There are different levels of government

B. There is one central authority in which all governmental power is vested

C. The national government cannot operate except with the consent of the governed

D. Elections are held at stated periodic times, rather than as called by the head of the government

Answer: A. There are different levels of government.
The United States is composed of fifty states, each responsible for its own affairs, but united under a federal government. (B) A centralized system is the opposite of a federal system. (C) That national government cannot operate except with the consent of the governed is a founding principle of American politics. It is not a political system like federalism. A centralized democracy could still be consensual, but would not be federal. (D) This is a description of electoral procedure, not a political system like federalism.

123. **The U.S. Constitution, adopted in 1789, provided for:**
(Skill 29.11) (Rigorous)

A. Direct election of the President by all citizens

B. Direct election of the President by citizens meeting a standard of wealth

C. Indirect election of the President by electors

D. Indirect election of the President by the U.S. Senate

Answer: C. Indirect election of the President by electors
The United States Constitution has always arranged for the indirect election of the President by electors. The question, by mentioning the original date of adoption, might mislead someone to choose B, but while standards of citizenship have been changed by amendment, the President has never been directly elected. Nor does the Senate have anything to do with presidential elections. The House of Representatives, not the Senate, settles cases where neither candidate wins in the Electoral College.

124. **From about 1870 to 1900 the settlement of America's "last frontier," the West, was completed. One attraction for settlers was free land, but it would have been to no avail without:**
(Skill 29.10) (Rigorous)

A. Better farming methods and technology

B. Surveying to set boundaries

C. Immigrants and others to seek new land

D. The railroad to get them there

Answer: D. The railroad to get them there
From about 1870 to 1900, the settlement of America's "last frontier" in the West was made possible by the building of the railroad. Without the railroad, the settlers never could have traveled such distances in an efficient manner.

125. **Slavery arose in the Southern Colonies partly as a perceived economical way to:**
(Skill 29.13) (Average)

A. Increase the owner's wealth through human beings used as a source of exchange

B. Cultivate large plantations of cotton, tobacco, rice, indigo, and other crops

C. Provide Africans with humanitarian aid, such as health care, Christianity, and literacy

D. Keep ships' holds full of cargo on two out of three legs of the "triangular trade" voyage.

Answer: B. Cultivate large plantations of cotton, tobacco, rice, indigo, and other crops.
The Southern states, with their smaller populations, were heavily dependent on slave labor as a means of being able to fulfill their role and remain competitive in the greater U.S. economy. (A) When slaves arrived in the South, the vast majority would become permanent fixtures on plantations, intended for work, not as a source of exchange. (C) While some slave owners instructed their slaves in Christianity, provided health care or some level of educations, such attention were not their primary reasons for owning slaves – a cheap and ready labor force was their reason. (D) Whether or not ships' holds were full on two or three legs of the triangular journey was not the concern of Southerners as the final purchasers of slaves. Such details would have concerned the slave traders.

126. **The post-Civil War years were a time of low public morality, a time of greed, graft, and dishonesty. Which one of the reasons listed would not be accurate?** *(Skill 29.15) (Rigorous)*

A. The war itself, because of the money and materials needed to conduct the War

B. The very rapid growth of industry and big business after the War

C. The personal example set by President Grant

D. Unscrupulous heads of large impersonal corporations

Answer: C. The personal example set by President Grant
The post-Civil War years were a particularly difficult time for the nation, and public morale was especially low. The war had plunged the country into debt, and ultimately into a recession by the 1890s. Racism was rampant throughout the South and the North, where freed Blacks were taking jobs for low wages. The rapid growth of industry and big business caused a polarization of rich and poor, workers and owners. Many people moved into the urban centers to find work in the new industrial sector. These jobs typically paid low wages, required long hours, and offered poor working conditions. The heads of large impersonal corporations treated their workers inhumanely, letting morale drop to a record low. The heads of corporations tried to prevent and disband labor unions.

127. **A number of women worked hard in the first half of the 19th century for women's rights, but decisive gains did not come until after 1850. The earliest accomplishments were in:**
(Skill 29.16) (Average)

A. Medicine

B. Education

C. Writing

D. Temperance

Answer: B. Education
Although women worked hard in the early nineteenth century to make gains in medicine, writing, and temperance movements, the most prestigious accomplishments of the early women's movement were in the field of education. Women such as May Wollstonecraft (1759-1797), Alice Palmer (1855-1902), and, of course, Elizabeth Blackwell (1821-1910) led the way for women, particularly in the area of higher education.

128. **Of all the major causes of both World Wars I and II, the most significant one is considered to be:**
(Skill 29.19) (Average)

A. Extreme nationalism

B. Military buildup and aggression

C. Political unrest

D. Agreements and alliances

Answer: A. Extreme nationalism
Although military buildup and aggression, political unrest, and agreements and alliances were all characteristic of the world climate before and during World War I and World War II, the most significant cause of both wars was extreme nationalism. Nationalism is the idea that the interests and needs of a particular nation are of the utmost and primary importance above all else. Some nationalist movements could be liberation movements while others were oppressive regimes, much depends on their degree of nationalism. The nationalism that sparked WWI included a rejection of German, Austro-Hungarian, and Ottoman imperialism by Serbs, Slavs and others culminating in the assassination of Archduke Ferdinand by a Serb nationalist in 1914. Following WWI and the Treaty of Versailles, many Germans and others in the Central Alliance Nations, malcontent at the concessions and reparations of the treaty started a new form of nationalism. Adolf Hitler and the Nazi regime led this extreme nationalism. Hitler's ideas were an example of extreme, oppressive nationalism combined with political, social and economic scapegoating and was the primary cause of WWII.

129. **Meridians, or lines of longitude, not only help in pinpointing locations but are also used for:**
(Skill 30.1) (Rigorous)

A. Measuring distance from the Poles

B. Determining direction of ocean currents

C. Determining the time around the world

D. Measuring distance on the equator

Answer: C. Determining the time around the world
Meridians, or lines of longitude, are the determining factor in separating time zones and determining time around the world.

130. **The study of the ways in which different societies around the world deal with the problems of limited resources and unlimited needs and wants is in the area of:**
(Skill 31.2) (Average)

A. Economics

B. Sociology

C. Anthropology

D. Political Science

Answer: A. Economics
The study of the ways in which different societies around the world deal with the problems of limited resources and unlimited needs and wants is a study of Economics. Economists consider the law of supply and demand as fundamental to the study of the economy. However, Sociology and Political Science also consider the study of economics and its importance in understanding social and political systems.

131. **Capitalism and communism are alike in that they are both:**
(Skill 31.3) (Easy)

A. Organic systems

B. Political systems

C. Centrally planned systems

D. Economic systems

Answer: D. Economic systems
While economic and (B) political systems are often closely connected, capitalism and communism are primarily (D) economic systems. Capitalism is a system of economics that allows the open market to determine the relative value of goods and services. Communism is an economic system where the market is planned by a central state. While communism is a (C) centrally planned system, this is not true of capitalism. (A) Organic systems are studied in biology, a natural science.

132. **The purchase of goods or services on one market for immediate resale on another market is:**
(Skill 31.3) (Average)

A. Output

B. Enterprise

C. Arbitrage

D. Mercantile

Answer: C. Arbitrage
Output is an amount produced or manufactured by an industry. Enterprise is simply any business organization. Mercantile is one of the first systems of economics in which goods were exchanged. Therefore, arbitrage is an item or service that an industry produces. The dictionary definition of arbitrage is the purchase of securities on one market for immediate resale on another market in order to profit from a price discrepancy.

133. **The economic system promoting individual ownership of land, capital, and businesses with minimal governmental regulations is called:**
(Skill 31.3) (Easy)

A. Macro-economy

B. Micro-economy

C. Laissez-faire

D. Free enterprise

Answer: D. Free enterprise
(D) Free enterprise or capitalism is the economic system that promotes private ownership of land, capital, and business with minimal government interference. (C) Laissez-faire is the idea that an "invisible hand" will guide the free enterprise system to the maximum potential efficiency.

134. **The American Labor Union movement started gaining new momentum:**
(Skill 31.5) (Rigorous)

A. During the building of the railroads

B. After 1865 with the growth of cities

C. With the rise of industrial giants such as Carnegie and Vanderbilt

D. During the war years of 1861-1865

Answer: B. After 1865 with the growth of cities
The American Labor Union movement had been around since the late 18th and early 19th centuries. The Labor movement began to first experience persecution by employers in the early 1800s. The American Labor Movement remained relatively ineffective until after the Civil War. In 1866, the National Labor Union was formed, pushing such issues as the eight-hour workday and new policies of immigration. This gave rise to the Knights of Labor and eventually the American Federation of Labor (AFL) in the 1890s and the Industrial Workers of the World (1905). Therefore, it was the period following the Civil War that empowered the labor movement in terms of numbers, militancy, and effectiveness.

135. **It can be reasonably stated that the change in the United States from primarily an agricultural country into an industrial power was due to all of the following except:**
(Skill 31.13) (Average)

A. Tariffs on foreign imports

B. Millions of hardworking immigrants

C. An increase in technological developments

D. The change from steam to electricity for powering industrial machinery

Answer: A. Tariffs on foreign imports
It can be reasonably stated that the change in the United States from primarily an agricultural country into an industrial power was due to a great degree of three of the reasons listed above. It was a combination of millions of hard-working immigrants, an increase in technological developments, and the change from steam to electricity for powering industrial machinery. The only reason given that really had little effect was the tariffs on foreign imports.

136. **There is no doubt that there was a vast improvement of the US Constitution over the Articles of Confederation. Which one of the four accurate statements below is a unique yet eloquent description of the document?**
(Skill 32.4) (Rigorous)

   A. The establishment of a strong central government in no way lessened or weakened the individual states.

   B. Individual rights were protected and secured.

   C. The Constitution is the best representation of the results of the American genius for compromise.

   D. Its flexibility and adaptation to change gives it a sense of timelessness.

   Answer: C. The Constitution is the best representation of the results of the American genius for compromise.
   The U.S. Constitution was indeed a vast improvement over the Articles of Confederation and the authors of the document took great care to assure longevity. It clearly stated that the establishment of a strong central government in no way lessened or weakened the individual states. In the Bill of Rights, citizens were assured that individual rights were protected and secured. Possibly the most important feature of the new Constitution was its flexibility and adaptation to change which assured longevity.

137. **"Marbury vs. Madison (1803)" was an important Supreme Court case which set the precedent for:**
(Skill 32.9) (Rigorous)

   A. The elastic clause

   B. Judicial review

   C. The supreme law of the land

   D. Popular sovereignty in the Territories

   Answer: B. Judicial review
   Marbury vs. Madison (1803) was an important case for the Supreme Court as it established judicial review. In that case, the Supreme Court set precedence to declare laws passed by Congress as unconstitutional. Popular sovereignty in the territories was a failed plan pushed by Stephen Davis to allow states to decide the slavery question for themselves. In his attempt to appeal to the masses in the pre-Civil War elections. The supreme law of the land is just that, the law that rules. The elastic clause is not a real term.

138. **Which one of the following is not a function or responsibility of the US political parties?**
(Skill 32.10) (Rigorous)

A. Conducting elections or the voting process

B. Obtaining funds needed for election campaigns

C. Choosing candidates to run for public office

D. Making voters aware of issues and other public affairs information

Answer: A. Conducting elections or the voting process
The US political parties have numerous functions and responsibilities. Among them are obtaining funds needed for election campaigns, choosing the candidates to run for office, and making voters aware of the issues. The political parties, however, do not conduct elections or the voting process, as that would be an obvious conflict of interest.

139. **Which of the following lists elements usually considered to be responsibilities of citizenship under the American system of government?**
(Skill 32.14) (Easy)

A. Serving in public office, voluntary government service, military duty

B. Paying taxes, jury duty, upholding the Constitution

C. Maintaining a job, giving to charity, turning in fugitives

D. Quartering of soldiers, bearing arms, government service

Answer: B. Paying taxes, jury duty, upholding the Constitution
Only paying taxes, jury duty and upholding the Constitution are responsibilities of citizens as a result of rights and commitments outlined in the Constitution; for example, the right of citizens to a jury trial in the Sixth and Seventh Amendments and the right of the federal government to collect taxes in Article 1, Section 8. (A) Serving in public office, voluntary government service and military duty, (C) maintaining a job, giving to charity and turning in fugitives are all considered purely voluntary actions, even when officially recognized and compensated. The United States has none of the compulsory military or civil service requirements of many other countries. (D) The quartering of soldiers is an act which, according to Amendment III of the Bill of Rights, requires a citizen's consent. Bearing arms is a right guaranteed under Amendment II of the Bill of Rights.

140. **In which of the following disciplines would the study of physical mapping, modern or ancient, and the plotting of points and boundaries be least useful?**
(Skill 34.1) (Average)

A. Sociology

B. Geography

C. Archaeology

D. History

Answer: A. Sociology
In geography, archaeology, and history, the study of maps and plotting of points and boundaries is very important as all three of these disciplines hold value in understanding the spatial relations and regional characteristics of people and places. Sociology, however, mostly focuses on the social interactions of people and while location is important, the physical location is not as important as the social location such as the differences between studying people in groups or as individuals.

141. **The study of the exercise of power and political behavior in human society today would be conducted by experts in:**
(Skill 34.2) (Average)

A. History

B. Sociology

C. Political Science

D. Anthropology

Answer: C. Political Science
Experts in the field of political science today would likely conduct the study of exercise of power and political behavior in human society. However, it is also reasonable to suggest that such studies would be important to historians (study of the past, often in an effort to understand the present), sociologists (often concerned with power structure in the social and political worlds), and even some anthropologists (study of culture and their behaviors).

142. **This writer and scientist was a delegate to the Continental Congress and a signer of the Declaration of Independence.**
(Average) (Skill 29.9)

A. George Washington

B. Benjamin Franklin

C. Orville Wright

D. Thomas Jefferson

Answer: B. Benjamin Franklin
Benjamin Franklin (1706-1790) was a writer, scientist, delegate to the Continental Congress and a signer of the Declaration of Independence.

143. **This high rugged mountain chain stretches from Alaska into Mexico.**
(Average) (Skill 30.1)

A. Rocky Mountains

B. The Pocono Mountains

C. Yosemite National Mountains

D. Coast Ranges

Answer: A. Rocky Mountains
This chain of mountains stretches from Alaska into Mexico.

144. **Land made from soil left behind in a river as it drains into a larger body of water is known as this:** *(Average) (Skill 30.1)*

   A. plain

   B. dam

   C. tributary

   D. delta

   Answer: D. delta
   A delta is and made from soil left behind in a river as it drains into a larger body of water

145. **Part of an ocean or a lake that extends into land is known as this:** *(Average) (Skill 30.3)*

   A. bay

   B. harbor

   C. tributary

   D. oasis

   Answer: A. bay
   A bay is part of an ocean or a lake that extends into land.

146. **This continent is located in the Southern hemisphere:** *(Easy) (Skill 30.1)*

   A. North America

   B. Europe

   C. Asia

   D. Antarctica

   Answer: D. Antarctica
   Antarctica is located in the Southern hemisphere of the Earth.

147. **The United States has which type of economy?** *(Average) (Skill 31.2)*

A. A market economy

B. A centrally planned economy

C. A market socialist economy

D. None of the above

Answer: A. A market economy
A market economy is one that is dependent on forces in the marketplace to determine what goods are manufactured and how they are distributed.

148. **Which of the following is a primary source document?**
(Average) (Skill 35.9)

A. A book recounting the events surrounding the 1932 kidnapping of aviator Charles Lindbergh's son

B. A newspaper story about the Wall Street crash of 1987

C. The text of Franklin D. Roosevelt's address to Congress of December 8, 1941, requesting a declaration of war against Japan

D. A movie dramatizing the life of a fictional family living in Poland during the German invasion of 1939

Answer: C. The text of Franklin D. Roosevelt's address to Congress of December 8, 1941, requesting a declaration of war against Japan
A book or a newspaper story describing a historical event are secondary sources. A movie can only be a primary source if it presents primary source materials—such as a documentary that presents archival photographs and interviews with actual survivors of a historical event.

149. **Which of the following is an example of a historical concept?**
(Rigorous) (Skill 29.1)

   A. Capitalism

   B. Racism

   C. Globalization

   D. All of the above

   Answer: D. All of the above
   Historical concepts are movements, belief systems, or other phenomena that can be identified and examined individually or as part of a historical theme. Capitalism, communism, democracy, racism, and globalization are all examples of historical concepts. Historical concepts can be interpreted as part of larger historical themes and provide insight into historical events by placing them in a larger historical context.

150. **What are two factors that can generate and affect landforms?**
(Average) (Skill 30.5)

   A. Observing a plateau at various scales

   B. Erosion and deposition

   C. The presence of oceans, lakes, seas, and canals

   D. The dry nature of some plateaus

   Answer: B. Erosion and deposition
   Observing plateaus at various scales, the presence of bodies of water, and the dry nature of some plateaus are important to geography, but are not considered to be factors that generate and affect landforms.

151. **Denver is called the "mile-high city" because it is:**
(Average) (Skill 30.1)

A. Located approximately one mile above the plains of eastern Colorado

B. Located exactly one mile above the base of Cheyenne Mountain

C. Located approximately one mile above sea level

D. The city with the tallest buildings in Colorado

Answer: C. Located approximately one mile above sea level
Elevations of cities are calculated according to their height above sea level. That fact negates all answers except C.

152. **_____ is the southernmost continent in the world.**
(Easy) (Skill 30.1)

A. Australia

B. New Zealand

C. The Arctic

D. Antarctica

Answer: D. Antarctica
Antarctica is the southernmost continent. It surrounds the South Pole. Australia is a continent in the southern hemisphere but it lies north of Antarctica. New Zealand is made up of two large islands but it is not a continent. The Arctic is a region that includes parts of several continents but it is not in and of itself a continent. In fact, much of the Arctic is ice-covered ocean.

153. **Human bones found during construction near an American Civil War battlefield would most likely be delivered to which of the following for study? (Average) (Skill 33.9)**

A. The Department of Veterans Affairs

B. A state medical examiner

C. A homicide detective

D. An anthropologist

Answer: D. An anthropologist
Anthropologists study bones that are found during construction excavations. The Department of Veterans Affairs might be the final recipient of Civil War bones, but the bones would initially go to an anthropologist for identification. A medical examiner and a homicide detective would not be interested because Civil War dead are not murder victims.

154. **States that are near the Rocky Mountains, such as Montana, have exceptional trout fishing because of which of the following: (Average) (Skill 30.5)**

A. Lakes in mountain regions have warm water that trout enjoy

B. Mountain regions are the only places that have large numbers of the aquatic insects trout like to eat

C. There are fewer people in these areas, so the fishing pressure is light

D. Trout thrive in the cold, clean rivers found in mountainous regions

Answer: D. Trout thrive in the cold, clean rivers found in mountainous regions
Trout cannot live in warm water. Aquatic insects eaten by trout are found in rivers all over the United States, not only in mountain regions. It is true that some mountain regions have low human populations, but the cold, clean water originating in mountain snowmelt is the best environment for trout.

155. **Our present-day alphabet comes from which of the following:**
(Average) (Skill 33.1)

A. Cuneiform

B. The Greek alphabet

C. Hieroglyphic writing

D. Hebrew Scriptures

Answer: B. The Greek alphabet
Cuneiform was introduced by the Sumerians. Hieroglyphics were created by the Egyptians. Hebrew Scriptures were introduced by the Hebrew people.

156. **The Cold War involved which two countries that both emerged as world powers?**
(Rigorous) (Skill 29.2)

A. China and Japan

B. The United States and the Soviet Union

C. England and Brazil

D. Afghanistan and the United States

Answer: B. The United States and the Soviet Union
After World War II, the United States and the Soviet Union constantly competed in space exploration and the race to develop nuclear weapons.

157. **Cultural diffusion is:**
(Rigorous) (Skill 29.4)

A. The process that individuals and societies go through in changing their behavior and organization to cope with social, economic, and environmental pressures

B. The complete disappearance of a culture

C. The exchange or adoption of cultural features when two cultures come into regular direct contact

D. The movement of cultural ideas or materials between populations independent of the movement of those populations

Answer: D. The movement of cultural ideas or materials between populations independent of the movement of those populations
By definition, cultural diffusion is the movement of cultural ideas or materials between populations independent of the movement of those populations.

158. **The Great Plains in the United States are an excellent place to grow corn and wheat for all of the following reasons EXCEPT:**
(Average) (Skill 30.10)

A. Rainfall is abundant and the soil is rich

B. The land is mostly flat and easy to cultivate

C. The human population is modest in size, so there is plenty of space for large farms

D. The climate is semitropical

Answer: D. The climate is semitropical
The climate on the Great Plains is not semitropical. It is temperate, with harsh winters. Rainfall and soil conditions are good. The land is fl at. The human population is not overcrowded; there is room for large farms.

Rationales with Sample Questions: Science

159. **When teaching Science rules pertaining to safety, Mrs. Miller explains to her students that chemicals should be stored**
    (Easy) (Skill 36.2)

    A. in the principal's office.

    B. in a dark room.

    C. in an off-site research facility.

    D. according to their reactivity with other substances.

    Answer: D. According to their reactivity with other substances.
    Chemicals should be stored with other chemicals of similar properties (e.g. acids with other acids), to reduce the potential for either hazardous reactions in the store-room, or mistakes in reagent use. Certainly, chemicals should not be stored in anyone's office, and the light intensity of the room is not very important because light-sensitive chemicals are usually stored in dark containers. In fact, good lighting is desirable in a store-room, so that labels can be read easily. Chemicals may be stored off-site, but that makes their use inconvenient. Therefore, the best answer is (D).

160. **Mr. Michalak's lab groups are measuring a liquid using graduated cylinders. Before expecting the students to accurately measure, he must teach them to read each measurement in the floowing way:**
    (Average Rigor) (Skill 37.2)

    A. At the highest point of the liquid.

    B. At the bottom of the meniscus curve.

    C. At the closest mark to the top of the liquid

    D. At the top of the plastic safety ring.

    Answer: B. At the bottom of the meniscus curve.
    To measure water in glass, you must look at the top surface at eye-level, and ascertain the location of the bottom of the meniscus (the curved surface at the top of the water). The meniscus forms because water molecules adhere to the sides of the glass, which is a slightly stronger force than their cohesion to each other. This leads to a U-shaped top of the liquid column, the bottom of which gives the most accurate volume measurement. (Other liquids have different forces, e.g. mercury in glass, which has a convex meniscus.) This is consistent only with answer (B).

161. **When is a hypothesis formed?**
(Easy) (Skill 38.2)

A. Before the data is taken.

B. After the data is taken.

C. After the data is analyzed.

D. Concurrent with graphing the data.

Answer: A. Before the data is taken.
A hypothesis is an educated guess, made before undertaking an experiment. The hypothesis is then evaluated based on the observed data. Therefore, the hypothesis must be formed before the data is taken, not during or after the experiment. This is consistent only with answer (A).

162. **Which of the following is the most accurate definition of a non-renewable resource?**
(Average Rigor) (Skill 39.5)

A. A nonrenewable resource is never replaced once used.

B. A nonrenewable resource is replaced on a timescale that is very long relative to human life-spans.

C. A nonrenewable resource is a resource that can only be manufactured by humans.

D. A nonrenewable resource is a species that has already become extinct.

Answer: B. A nonrenewable resource is replaced on a timescale that is very long relative to human life-spans.
Renewable resources are those that are renewed, or replaced, in time for humans to use more of them. Examples include fast-growing plants, animals, or oxygen gas. (Note that while sunlight is often considered a renewable resource, it is actually a nonrenewable but extremely abundant resource.) Nonrenewable resources are those that renew themselves only on very long timescales, usually geologic timescales. Examples include minerals, metals, or fossil fuels. Therefore, the correct answer is (B).

163. **A middle school science class is reviewing an experiment in which a scientist exposes mice to cigarette smoke, and notes that their lungs develop tumors. Mice that were not exposed to the smoke do not develop as many tumors. Which of the following conclusions may be drawn from these results?** *(Rigorous) (Skill 40.2)*

I. Cigarette smoke causes lung tumors.
II. Cigarette smoke exposure has a positive correlation with lung tumors in mice.
III. Some mice are predisposed to develop lung tumors.
IV. Cigarette smoke exposure has a positive correlation with lung tumors in humans.

A. I and II only.

B. II only.

C. I , II, III and IV.

D. II and IV only.

Answer: B. II only.
Although cigarette smoke has been found to cause lung tumors (and many other problems), this particular experiment shows only that there is a positive correlation between smoke exposure and tumor development in these mice. It may be true that some mice are more likely to develop tumors than others, which is why a control group of identical mice should have been used for comparison. Mice are often used to model human reactions, but this is as much due to their low financial and emotional cost as it is due to their being a "good model" for humans, and thus this scientist cannot make the conclusion that cigarette smoke exposure has a positive correlation with lung tumors in humans based on this data alone. Therefore, the answer must be (B).

164. Which of the following is a correct explanation for an astronaut's 'weightlessness'?
(Average Rigor) (Skill 41.1)

A. Astronauts continue to feel the pull of gravity in space, but they are so far from planets that the force is small.

B. Astronauts continue to feel the pull of gravity in space, but spacecraft have such powerful engines that those forces dominate, reducing effective weight.

C. Astronauts do not feel the pull of gravity in space, because space is a vacuum.

D. The cumulative gravitational forces, that the astronaut is experiencing, from all sources in the solar system equal out to a net gravitational force of zero.

Answer: A. Astronauts continue to feel the pull of gravity in space, but they are so far from planets that the force is small.
Gravity acts over tremendous distances in space (theoretically, infinite distance, though certainly at least as far as any astronaut has traveled). However, gravitational force is inversely proportional to distance squared from a massive body. This means that when an astronaut is in space, s/he is far enough from the center of mass of any planet that the gravitational force is very small, and s/he feels 'weightless'. Space is mostly empty (i.e. vacuum), and spacecraft do have powerful engines. However, none of these has the effect attributed to it in the incorrect answer choices (B), or (C). Although, theoretically there is a point in space where the cumulative gravitational forces of sources within the solar system would equal a net force of zero, that point would be in constant motion and difficult to find, making answer D unlikely at best and but more accurately near impossible to keep an astronaught at this point. The answer to this question must therefore be (A).

165.   **Physical properties are observable characteristics of a substance in its natural state. Which of the following are considered physical properties.**
        (Rigorous) (Skill 42.1)

I. Color
II. Density
III. Specific gravity
IV. Melting Point

A. I only

B. I and II only

C. I, II, and III only

D. III and IV only

Answer: C. I, II, and III only
Of the possibilities only the melting point of a substance cannot be found without altering the substance itself. Color is readily observable. Density can be measured without changing a substances form or structure, and specific gravity is a ratio based on density, so once one is known the other can be calculated. Thus answer (C) is the only possible answer.

166.   **Intermediate students in Mr. Lang's class are focusing on weather. The students are completing experiments using water in various forms. When the teacher boils water, he explains that the change in phase from liquid to gas is called:**
        (Rigorous) (Skill 42.2)

A. Evaporation.

B. Condensation.

C. Vaporization.

D. Boiling.

Answer: A. Evaporation
Condensation is the change in phase from a gas to a liquid; vaporization is the conversion of matter to vapor- not all gases are vapors. Boiling is one method of inducing the change from a liquid to a gas; the process is evaporation. The answer is (A).

167. **Which of the following statements is true of all transition elements?**
(Rigorous) (Skill 43.3)

A. They are all hard solids at room temperature.

B. They tend to form salts when reacted with Halogens.

C. They all have a silvery appearance in their pure state.

D. All of the Above

Answer: B. They tend to form salts when reacted with Halogens
Answer (A) is incorrect because Mercury, which has a low melting point, is a liquid at room temperature. Answer (C) is incorrect because Copper and Gold do not have a silvery appearance in the natural states. Since answers (A) and (C) are not correct then answer (D) cannot be correct either. This leaves only answer (B).

168. **A boulder sitting on the edge of a cliff has which type of energy?**
(Easy) (Skill 44.1)

A. Kinetic energy

B. Latent Energy

C. No energy

D. Potential Energy

Answer: D. Potential Energy
Answer (A) would be true if the boulder fell off the cliff and started falling. Answer (C) would be a difficult condition to find since it would mean that no outside forces where operating on an object, and gravity is difficult to avoid. Answer (B) might be a good description of answer (D) which is the correct energy. The boulder has potential energy is imparted from the force of gravity.

169. **A converging lens produces a real image _____.**
(*Rigorous*) *(Skill 44.4)*

A. always.

B. never.

C. when the object is within one focal length of the lens.

D. when the object is further than one focal length from the lens.

Answer: D. when the object is further than one focal length from the lens.
A converging lens produces a real image whenever the object is far enough from the lens (outside one focal length) so that the rays of light from the object can hit the lens and be focused into a real image on the other side of the lens. When the object is closer than one focal length from the lens, rays of light do not converge on the other side; they diverge. This means that only a virtual image can be formed, i.e. the theoretical place where those diverging rays would have converged if they had originated behind the object. Thus, the correct answer is (D).

170. **Which of the following is not a factor in how different materials will conduct seismic waves?**
(*Average Rigor*) *(Skill 44.6)*

A. Density

B. Incompressiblity

C. Rigidity

D. Tensile strength

Answer: D. Tensile strength
Density affects the speed at which seismic waves travel through the material. Incompressibilty has to do with how quickly a material compresses and rebounds as the waves hit it. The more compressable a material (and thus the slower the rebound) the slower the wave travels trhough the material. Seismic waves create a shearing force as they travel through a material, rigidity is the measure of the material's resistance to that shearing force. Tensile strength measures how far something can be stretched before breaking. Since seismic waves compress materials and are not stretching them that makes answer (D) the correct answer.

171. **The Law of Conservation of Energy states that _____.**
   (Average Rigor) (Skill 45.2)

   A. There must be the same number of products and reactants in any chemical equation.

   B. Mass and energy can be interchanged.

   C. Energy is neither created nor destroyed, but may change form.

   D. One form energy must remain intact (or conserved) in all reactions

   Answer: C. Energy is neither created nor destroyed, but may change form.
   Answer (C) is a summary of the Law of Conservation of Energy (for non-nuclear reactions). In other words, energy can be transformed into various forms such as kinetic, potential, electric, or heat energy, but the total amount of energy remains constant. Answer (A) is untrue, as demonstrated by many synthesis and decomposition reactions. Answers (B) and (D) may be sensible, but they are not relevant in this case. Therefore, the answer is (C).

172. **When you step out of the shower, the floor feels colder on your feet than the bathmat. Which of the following is the correct explanation for this phenomenon?**
(Rigorous) (Skill 45.5)

A. The floor is colder than the bathmat.

B. The bathmat is smaller so that the floor quickly reaches equilibrium with your body temperature.

C. Heat is conducted more easily into the floor.

D. Water is absorbed from your feet into the bathmat. It doesn't evaporate as quickly as it does off the floor, therefore not cooling the bathmat as quickly.

Answer: C. Heat is conducted more easily into the floor.
When you step out of the shower and onto a surface, the surface is most likely at room temperature, regardless of its composition (eliminating answer (A)). The bathmat is likely a good insulator and is unlikely to reach equilibrium with your body temperature after a short exposure so answer (B) is incorrect. Although evaporation does have a cooling effect, in the short time it takes you to step from the bathmat to the floor, it is unlikely to have a significant effect on the floor temperature (eliminating answer (D)). Your feet feel cold when heat is transferred from them to the surface, which happens more easily on a hard floor than a soft bathmat. This is because of differences in specific heat (the energy required to change temperature, which varies by material). Therefore, the answer must be (C), i.e. heat is conducted more easily into the floor from your feet.

173. **Identify the correct sequence of organization of living things from lower to higher order:**
(Average Rigor) (Skill 46.3)

    A. Cell, Organelle, Organ, Tissue, System, Organism.

    B. Cell, Tissue, Organ, Organelle, System, Organism.

    C. Organelle, Cell, Tissue, Organ, System, Organism.

    D. Organelle, Tissue, Cell, Organ, System, Organism.

    Answer: C. Organelle, Cell, Tissue, Organ, System, Organism.
    Organelles are parts of the cell; cells make up tissue, which makes up organs. Organs work together in systems (e.g. the respiratory system), and the organism is the living thing as a whole. Therefore, the answer must be (C).

174. **Catalysts assist reactions by _____ .**
(Easy) (Skill 46.5)

    A. lowering required activation energy.

    B. maintaining precise pH levels.

    C. keeping systems at equilibrium.

    D. changing the starting amounts of reactants.

    Answer: A. lowering required activation energy.
    Chemical reactions can be enhanced or accelerated by catalysts, which are present both with reactants and with products. They induce the formation of activated complexes, thereby lowering the required activation energy—so that less energy is necessary for the reaction to begin. Catalysts may require a well maintained pH to operate effectively, however they do not do this themselves. A catalyst, by lowering activation energy, may change a reaction's equilibrium point however it does not maintain a system at equilibrium. The starting level of reactants is controlled separately from the addition of the catalyst, and has no direct correlation. Thus the correct answer is (A).

175. **Which process result in a haploid chromosome number?**
(Rigorous) (Skill 47.2)

A. Mitosis.

B. Meiosis I.

C. Meiosis II.

D. Neither mitosis nor meiosis.

Answer: C. Meiosis II.
Meiosis is the division of sex cells. The resulting chromosome number is half the number of parent cells, i.e. a 'haploid chromosome number'. Meiosis I mirrors Mitosis, resulting in diploid cells. It is only during Meiosis II that the number of chromosomes is halved. Mitosis, however, is the division of other cells, in which the chromosome number is the same as the parent cell chromosome number. Therefore, the answer is (C).

176. **A carrier of a genetic disorder is heterozygous for a disorder that is recessive in nature. Hemophilia is a sex-linked disorder. This means that:**
(Easy) (Skill 47.4)

A. Only females can be carriers

B. Only males can be carriers.

C. Both males and females can be carriers.

D. Neither females nor males can be carriers.

Answer: A. Only females can be carriers
Since hemophilia is a sex-linked disorder the gene only appears on the X chromosome, with no counterpart on the Y chromosome. Since males are XY they cannot be heterozygous for the trait, what ever is on the single X chromosome will be expressed. Females being XX can be heterozygous. Answer (C) would describe a genetic disorder that is recessive and expressed on one of the somatic chromosomes (not sex-linked). Answer (D) would describe a genetic disorder that is dominant and expressed on any of the chromosomes. An example of answer (C) is sickle cell anemia. An example of answer (D) is Achondroplasia (the most common type of short-limbed dwarfism). For this condition, people that are homozygous dominant for the gene that creates the disorder usually have severe health problems if they live past infancy; hence, almost all individuals with this disorder are carriers.

177. **During a field trip to the local zoo, a student in Mrs. Meyer's class comments that the giraffe they are observing is as tall as a tree. Using this as a teachable moment, Mrs. Meyers should explain which of the following for scientific biological adaptation?**
(Average Rigor) (Skill 48.2)

   A. Giraffes need to reach higher for leaves to eat, so their necks stretch. The giraffe babies are then born with longer necks. Eventually, there are more long-necked giraffes in the population.

   B. Giraffes with longer necks are able to reach more leaves, so they eat more and have more babies than other giraffes. Eventually, there are more long-necked giraffes in the population.

   C. Giraffes want to reach higher for leaves to eat, so they release enzymes into their bloodstream, which in turn causes fetal development of longer-necked giraffes. Eventually, there are more long-necked giraffes in the population.

   D. Giraffes with long necks are more attractive to other giraffes, so they get the best mating partners and have more babies. Eventually, there are more long-necked giraffes in the population.

Answer: B. Giraffes with longer necks are able to reach more leaves, so they eat more and have more babies than other giraffes. Eventually, there are more long-necked giraffes in the population.
Although evolution is often misunderstood, it occurs via natural selection. Organisms with a life/reproductive advantage will produce more offspring. Over many generations, this changes the proportions of the population. In any case, it is impossible for a stretched neck (A) or a fervent desire (C) to result in a biologically mutated baby. Although there are traits that are naturally selected because of mate attractiveness and fitness (D), this is not the primary situation here, so answer (B) is the best choice.

178. **An animal choosing its mate because of attractive plumage or a strong mating call is an example of:**
(Average Rigor) (Skill 48.4)

A. Sexual Selection.

B. Natural Selection.

C. Mechanical Isolation.

D. Linkage

Answer: A. Sexual Selection.
The coming together of genes determines the makeup of the gene pool. Sexual selection, the act of choosing a mate, allows animals to have some choice in the breeding of its offspring. The answer is (A).

179. **Many male birds sing long complicated songs that describe thier identity and the area of land that they claim. Which of the answers below is the best decription of this behavior?**
(Rigorous) (Skill 49.1)

A. Innate territorial behavior

B. Learned competitve behavior

C. Innate mating behavior

D. Learned territorial behavior

Answer: D. Learned territorial behavior
Birds often learn their songs, through a combination of trial and error, and listening to the songs of other members of their species (in some cases, this is called mimicry). Thus answers (A) and (C) are not correct. Typically, a male bird will use a short song to impress a mate. The longer song is territorial because it is trying to convey to other males both identity and the territory that it claims.

180.   **A wrasse (fish) cleans the teeth of other fish by eating away plaque. This is an example of _____ between the fish.**
   (Average Rigor) (Skill 50.2)

   A. parasitism

   B. symbiosis (mutualism)

   C. competition

   D. predation

   Answer: B. symbiosis (mutualism)
   When both species benefit from their interaction in their habitat, this is called 'symbiosis', or 'mutualism'. In this example, the wrasse benefits from having a source of food, and the other fish benefit by having healthier teeth. Note that 'parasitism' is when one species benefits at the expense of the other; 'competition' is when two species compete with one another for the same habitat or food, and 'predation' is when one species feeds on another. Therefore, the answer is (B).

181.   **Which of the following causes the Aurora Borealis?**
   (Rigorous) (Skill 51.3)

   A. gases escaping from earth

   B. particles from the sun

   C. particles from the moon

   D. electromagnetic discharges from the North pole.

   Answer: B. particles from the sun
   Aurora Borealis is a phenomenon caused by particles escaping from the sun. The particles escaping from the sun include a mixture of gases, electrons and protons, and are sent out at a force that scientists call solar wind. When conditions are right, the build-up of pressure from the solar wind creates an electric voltage that pushes electrons into the ionosphere. Here they collide with gas atoms, causing them to release both light and more electrons.

182. **The transfer of heat from the earth's surface to the atmosphere is called** *(Average Rigor) (Skill 51.6)*

A. Convection

B. Radiation

C. Conduction

D. Advection

Answer: C. Conduction
Radiation is the process of warming through rays or waves of energy, such as the Sun warms earth. The Earth returns heat to the atmosphere through conduction. This is the transfer of heat through matter, such that areas of greater heat move to areas of less heat in an attempt to balance temperature.

183. **Mrs. Miller's class creates models of the water cycle and the students are required to describe each step. What is the most accurate description of the Water Cycle?**
(Rigorous) (Skill 52.2)

A. Rain comes from clouds, filling the ocean. The water then evaporates and becomes clouds again.

B. Water circulates from rivers into groundwater and back, while water vapor circulates in the atmosphere.

C. Water is conserved except for chemical or nuclear reactions, and any drop of water could circulate through clouds, rain, ground-water, and surface-water.

D. Water flows toward the oceans, where it evaporates and forms clouds, which causes rain, which in turn flow back to the oceans after it falls.

Answer: C. Water is conserved except for chemical or nuclear reactions, and any drop of water could circulate through clouds, rain, ground-water, and surface-water.
All natural chemical cycles, including the Water Cycle, depend on the principle of Conservation of Mass. (For water, unlike for elements such as Nitrogen, chemical reactions may cause sources or sinks of water molecules.) Any drop of water may circulate through the hydrologic system, ending up in a cloud, as rain, or as surface- or ground-water. Although answers (A), (B) and (D) describe parts of the water cycle, the most comprehensive and correct answer is (C).

184. **What makes up the largest abiotic portion of the Nitrogen Cycle?**
(Average Rigor) (Skill 52.3)

A. Nitrogen Fixing Bacteria.

B. Nitrates.

C. Decomposers.

D. Atomsphere.

Answer: D. Atomsphere.
Since answers (A) and (C) are both examples of living organisms they are biotic components of the nitrogen cycle. Nitrates are one type of nitrogen compond, (making it abiotic) that can be found in soil and in living organisms, however it makes up a small portion of the avaible nitrogen. The atmosphere being 78% Nitrogen gas (an abiotic component) makes up the largest source available to the Nitrogen Cycle.

185. **What are the most significant and prevalent elements in the biosphere?**
(Easy) (Skill 52.5)

A. Carbon, Hydrogen, Oxygen, Nitrogen, Phosphorus.

B. Carbon, Hydrogen, Sodium, Iron, Calcium.

C. Carbon, Oxygen, Sulfur, Manganese, Iron.

D. Carbon, Hydrogen, Oxygen, Nickel,Sodium, Nitrogen.

Answer: A. Carbon, Hydrogen, Oxygen, Nitrogen, Phosphorus.
Organic matter (and life as we know it) is based on Carbon atoms, bonded to Hydrogen and Oxygen. Nitrogen and Phosphorus are the next most significant elements, followed by Sulfur and then trace nutrients such as Iron, Sodium, Calcium, and others. Therefore, the answer is (A). If you know that the formula for any carbohydrate contains Carbon, Hydrogen, and Oxygen, that will help you narrow the choices to (A) and (D) in any case.

186. **"Neap Tides" are especially weak tides that occur when the Sun and Moon are in a perpendicular arrangement to the Earth, and "Spring Tides" are especially strong tides that occur when the Sun and Moon are in line. At which combination of lunar phases do these tides occur (respectively)?** *(Rigorous) (Skill 53.5)*

A. Half Moon, and Full Moon

B. Quarter Moon, and New Moon

C. Gibbous Moon, and Quarter Moon

D. Full Moon and New Moon

Answer: B. Quarter Moon, and New Moon
"Spring tides" are especially strong tides that occur when the Earth, Sun and Moon are in line, allowing both the Sun and the Moon to exert gravitational force on the Earth and increase tidal bulge height. These tides occur during the full moon and the new moon. "Neap tides" occur during quarter moons, when the sun is illuminating half of the Moon's surface, (the term quarter is used to refer to the fact that the Moon has traveled 1/2 of its way through the cycle, not the amount of the surface illuminated by the Sun.) A Gibbous Moon describes the Moon between Full and Quarter.

187. **The planet with true retrograde rotation is:** *(Rigorous) (Skill 54.1)*

A. Pluto

B. Neptune

C. Venus

D. Saturn

Answer: C. Venus
Venus has an axial tilt of only 3 degrees and a very slow rotation. It spins in the direction opposite of its counterparts (who spin in the same direction as the Sun). Uranus is also tilted and orbits on its side. However, this is thought to be the consequence of an impact that left the previously prograde rotating planet tilted in such a manner.

188. **The phases of the moon are the result of its _____ in relation to the sun.** *(Average Rigor) (Skill 54.2)*

A. revolution

B. rotation

C. position

D. inclination

Answer: C. position
The moon is visible in varying amounts during its orbit around the earth. One half of the moon's surface is always illuminated by the Sun (appears bright), but the amount observed can vary from full moon to none.

189. **The end of a geologic era is most often characterized by?** *(Average Rigor) (Skill 55.1)*

A. A general uplifting of the crust.

B. The extinction of the dominant plants and animals

C. The appearance of new life forms.

D. All of the above.

Answer: D. All of the above.
Any of these things can be used to characterize the end of a geologic era, and often a combination of factors are applied to determining the end of an era.

190. **While studying how animals of the past have changed, students in Ms. Kripa's class spend time at their local museum. While there, they learn that the best preserved animal remains have been discovered in:**
(Rigorous) (Skill 55.4)

A. Resin

B. Fossil Mold

C. Tar pits

D. Glacial Ice

Answer: C. Tar pits.
Tar pits provide a wealth of information when it comes to fossils. Tar pits are oozing areas of asphalt, which were so sticky as to trap animals. These animals, without a way out, would die of starvation or be preyed upon. Their bones would remain in the tar pits, and be covered by the continued oozing of asphalt. Because the asphalt deposits were continuously added, the bones were not exposed to much weathering, and we have found some of the most complete and unchanged fossils from these areas, including mammoths and saber toothed cats.

191. **Which type of student activity is most likely to expose a student's misconceptions about science?**
(Average Rigor) (Skill 56.4)

    A. Multiple-Choice and fill-in-the-blank worksheets.

    B. Laboratory activities, where the lab is laid out step by step with no active thought on the part of the student.

    C. Teacher- lead demonstrations.

    D. Laboratories in which the student are forced to critically consider the steps taken and the results.

    Answer: D. Laboratories in which the student are forced to critically consider the steps taken and the results.
    Answer (A) is a typical retain and repeat exercise, where a student just needs to remember the answer and doesn't need to understand it. Answer (B) is often called a cookie cutter lab because everything fits to a specific plan. Students are often able to guess the right answer without understanding the process. Teacher lead demonstrations can be interesting for the students, and may challenge a student's misconceptions. Misconceptions are often firmly routed and will require critical thought and reflection by the student for it to change. Often an attempt to illuminate a student's misconception doesn't get rid of it, but gets incorporated into their inaccurate understanding of the universe. Answer (D) requires active mental participation on the behalf of the student and thus is most likely to alter their personal understanding. These types of labs are often referred to as guided discovery laboratories.

192. As Mrs. Poshing demonstrates the dfifference between independent and dependent variables in her eighth grade science class, she shows the students a previously conducted medical experiment that involved petri dishes. She then asked them the following: In an experiment measuring the effect of different antibiotic discs on bacteria grown in Petri dishes, what are the independent and dependent variables respectively?
(Rigorous) (Skill 57.6)

A. Number of bacterial colonies and the antibiotic type.

B. Antibiotic type and the distance between antibiotic and the closest colony.

C. Antibiotic type and the number of bacterial colonies.

D. Presence of bacterial colonies and the antibiotic type.

Answer: B. Antibiotic type and the distance between antibiotic and the closest colony.
To answer this question, recall that the independent variable in an experiment is the entity that is changed by the scientist, in order to observe the effects the dependent variable. In this experiment, antibiotic used is purposely changed so it is the independent variable. Answers A and D list antibiotic type as the dependent variable and thus cannot be the answer, leaving answers B and C as the only two viable choices. The best answer is B, because it measures at what concentration of the antibiotic the bacteria are able to grow at, (as you move from the source of the antibiotic, the concentration decreases). Answer C is not as effective because it could be interpreted that a plate that shows a large number of colonies at a greater distance from the antibiotic is a less effective antibiotic than a plate with a smaller number of colonies in close proximity to the antibiotic disc, which is reverse of the actual result.

193. **Which is the correct order of the scientific method?**
(Easy) (Skill 38.1)

    1. collecting data
    2. planning a controlled experiment
    3. drawing a conclusion
    4. hypothesizing a result
    5. re-visiting a hypothesis to answer a question

    A. 1,2,3,4,5

    B. 4,2,1,3,5

    C. 4,5,1,3,2

    D. 1,3,4,5,2

Answer: B. 4,2,1,3,5
The correct methodology for the scientific method is first to make a meaningful hypothesis (educated guess), then plan and execute a controlled experiment to test that hypothesis. Using the data collected in that experiment, the scientist then draws conclusions and attempts to answer the original question related to the hypothesis. This is consistent only with answer (B).

194. **For her first project of the year, a student is designing a science experiment to test the effects of light and water on plant growth. You should recommend that she _____**
(Average Rigor) (Skill 38.1)

    A. manipulate the temperature also.

    B. manipulate the water pH also.

    C. determine the relationship between light and water unrelated to plant growth.

    D. omit either water or light as a variable.

Answer: D. omit either water or light as a variable.
As a science teacher for middle-school-aged students, it is important to reinforce the idea of "constant" vs. "variable" in science experiments. At this level, it is wisest to have only one variable examined in each science experiment.
(Later, students can hold different variables constant while investigating others.) Therefore, it is counterproductive to add other variables answers (A) or (B). It is also irrelevant to determine the light-water interactions aside from plant growth (C). So the only possible answer is (D).

195. **When designing a scientific experiment, a student considers all the factors that may influence the results. The process goal is to _____**
(Average Rigor) (Skill 38.2)

   A. recognize and manipulate independent variables.

   B. recognize and record independent variables.

   C. recognize and manipulate dependent variables.

   D. recognize and record dependent variables.

   Answer: A. recognize and manipulate independent variables.
   When a student designs a scientific experiment, s/he must decide what to measure and what independent variables will play a role in the experiment. S/he must determine how to manipulate these independent variables to refine his/her procedure and to prepare for meaningful observations. Although s/he will eventually record dependent variables (D), this does not take place during the experimental design phase. Although the student will likely recognize and record the independent variables (B), this is not the process goal, but a helpful step in manipulating the variables. It is unlikely that the student will manipulate dependent variables directly in his/her experiment (C), or the data would be suspect. Thus, the answer is (A).

196. **Which of the following is not an acceptable way for a student to acknowledge sources in a laboratory report?**
(Rigorous) (Skill 38.8)

   A. The student tells his/her teacher what sources s/he used to write the report.

   B. The student uses footnotes in the text, with sources cited, but not in correct MLA format.

   C. The student uses endnotes in the text, with sources cited, in correct MLA format.

   D. The student attaches a separate bibliography, noting each use of sources.

   Answer: A. The student tells his/her teacher what sources s/he used to write the report.
   It may seem obvious, but students are often unaware that scientists need to cite all sources used. For the young adolescent, it is not always necessary to use official MLA format (though this should be taught at some point). Students may properly cite references in many ways, but these references must be in writing, with the original assignment. Therefore, the answer is (A).

197. **Factor that is changed in an experiment:**
(Average) (Skill 38.1)

A. independent variable

B. dependent variable

C. inquiry

D. control

Answer: D. control
Designing an experiment involves identifying a control, constants, independent variables, and dependent variables. Independent variables are factors that are changed in an experiment. There should always be more constants than variables to obtain reproducible results in an experiment.

198. **Which of these is the best example of "negligence"?**
(Easy) (Skill 38.5)

A. A teacher fails to give oral instructions to those with reading disabilities.

B. A teacher fails to exercise ordinary care to ensure safety in the classroom.

C. A teacher does not supervise a large group of students.

D. A teacher reasonably anticipates that an event may occur, and plans accordingly.

Answer: B. A teacher fails to exercise ordinary care to ensure safety in the classroom.
"Negligence" is the failure to "exercise ordinary care" to ensure an appropriate and safe classroom environment. It is best for a teacher to meet all special requirements for disabled students and to be good at supervising large groups. However, if a teacher can prove that s/he has done a reasonable job to ensure a safe and effective learning environment, then it is unlikely that she/he would be found negligent. Therefore, the answer is (B).

199. **Formaldehyde should not be used in school laboratories for the following reason:**
(Average Rigor) (Skill 37.1)

A. It smells unpleasant.

B. It is a known carcinogen.

C. It is expensive to obtain.

D. It is explosive.

Answer: B. It is a known carcinogen.
Formaldehyde is a known carcinogen, so it is too dangerous for use in schools. In general, teachers should not use carcinogens in school laboratories. Although formaldehyde also smells unpleasant, a smell alone is not a definitive marker of danger. For example, many people find the smell of vinegar to be unpleasant, but vinegar is considered a very safe classroom/laboratory chemical. Furthermore, some odorless materials are toxic. Formaldehyde is neither particularly expensive nor explosive. Thus, the answer is (B).

200. **Experiments may be done with any of the following animals except**

_____
(Rigorous) (Skill 38.5)

A. birds.

B. invertebrates.

C. lower order life.

D. frogs.

Answer: A. Birds.
No dissections may be performed on living mammalian vertebrates or birds. Lower order life and invertebrates may be used. Biological experiments may be done with all animals except mammalian vertebrates or birds. Therefore the answer is (A).

TExES Core Subjects 4-8
SAMPLE TEST 2

LANGUAGE ARTS

1. **Which of the following is NOT characteristic of a good reader?** *(Average) (Skill 1.8)*

   A. When faced with unfamiliar words, they skip over them unless meaning is lost

   B. They formulate questions that they predict will be answered in the text

   C. They establish a purpose before reading

   D. They go back to reread when something doesn't make sense

2. **Phonological awareness includes all of the following skills except:** *(Average) (Skill 1.1)*

   A. Rhyming and syllabification

   B. Blending sounds into words

   C. Understanding the meaning of the root word

   D. Removing initial sounds and substituting others

3. **If a student's fluency rate is low, which of the following may occur:** *(Easy) (Skill 3.2)*

   A. The student's vocabulary level will be low.

   B. He or she will have difficulty with grammar skills.

   C. The student will have difficulty remembering what has been read.

   D. There will be no negative consequences stemming from a low fluency rate.

4. **Which of the following is NOT utilized by a reader when trying to comprehend the meaning behind the literal text?** *(Rigorous) (Skill 4.1)*

   A. Pictures and graphics in the text

   B. Background knowledge about a topic

   C. Knowledge of different types of text structure

   D. Context clues

5. **Which is NOT a true statement concerning informational texts?** *(Rigorous) (Skill 5.3)*

A. They contain concepts or phenomena

B. They could explain history

C. They are based on research

D. They are presented in a very straightforward, choppy manner

6. **What does the word** *convoluted* **mean in the sentence below?** *(Easy) (Skill 3.4)*

Misty listened to Marty intently. But as Marty revealed more of her plan, Misty wasn't sure she wanted anything to do with it. Marty's plan was <u>convoluted</u> and twisted and, quite frankly, Misty was worried about her own safety.

A. Strange

B. Straight

C. Thorough

D. Polluted

7. **Which of the following contains a subordinating conjunction?** *(Rigorous) (Skill 6.1)*

A. Matthew is a great student, but his handwriting is poor.

B. As I have already stated, you may have this one or that one.

C. Do you want pizza, or would you rather have a sub?

D. Anthony's mom is a dentist, and Brian's mom is an attorney.

8. **All of the following are true about an expository essay EXCEPT:** *(Average) (Skill 7.5)*

A. Its purpose is to make an experience available through one of the five senses

B. It is not interested in changing anyone's mind

C. It exists to give information

D. It is not trying to get anyone to take a certain action

9. **All of the following are stages of the writing process EXCEPT:** *(Average) (Skill 7.1)*

A. Prewriting

B. Revising

C. Organizing

D. Presenting

10. **Which of the following sentences is a compound sentence?**
(Easy) (Skill 6.2)

A. Elizabeth took Gracie to the dog park but forgot to bring the leash.

B. We thoroughly enjoyed our trip during Spring Break and will plan to return next year.

C. We were given two choices: today or tomorrow.

D. By the end of the evening, we were thoroughly exhausted; we decided to forego the moonlight walk.

11. **Topic sentences, transition words, and appropriate vocabulary are used by writers to:**
(Easy) (Skill 6.4)

A. Meet various purposes

B. Organize a multi-paragraph essay

C. Express an attitude on a subject

D. Explain the presentation of ideas

12. **When speaking on a formal platform, students should do all of the following EXCEPT:**
(Average) (Skill 1.10)

A. Use no contractions

B. Have longer sentences

C. Connect with the audience

D. Strictly organize longer segments

13. **Good listeners do which of the following:**
(Average) (Skill 1.3)

A. Make eye contact with the speaker

B. Avoid jumping to conclusions.

C. Ask clarifying questions only at an appropriate time.

D. All of the above.

14. **Four of Ms. Wolmark's students have lived in other countries. She is particularly pleased to be studying Sumerian proverbs with them as part of the fifth grade unit in analyzing the sayings of other cultures because:**
(Rigorous) (Skill 1.7)

A. This gives her a break from teaching, and the children can share sayings from other cultures they and their families have experienced

B. This validates the experiences and expertise of ELL learners in her classroom

C. This provides her children from the U.S. with a lens on other cultural values

D. All of the above

15. **What does the word *pang* mean in the sentence below?**
(Easy) (Skill 3.7)

*Standing outside of her homeroom, Lauren watched other children enter the room and overheard them sharing stories about their summer adventures. She couldn't help but feel a **pang** of loneliness as she thought of her best friend Morgan back in Colorado.*

A. Pain

B. Hint

C. Depression

D. Song

16. **A strong topic sentence will:**
(Average) (Skill 7.8)

A. Be phrased as a question.

B. Always be the first sentence in a paragraph.

C. Both A and B

D. Neither A nor B

17. **Which of the following is true about semantics?**
(Average) (Skill 3.3)

   A. Semantics will sharpen the effect and meaning of a text

   B. Semantics refers to the meaning expressed when words are arranged in a specific way

   C. Semantics is a vocabulary instruction technique

   D. Semantics is representing spoken language through the use of symbols

18. **John Bunyan, Coleridge, Shakespeare, Homer, and Chaucer all contributed to what genre of literature?**
(Average) (Skill 4.1)

   A. Children's literature

   B. Preadolescent literature

   C. Adolescent literature

   D. Adult literature

19. **Which of the following is NOT true of slant rhyme?**
(Rigorous) (Skill 5.9)

   A. This occurs when a rhyme is not exact

   B. Words are used to evoke meaning by their sounds

   C. The final consonant sounds are the same, but the vowels are different

   D. It occurs frequently in Welsh verse

20. **Which of the following should students use to improve coherence of ideas within an argument?**
(Rigorous) (Skill 6.6)

   A. Transitional words or phrases to show relationship of ideas

   B. Conjunctions like "and" to join ideas together

   C. Use direct quotes extensively to improve credibility

   D. Adjectives and adverbs to provide stronger detail

21. Which of the following are punctuated correctly?
(Rigorous) (Skill 6.5)

I. The teacher directed us to compare Faulkner's three symbolic novels *Absalom, Absalom; As I Lay Dying;* and *Light in August.*

II. Three of Faulkner's symbolic novels are: *Absalom, Absalom; As I Lay Dying;* and *Light in August.*

III. The teacher directed us to compare Faulkner's three symbolic novels: *Absalom, Absalom; As I Lay Dying;* and *Light in August.*

IV. Three of Faulkner's symbolic novels are *Absalom, Absalom; As I Lay Dying;* and *Light in August.*

A. I and II only

B. II and III only

C. III and IV only

D. IV only

22. Being competent in _____, a reader is able to understand what the writer is trying to convey to the audience.
(Average) (Skill 4.3)

A. Semantics

B. Pragmatics

C. Morphemes

D. Phonemes

23. Which of the following is NOT utilized by a reader when trying to comprehend the meaning behind the literal text?
(Rigorous) (Skill 4.3)

A. Pictures and graphics in the text

B. Background knowledge about a topic

C. Knowledge of different types of text structure

D. Context clues

24. To make an inference a reader must:
(Average) (Skill 3.15)

A. Make a logical guess as to the next event.

B. Find a line of reasoning on which to rely.

C. Make a decision based on an observation.

D. Use prior knowledge and apply it to the current situation.

25. Which of the following is NOT utilized by a reader when trying to comprehend the meaning behind the literal text?
(Rigorous) (Skill 2.3)

A. Pictures and graphics in the text

B. Background knowledge about a topic

C. Knowledge of different types of text structure

D. Context clues

26. All of the following are true about schemata EXCEPT:
(Rigorous) (Skill 4.1)

A. Used as a basis for literary response

B. Structures that represent concepts stored in our memories

C. A generalization that is proven with facts

D. Used together with prior knowledge for effective reading comprehension

27. Asking a child if what he or she has read makes sense to him or her, is prompting the child to use:
(Average) (Skill 3.6)

A. Phonics cues

B. Syntactic cues

C. Semantic cues

D. Prior knowledge

28. Which of the following indicates that a student is a fluent reader?
(Rigorous) (Skill 3.1)

A. Reads texts with expression or prosody

B. Reads word-to-word and haltingly

C. Must intentionally decode a majority of the words

D. In a writing assignment, sentences are poorly-organized, structurally

29. To decode is to:
(Average) (Skill 2.2)

A. Construct meaning

B. Sound out a printed sequence of letters

C. Use a special code to decipher a message

D. None of the above

30. **John Bunyan, Coleridge, Shakespeare, Homer, and Chaucer all contributed to what genre of literature?**
(Average) (Skill 5.13)

A. Children's literature

B. Preadolescent literature

C. Adolescent literature

D. Adult literature

31. **All of the following are true about graphic organizers EXCEPT:**
(Rigorous) (Skill 5.8)

A. Solidify a visual relationship among various reading and writing ideas

B. Organize information for an advanced reader

C. Provide scaffolding for instruction

D. Activate prior knowledge

32. **Identify the type of appeal used by Molly Ivins's in this excerpt from her essay "Get a Knife, Get a Dog, But Get Rid of Guns."**
(Rigorous) (Skill 5.14)

As a civil libertarian, I, of course, support the Second Amendment. And I believe it means exactly what it says:

"A well regulated militia being necessary to the security of a free state, the right of the people to keep and bear arms shall not be infringed."

A. Appeal based on writer's credibility

B. Appeal to logic

C. Appeal to the emotion

D. Appeal to the reader

33. **"What is the point?" is the first question to be asked when:**
(Average) (Skill 5.12)

A. Reading a written piece

B. Listening to a presentation

C. Writing a composition

D. All of the above

34. **All of the following are true about writing an introduction EXCEPT:** *(Average) (Skill 7.11)*

    A. It should be written last

    B. It should lead the audience into the discourse

    C. It is the point of the paper

    D. It can take up a large percentage of the total word count

35. **Which of the following is an important feature of vocabulary instruction, according to the National Reading Panel?** *(Average) (Skill 7.2)*

    A. Repetition of vocabulary items

    B. Keeping a consistent task structure at all times

    C. Teaching vocabulary in more than one language

    D. Isolating vocabulary instruction from other subjects

36. **Isaac is mimicking the way his father is writing. He places a piece of paper on the table and holds the pencil in his hand correctly, but he merely draws lines and makes random marks on the paper. What type of writer is he?** *(Average) (Skill 7.2)*

    A. Role play writer

    B. Emergent writer

    C. Developing writer

    D. Beginning writer

37. **The following sentences are correct EXCEPT:** *(Rigorous) (Skill 7.4)*

    A. One of the boys was playing too rough.

    B. A man and his dog were jogging on the beach.

    C. The House of Representatives has adjourned for the holidays.

    D. Neither Don nor Joyce has missed a day of school this year.

38. **To determine an author's purpose a reader must:** *(Average) (Skill 5.2)*

    A. Use his or her own judgment.

    B. Verify all the facts.

    C. Link the causes to the effects.

    D. Rely on common sense.

39. Which of the following skills can help students improve their listening comprehension? *(Rigorous) (Skill 4.2)*

    I.   Tap into prior knowledge.
    II.   Look for transitions between ideas.
    III. Ask questions of the speaker.
    IV.   Discuss the topic being presented.

    A. I and II only

    B. II and IV only

    C. II and IV only

    D. IV only

40. Academically, appropriate literature primarily helps students to _____. *(Rigorous) (Skill 5.17)*

    A. Become better readers

    B. See how the skills they learned are applied to writing

    C. Enjoy library time

    D. Increase academic skills in other content areas

41. While standing in line at the grocery store, three-year-old Megan says to her mother in a regular tone of voice, "Mom, why is that woman so fat?" What does this indicate a lack of understanding of? *(Average) (Skill 1.1)*

    A. Syntax

    B. Semantics

    C. Morphology

    D. Pragmatics

42. Oral language development can be enhanced by which of the following? *(Easy) (Skill 1.4)*

    A. Meaningful conversation

    B. Storytelling

    C. Alphabet songs

    D. All of the above

43. **Ms. Chomski is presenting a new story to her class of first graders. In the story, a family visits their grandparents, where they all gather around a record player and listen to music. Many students do not understand what a record player is, especially some children for whom English is not their first language. Which of the following would be best for Ms. Chomski to do?** *(Rigorous) (Skill 1.5)*

A. Discuss what a record player is with her students

B. Compare a record player with a CD player

C. Have students look up *record player* in a dictionary

D. Show the students a picture of a record player

44. **Reading aloud correlates with all of the following EXCEPT:** *(Rigorous) (Skill 1.7)*

A. Reader self-confidence

B. Better reading comprehension

C. Literacy development

D. Overall school success

45. **Mr. Johns is using an activity that involves having students analyze the public speaking of others. All of the following would be guidelines for this activity EXCEPT:** *(Rigorous) (Skill 1.10)*

A. The speeches to be evaluated are not given by other students

B. The rubric for evaluating the speeches includes pace, pronunciation, body language, word choice, and visual aids

C. The speeches to be evaluated are best presented live to give students a more engaging learning experience

D. One of Mr. Johns's goals with this activity is to help students improve their own public speaking skills

46. **All of the following are true about phonological awareness EXCEPT:** *(Average) (Skill 2.1)*

A. It may involve print

B. It is a prerequisite for spelling and phonics

C. Activities can be done by the children with their eyes closed

D. It starts before letter recognition is taught

47. **Which of the following explains a significant difference between phonics and phonemic awareness?**
(Rigorous) (Skill 2.1)

 A. Phonics involves print, while phonemic awareness involves language

 B. Phonics is harder than phonemic awareness

 C. Phonics involves sounds, while phonemic awareness involves letters

 D. Phonics is the application of sounds to print, while phonemic awareness is oral

48. **Theorist Marilyn Jager Adams, who researches early reading, has outlined five basic types of phonemic awareness tasks. Which of the following is NOT one of the tasks noted by Jager Adams?**
(Average) (Skill 2.2)

 A. Ability to do oddity tasks

 B. Ability to orally blend words and split syllables

 C. Ability to sound out words when reading aloud

 D. Ability to do phonics manipulation tasks

49. **Activities that parents can practice at home to improve phonological and phonemic awareness include which of the following?**
(Average) (Skill 2.5)

 A. Play games with words that sound alike as you experience them in everyday home activities

 B. Demonstrate how sounds blend together in familiar words

 C. Play a game in which the goal is to find objects with names that begin with a certain initial sound

 D. All of the above

50. **The alphabetic principle can best be described by which of the following statements?**
(Rigorous) (Skill 3.1)

 A. Most reading skills need to be acquired through a regular teaching of the alphabet

 B. Written words are composed of patterns of letters that represent the sounds of spoken words

 C. Written words are composed of patterns that must be memorized in order to read well

 D. Spoken words (regular and irregular) lead to phonological reading

51. **Which of the following is NOT true about multisensory approaches to teaching the alphabetic principle?** *(Rigorous) (Skill 3.3)*

   A. Some children can only learn through multisensory techniques

   B. Multisensory techniques give multiple cues to enhance memory and learning

   C. Quilt book, rhyme time, letter path, and shape game are multisensory strategies

   D. Multisensory techniques require direct teaching and ongoing engagement

52. **Activities that facilitate learning the alphabetic principle include:** *(Average) (Skill 3.4)*

   A. Read alouds, alphabet art, concept books, and name sorts

   B. Read alouds, shared reading, concept books, and picture books

   C. Picture books, concept books, and alphabet books

   D. Alphabet art, name sorts, shared reading, and phonics

53. **Which of the following is a convention of print that children learn during reading activities?** *(Rigorous) (Skill 4.1)*

   A. The meaning of words

   B. The left-to-right motion

   C. The purpose of print

   D. The identification of letters

54. **Alphabet books are classified as:** *(Average) (Skill 4.6)*

   A. Concept books

   B. Easy-to-read books

   C. Board books

   D. Picture books

55. **To draw inferences and make conclusions, an** *(Average) (Skill 4.10)*

   A. Author's Purpose

   B. Author's Tone

   C. Main Idea

   D. Inference

56. **The process in which one takes different things and makes them one whole thing:**
(Average) (Skill 4.10)

   A. synthesis

   B. evaluation

   C. analysis

   D. context

57. **Contextual redefinition is a strategy that encourages children to use the context more effectively by presenting them with sufficient vocabulary _____ the reading of a text.**
(Rigorous) (Skill 5.2)

   A. After

   B. Before

   C. During

   D. none of the above

58. **What is the best place for students to find appropriate synonyms, antonyms, and other related words to enhance their writing?**
(Average) (Skill 5.6)

   A. Dictionary

   B. Spell check

   C. Encyclopedia

   D. Thesaurus

59. **An _____ is a story in verse or prose with characters representing virtues and vices.**
(Average) (Skill 5.9)

   A. Epistle

   B. Epic

   C. Essay

   D. allegory

60. **Which of the following reading strategies is NOT associated with fluent reading abilities?**
(Average) (Skill 6.1)

   A. Pronouncing unfamiliar words by finding similarities with familiar words

   B. Establishing a purpose for reading

   C. Formulating questions about the text while reading

   D. Reading sentences word by word

61. **Automaticity refers to all of the following EXCEPT:**
    (Rigorous) (Skill 6.2)

    A. Automatic whole-word identification

    B. Automatic recognition of syllable types

    C. Automatic reactions to the content of a paragraph

    D. Automatic identification of graphemes as they relate to four basic word types

62. **Which of the following activities are likely to improve fluency?**
    (Easy) (Skill 6.4)

    A. Partner reading and a reading theater

    B. Phrased reading

    C. Both A and B

    D. None of the above

63. **Students are about to read a text that contains words that will need to be understood for the students to understand the text. When should the vocabulary be introduced to students?**
    (Average) (Skill 7.2)

    A. Before reading

    B. During reading

    C. After reading

    D. It should not be introduced

64. **Which of the following is an important feature of vocabulary instruction, according to the National Reading Panel?**
    (Average) (Skill 7.2)

    A. Repetition of vocabulary items

    B. Keeping a consistent task structure at all times

    C. Teaching vocabulary in more than one language

    D. Isolating vocabulary instruction from other subjects

65. **The book *The Giver* by Lois Lowry is a great book. The characters are interesting and they are unique. Everyone who reads *The Giver* will enjoy it and not be able to put it down.**

    Is this a valid or invalid argument?
    (Average) (Skill 5.1)

    A. Valid

    B. Invalid

66. **Which of the following is not a strategy of teaching reading comprehension?**
(Rigorous) (Skill 7.7)

A. Asking questions

B. Utilizing graphic organizers

C. Focusing on mental images

D. Manipulating sounds

67. **The children's literature genre came into its own in the:**
(Easy) (Skill 7.11)

A. Seventeenth century

B. Eighteenth century

C. Nineteenth century

D. Twentieth century

68. **When evaluating reference sources, students should do all of the following EXCEPT:**
(Rigorous) (Skill 8.1)

A. Look for self-published books by the author as evidence of expert status

B. Examine the level of detail provided by the source

C. Review the references at the end of the book or article

D. See if the author presents both sides of an argument or viewpoint

69. **Graphic organizers:**
(Average) (Skill 8.2)

A. are used primarily in grades K-3

B. work better with poetry than other forms of writing

C. help readers think critically by pulling out the main idea and supporting details

D. generally aren't helpful to ELL students

70. **Which of the following helps students in a way that is similar to using a glossary?**
(Average) (Skill 8.4)

A. Information in the text such as charts, graphs, maps, diagrams, captions, and photos

B. Prewriting

C. Classroom discussion of the main idea

D. Paired reading

71. **Which of these describes the best way to teach spelling?**
(Rigorous) (Skill 9.4)

    A. At the same time that grammar and sentence structure are taught

    B. Within the context of meaningful language experiences

    C. Independently so that students can concentrate on spelling

    D. In short lessons, as students pick up spelling almost immediately

72. **Which of the following sentences contains an error in agreement?**
(Rigorous) (Skill 9.8)

    A. Jennifer is one of the women who writes for the magazine.

    B. Each one of their sons plays a different sport.

    C. This band has performed at the Odeum many times.

    D. The data are available online at the listed Web site.

73. **All of the following are correctly punctuated EXCEPT:**
(Rigorous) (Skill 9.8)

    A. "The airplane crashed on the runway during takeoff."

    B. I was embarrassed when Ms. White said, "Your slip is showing!"

    C. "The middle school readers were unprepared to understand Bryant's poem 'Thanatopsis.'"

    D. The hall monitor yelled, "Fire! Fire!"

74. **Which of the following is not a technique of prewriting?**
(Average) (Skill 10.4)

    A. Clustering

    B. Listing

    C. Brainstorming

    D. Proofreading

MATHEMATICS

75. **Which of the following statements best characterizes the meaning of "absolute value of x"?** *(Average) (Skill 15.1)*

   A. The square root of x

   B. The square of x

   C. The distance on a number line between x and $-x$

   D. The distance on a number line between 0 and x

76. **Which of the following terms most accurately describes the set of numbers below?**

   $$\{3, \sqrt{16}, \pi^0, 6, \frac{28}{4}\}$$

   (Average) (Skill 10.2)

   A. Rationals

   B. Irrationals

   C. Complex

   D. Whole numbers

77. **Calculate the value of the following expression.**

   $$\left(\frac{6}{3} + 1 \cdot 5\right)^2 \cdot \left(\frac{1}{7}\right) + (3 \cdot 2 - 1)$$

   (Average) (Skill 11.3)

   A. 6

   B. 10

   C. 12

   D. 294

78. **What is the GCF of 12, 30, 56, and 144?**
   (Rigorous) (Skill 11.1)

   A. 2

   B. 3

   C. 5

   D. 7

79. **What is the value of the following expression?**

   $$\frac{25 - 2(6 - 2 \bullet 3)}{^-5(2 + 2 \bullet 4)}$$

   (Rigorous) (Skill 11.2)

   A. 0.5

   B. 5.0

   C. -0.5

   D. 3.4

80. The final cost of an item (with sales tax) is \$8.35. If the sales tax is 7%, what was the pre-tax price of the item? *(Average) (Skill 12.5)*

A. \$7.80

B. \$8.00

C. \$8.28

D. \$8.93

81. Which expression best characterizes the shaded area in the graph below?

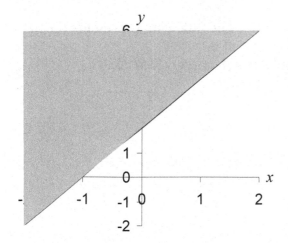

(Rigorous) (Skill 14.1)

A. $y \leq -x + 2$

B. $y \geq 2x + 2$

C. $y = 2x + 2$

D. $y \geq 2x - 1$

82. Solve for L:

$$R = r + \frac{400(W - L)}{N}$$

(Rigorous) (Skill 10.4)

A. $L = W - \frac{N}{400}(R - r)$

B. $L = W + \frac{N}{400}(R - r)$

C. $L = W - \frac{400}{N}(R - r)$

D. $L = \frac{NR}{r} - 400W$

83. A burning candle loses ½ inch in height every hour. If the original height of the candle was 6 inches, which of the following equations describes the relationship between the height h of the candle and the number of hours t since it was lit? *(Average) (Skill 13.4)*

A. $2h + t = 12$

B. $2h - t = 12$

C. $h = 6 - t$

D. $h = 0.5t + 6$

84. **Which set cannot be considered "dense"?**
(Rigorous)(Skill 11.5)

 A. Integers

 B. Rationals

 C. Irrationals

 D. Reals

85. **Which of the following expressions are equivalent to 28 − 4 • 6 +12?**
(Average) (Skill 14.2)

 I. $(28 − 4) • 6 +12$
 II. $28 − (4 • 6) +12$ √
 III. $(28 − 4) • (6 +12)$
 IV. $(28 + 12) − (4 • 6)$
 V. $28 − 4 • 12 + 6$

 A. I and V

 B. II and IV

 C. III and V

 D. IV and V

86. **A recipe makes 6 servings and calls for $1\frac{1}{2}$ cups of rice. How much rice is needed to make 10 servings?**
(Average)(Skill 10.5)

 A. 2 cups

 B. $2\frac{1}{4}$ cups

 C. $2\frac{1}{2}$ cups

 D. $2\frac{3}{4}$ cups

87. **The following represents the net of a**
(Average) (Skill 18.3)

 A. Cube

 B. Tetrahedron

 C. Octahedron

 D. Dodecahedron

88. Ginny and Nick head back to their respective colleges after being home for the weekend. They leave their house at the same time and drive for 4 hours. Ginny drives due south at the average rate of 60 miles per hour and Nick drives due east at the average rate of 60 miles per hour. What is the straight-line distance between them, in miles, at the end of the 4 hours? *(Rigorous)(Skill 15.8)*

A. 169.7 miles

B. 240 miles

C. 288 miles

D. 339.4 miles

89. A school band has 200 members. Looking at the pie chart below, determine which statement is true about the band. *(Average)(Skill 21.1)*

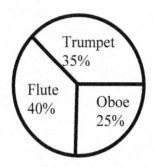

A. There are more trumpet players than flute players

B. There are fifty oboe players in the band

C. There are forty flute players in the band

D. One-third of all band members play the trumpet

90. A restaurant offers the following menu choices.

Green Vegetable	Yellow Vegetable
Asparagus	Carrots
Broccoli	Corn
Peas	Squash
Spinach	

If a customer chooses a green vegetable and a yellow vegetable at random, what is the probability that the customer will order neither asparagus nor corn?
(Rigorous)(Skill 21.3)

A. $\frac{1}{12}$

B. $\frac{1}{6}$

C. $\frac{1}{3}$

D. $\frac{1}{2}$

91. A music store owner wants to change the window display every week. Only 4 out of 6 instruments can be displayed in the window at the same time. How many weeks will it be before the owner must repeat the same arrangement (in the same order) of instruments in the window display?
(Rigorous)(Skill 21.3)

A. 24 weeks

B. 36 weeks

C. 120 weeks

D. 360 weeks

92. Half the students in a class scored 80% on an exam; one student scored 10%; and the rest of the class scored 85%. Which would be the best measure of central tendency for the test scores?
(Rigorous)(Skill 21.4)

A. Mean

B. Median

C. Mode

D. Either the median or the mode because they are equal

93. Which of the following is an example of a multiplicative inverse?
(Average) (Skill 15.2)

A. $x^2 - x^2 = 0$

B. $(y-3)^0 = 1$

C. $\dfrac{1}{e^{3z}} e^{3z} = 1$

D. $f^2 = \dfrac{1}{g}$

94. Based upon the following examples, can you conclude that the sum of two prime numbers is also a prime number? Why or why not?
(Rigorous)(Skill 15.4)

$2 + 3 = 5$
$2 + 5 = 7$
$11 + 2 = 13$

A. Yes; there is a pattern

B. Yes; there are many more examples, such as $17 + 2 = 19$ and $29 + 2 = 31$

C. No; there are many counterexamples

D. No; the sums are not prime numbers

95. Two farmers are buying feed for animals. One farmer buys eight bags of grain and six bales of hay for $105, and the other farmer buys three bags of grain and nine bales of hay for $69.75. How much is a bag of grain?
(Rigorous)(Skill 12.2)

A. $4.50

B. $9.75

C. $14.25

D. $28.50

96. Which of the following is correct?
(Easy) (Skill 11.7)

A. $2365 > 2340$

B. $0.75 > 1.25$

C. $3/4 < 1/16$

D. $-5 < -6$

97. **For which of the following is the additive inverse equal to the multiplicative inverse?**
(Rigorous) (Skill 12.1)

A. $\dfrac{2}{3} + \dfrac{3}{2}$

B. $\sqrt{-1}$

C. $\dfrac{1-\sqrt{2}}{1+\sqrt{2}}$

D. $(a+b)/(b-a)$

98. **Which of the statements below explain the error(s), if any, in the following calculation?**

$$\frac{18}{18} + 23 = 23$$

I. A number divided by itself is 1, not 0.
II. The sum of 1 and 23 is 24, not 23.
III. The 18s are "cancelled" and replaced by 0.

(Rigorous) (Skill 12.3)

A. I and II

B. II and III

C. I, II, and III

D. There is no error.

99. **What is the length of the shortest side of a right isosceles triangle if the longest side is 5 centimeters?**
(Rigorous) (Skill 19.1)

A. 2.24 centimeters

B. 2.5 centimeters

C. 3.54 centimeters

D. Not enough information

100. **What is the sample space for the sum of the outcomes for two rolls of a six-sided die?**
(Easy) (Skill 23.1)

A. {1, 2, 3, 4, 5, 6}

B. {1, 2, 3, 4, 5, 6, 7, 8, 9, 10, 11, 12}

C. {2, 3, 4, 5, 6, 7, 8, 9, 10, 11, 12}

D. {7, 8, 9, 10, 11, 12}

101. **What is the GCF of 12, 30, 56, and 144?**
(Rigorous) (Skill 11.4)

A. 2

B. 3

C. 5

D. 7

102. **A traveler uses a ruler and finds the distance between two cities to be 3.5 inches. If the legend indicates that 100 miles is the same as an inch, what is the distance in miles between the cities?**
(Average) (Skill 17.2)

A. 29 miles

B. 35 miles

C. 100 miles

D. 350 miles

103. **What is the area of the shaded region below, where the circle has a radius r?**
(Average) (Skill 18.4)

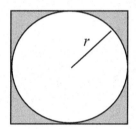

A. r^2

B. $(4-\pi)r^2$

C. $(2-\pi)r^2$

D. $4\pi r^2$

104. **Students in Mr. Anderson's class want to know which train car will hold more plastic apples: the long, thin car, or the square car. First, they fill the long, thin car with apples and record their answer. Then they fill the square car with apples and record their answer. Which math principles does this activity demonstrate?**
(Rigorous) (Skill 26.1)

A. Problem solving, subtraction

B. Subtraction, meaningful counting

C. Problem solving, number sense

D. Addition, problem solving

105. **Which of the following is a true statement regarding manipulatives in mathematics instruction?**
(Average) (Skill 13.4)

A. Manipulatives are materials that students can physically handle

B. Manipulatives help students make concrete concepts abstract

C. Manipulatives include fingers, tiles, paper folding, and ice cream sticks

D. Manipulatives help students make abstract concepts concrete

106. All of the following are tools that can strengthen students' mathematical understanding EXCEPT:
(Easy) (Skill 13.6)

A. Rulers, scales, and protractors

B. Calculators, counters, and measuring containers

C. Software and hardware

D. Money and software

107. Which of the following is not a good example of helping students make connections between the real world and mathematics?
(Average) (Skill 13.9)

A. Studying a presidential election from the perspective of the math involved

B. Using weather concepts to teach math

C. Having student helpers take attendance

D. Reviewing major mathematical theorems on a regular basis

108. Which of the following is an example of the associative property?
(Rigorous) (Skill 14.1)

A. $a(b + c) = ab + bc$

B. $a + 0 = a$

C. $(a + b) + c = a + (b + c)$

D. $a + b = b + a$

109. Simplify:

$$\frac{5^{-2} \times 5^3}{5^5 \times 5^{-7}}$$

(Average) (Skill 11.6)

A. 5^5

B. 125

C. $\dfrac{1}{125}$

D. 25

110. **Mathematical operations are done in the following order:**
(Rigorous) (Skill 14.4)

   A. Simplify inside grouping characters such as parentheses, brackets, square roots, fraction bars, etc.; multiply out expressions with exponents; do multiplication or division, from left to right; do addition or subtraction, from left to right

   B. Do multiplication or division, from left to right; simplify inside grouping characters such as parentheses, brackets, square roots, fraction bars, etc.; multiply out expressions with exponents; do addition or subtraction, from left to right

   C. Simplify inside grouping characters such as parentheses, brackets, square roots, fraction bars, etc.; do addition or subtraction, from left to right; multiply out expressions with exponents; do multiplication or division, from left to right

   D. None of the above

111. **Which of the following is an irrational number?**
(Rigorous) (Skill 14.5)

   A. .36262626262…

   B. 4

   C. 8.2

   D. -5

112. **The number "0" is a member of all of the following groups of numbers EXCEPT:**
(Rigorous) (Skill 14.5)

   A. Whole numbers

   B. Real numbers

   C. Natural numbers

   D. Integers

113. **4,087,361: What number represents the ten thousands' place?**
(Easy) (Skill 14.9)

   A. 4

   B. 6

   C. 0

   D. 8

114. Two mathematics classes have a total of 410 students. The 8:00 a.m. class has 40 more students than the 10:00 a.m. class. How many students are in the 10:00 a.m. class?
(Average) (Skill 15.3)

    A. 123.3

    B. 370

    C. 185

    D. 330

115. Three-dimensional figures in geometry are called:
(Easy) (Skill 16.1)

    A. Solids

    B. Cubes

    C. Polygons

    D. Blocks

116. The volume is:
(Easy) (Skill 16.2)

    A. Area of the faces excluding the bases

    B. Total area of all the faces, including the bases

    C. The number of cubic units in a solid

    D. The measure around the object

SOCIAL STUDIES

117. The state of Louisiana is divided into parishes. What type of region do the parishes represent?
(Rigorous) (Skill 30.1)

    A. Formal region

    B. Functional region

    C. Vernacular region

    D. Human region

118. Which continent is only one country?
(Easy) (Skill 30.2)

    A. Australia

    B. New Zealand

    C. The Arctic

    D. Antarctica

119. Anthropology is:
(Easy) (Skill 33.11)

    A. The profession that made the Leakey family famous

    B. The scientific study of human culture and humanity

    C. Not related to geography at all

    D. Margaret Mead's study of the Samoans

120. In the 1920s, Margaret Mead wrote *Coming of Age in Samoa*, relating her observations about this group's way of life. What of these types of geographical study best describes her method?
(Rigorous) (Skill 30.3)

A. Regional

B. Topical

C. Physical

D. Human

121. Which civilization laid the foundations of geometry?
(Average) (Skill 30.10)

A. Egyptian

B. Greek

C. Roman

D. Chinese

122. Consumers are, in effect, voting for the goods and services that they want with dollars, or what is called:
(Average) (Skill 31.4)

A. Economics

B. Scarcity

C. Dollar Voting

D. Profitability Voting

123. Which of the following are two agricultural innovations that began in China?
(Average) (Skill 31.3)

A. Using pesticides and fertilizer

B. Irrigation and cuneiform

C. Improving the silk industry and inventing gunpowder

D. Terrace farming and crop rotation

124. English and Spanish colonists took what from Native Americans?
(Easy) (Skill 29.2)

A. Land

B. Water rights

C. Money

D. Religious beliefs

125. In the events leading up to the American Revolution, which of these methods was effective in dealing with the British taxes?
(Rigorous) (Skill 31.6)

A. Boycotts

B. Strikes

C. Armed conflicts

D. Resolutions

126. How did the labor force change after 1830?
(Easy) (Skill 31.2)

A. Employers began using children

B. Employers began hiring immigrants

C. Employers began hiring women

D. Employers began hiring non-immigrant men

127. Which of these was not a result of World War I in the United States?
(Easy) (Skill 29.14)

A. Establishment of new labor laws.

B. Prosperous industrial growth.

C. Formation of the United Nations

D. Growth of the stock market.

128. Among civilized people:
(Easy) (Skill 32.1)

A. Strong government is not necessary

B. Systems of control are rudimentary at best

C. Government has no sympathy for individuals or for individual happiness

D. Governments began to assume more institutional forms

129. Which of the following was not a source of conflict in writing the U.S. Constitution?
(Average) (Skill 32.3)

A. Establishing a monarchy

B. Equalizing power between the small states and the large states

C. Dealing with slavery

D. Electing a president

130. Upon arrest, a person is read a "Miranda warning" which reads, in part, "You have the right to remain silent. Anything you say can and will be used against you in a court of law." Under what amendment in the Bill of Rights is this covered?
(Rigorous) (Skill 32.11)

A. The right against unreasonable search and seizures

B. The right to trial by jury and right to legal council

C. The right against self-incrimination

D. The right to jury trial for civil actions

131. **The equilibrium price:**
(Rigorous) (Skill 31.5)

A. Is the price that clears the markets

B. Is the price in the middle

C. Identifies a shortage or a surplus

D. Is an agricultural price support

132. **Capital is:**
(Average) (Skill 31.2)

A. Anyone who sells his or her ability to produce goods and services

B. The ability of an individual to combine the three inputs with his or her own talents to produce a viable good or service

C. Anything that is manufactured to be used in the production process

D. The land itself and everything occurring naturally on it

133. **Which of the following countries has historically operated in a market economy?**
(Rigorous) (Skill 31.13)

A. Great Britain

B. Cuba

C. Yugoslavia

D. India

134. **For their research paper on the use of technology in the classroom, students have gathered data that shows a sharp increase in the number of online summer classes over the past five years. What would be the best way for them to depict this information visually?**
(Average) (Skill 34.15)

A. A line chart

B. A table

C. A pie chart

D. A flow chart

135. **An example of something that is not a primary source is:**
(Easy) (Skill 34.5)

A. The published correspondence between Winston Churchill and Franklin D. Roosevelt during World War II

B. Martin Gilbert's biography of Winston Churchill

C. The diary of Field Marshal Sir Alan Brooke, the head of the British Army during World War II

D. Franklin D. Roosevelt's handwritten notes from the World War II era

136. **Mr. Phillips is creating a unit to study *To Kill a Mockingbird* and wants to familiarize his high school freshmen with the attitudes and issues of the historical period. Which activity would familiarize students with the attitudes and issues of the Depression-era South?** *(Rigorous) (Skill 35.9)*

    A. Create a detailed timeline of 15–20 social, cultural, and political events that focus on race relations in the 1930s

    B. Research and report on the life of its author Harper Lee; compare her background with the events in the book

    C. Watch the movie version and note language and dress

    D. Write a research report on the stock market crash of 1929 and its effects

137. **Which of the following are non-renewable resources?** *(Easy)(Skill 31.9)*

    A. Fish, coffee, and forests

    B. Fruit, water, and solar energy

    C. Wind power, alcohol, and sugar

    D. Coal, natural gas, and oil

138. **What people perfected the preservation of dead bodies?** *(Average) (Skill 33.2)*

    A. Sumerians

    B. Phoenicians

    C. Egyptians

    D. Assyrians

139. **Which major economic activity of the Southern colonies led to the growth of slavery?** *(Rigorous) (Skill 32.4)*

    A. Manufacturing

    B. Fishing

    C. Farming

    D. Coal mining

140. **In the fictional country of Nacirema, the government controls the means of production and directs resources. It alone decides what will be produced; as a result, there is an abundance of capital and military goods but a scarcity of consumer goods. What type of economy is this?** *(Rigorous) (Skill 31.7)*

    A. Market economy

    B. Centrally planned economy

    C. Market socialism

    D. Capitalism

141. Which of the following are secondary research materials?
(Average) (Skill 34.7)

A. The conclusions and inferences of other historians

B. Literature and nonverbal materials, novels, stories, poetry, and essays from the period, as well as coins, archaeological artifacts, and art produced during the period

C. Interviews and surveys conducted by the researcher

D. Statistics gathered as the result of the research's experiments

142. In December, Ms. Griffin asks her students to talk about their holiday traditions. Rebecca explains about lighting the nine candles during Chanukkah, Josh explains about the lighting of the seven candles during Kwanzaa, and Bernard explains about lighting the four candles during Advent. This is an example of:
(Rigorous) (Skill 33.9)

A. Cross-cultural exchanges

B. Cultural diffusion

C. Cultural identity

D. Cosmopolitanism

143. Socialism is:
(Rigorous) (Skill 32.5)

A. A system of government with a legislature

B. A system where the government is subject to a vote of "no confidence"

C. A political belief and system in which the state takes a guiding role in the national economy

D. A system of government with three distinct branches

144. The U.S. House of Representatives has:
(Average) (Skill 32.6)

A. 100 members

B. 435 members

C. Three branches

D. A president and a vice president

145. Which of the following was not a source of conflict in writing the U.S. Constitution?
(Average) (Skill 32.7)

A. Establishing a monarchy

B. Equalizing power between the small states and the large states

C. Dealing with slavery

D. Electing a president

146. **The existence of economics is based on:**
(Rigorous) (Skill 31.10)

A. The scarcity of resources

B. The abundance of resources

C. Little or nothing that is related to resources

D. Entrepreneurship

147. **Using graphics can enhance the presentation of social science information because:**
(Average) (Skill 19.3)

A. They can explain complex relationships among various data points

B. Charts and graphs summarize information well

C. Maps can describe geographic distribution of historical information

D. All of the above

148. **All of the following are key elements in planning a child-centered curriculum EXCEPT:**
(Rigorous) (Skill 19.5)

A. Referring students who need special tutoring

B. Identifying students' prior knowledge and skills

C. Sequencing learning activities

D. Specifying behavioral objectives

149. **The Texas Assessment of Knowledge and Skills (TAKS) test is an example of:**
(Average) (Skill 19.11)

A. Criterion-referenced assessment

B. Norm-referenced assessment

C. Performance-based assessment

D. Other type of assessment

150. **Ms. Gomez has a number of ESOL students in her class. In order to meet their specific needs as second-language learners, which of the following would NOT be an appropriate approach?**
(Easy) (Skill 19.11)

A. Pair students of different ability levels for English practice

B. Focus most of her instruction on teaching English rather than content

C. Provide accommodations during testing and with assignments

D. Use visual aids to help students make word links with familiar objects

151. Which one of the following is NOT a reason why Europeans came to the New World?
(Rigorous) (Skill 20.1)

    A. To find resources in order to increase wealth

    B. To establish trade

    C. To increase a ruler's power and importance

    D. To spread Christianity

152. Which of the following were results of the Age of Exploration?
(Easy) (Skill 20.1)

    A. More complete and accurate maps and charts

    B. New and more accurate navigational instruments

    C. Proof that the Earth is round

    D. All of the above

153. This is used to show the relationship between a unit of measurement on the map versus the real world measure on the Earth:
(Average) (Skill 30.2)

    A. Legend

    B. Grid

    C. Scale

    D. Title

154. Nationalism can be defined as the division of land and resources according to which of the following?
(Rigorous) (Skill 20.1)

    A. Religion, race, or political ideology

    B. Religion, race, or gender

    C. Historical boundaries, religion, or race

    D. Race, gender, or political ideology

155. The study of the social behavior of minority groups would be in the area of:
(Average) (Skill 20.8)

    A. Anthropology

    B. Psychology

    C. Sociology

    D. Cultural geography

156. "Participant observation" is a method of study most closely associated with and used in:
(Rigorous) (Skill 20.8)

    A. Anthropology

    B. Archaeology

    C. Sociology

    D. Political science

157. **For the historian studying ancient Egypt, which of the following would be least useful? (Rigorous) (Skill 20.11)**

   A. The record of an ancient Greek historian on Greek-Egyptian interaction

   B. Letters from an Egyptian ruler to his/her regional governors

   C. Inscriptions on stele of the fourteenth Egyptian dynasty

   D. Letters from a nineteenth-century Egyptologist to his wife

158. **The term *sectionalism* refers to: (Easy) (Skill 20.20)**

   A. Different regions of the continent

   B. Issues between the North and South

   C. Different regions of the country

   D. Different groups of countries

SCIENCE

159. **Which is the correct order for the layers of Earth's atmosphere? (Easy) (Skill 42.6)**

   A. Troposphere, stratosphere, mesosphere, and thermosphere

   B. Mesosphere, stratosphere, troposphere, and thermosphere

   C. Troposphere, stratosphere, thermosphere, and mesosphere

   D. Thermosphere, troposphere, stratosphere, mesosphere

160. **What type of rock can be classified by the size of the crystals in the rock? (Easy) (Skill 46.1)**

   A. Metamorphic

   B. Igneous

   C. Minerals

   D. Sedimentary

161. **What are solids with a definite chemical composition and a tendency to split along planes of weakness? (Easy) (Skill 40.1)**

   A. Ores

   B. Rocks

   C. Minerals

   D. Salts

162. **Which of the following objects in the universe is the largest?**
(Average)(Skill 40.5)

A. Pulsars

B. Quasars

C. Black holes

D. Nebulas

163. **Why is the winter in the southern hemisphere colder than winter in the northern hemisphere?**
(Average) (Skill 40.3)

A. Earth's axis of 24-hour rotation tilts at an angle of 23□°

B. The elliptical orbit of Earth around the Sun changes the distance of the Sun from Earth

C. The southern hemisphere has more water than the northern hemisphere

D. The greenhouse effect is greater for the northern hemisphere

164. **Which of the following processes and packages macromolecules?**
(Easy) (Skill 43.1)

A. Lysosomes

B. Cytosol

C. Golgi apparatus

D. Plastids

165. **Which of the following is not a property that eukaryotes have and prokaryotes do not have?**
(Average) (Skill 43.1)

A. Nucleus

B. Ribosomes

C. Chromosomes

D. Mitochondria

166. **What is the purpose of sexual reproduction?**
(Rigorous) (Skill 46.3)

A. Produce more organisms

B. Produce organisms that are genetically diverse

C. Give organisms the protection of male and female parents

D. Increase social cooperation between organisms

167. **In mitotic cell division, at what stage do the chromosomes line up in the cell?** *(Average) (Skill 46.2)*

A. Interphase

B. Anaphase

C. Prophase

D. Metaphase

168. **According to natural selection:** *(Easy) (Skill 48.1)*

    A. Individuals within a population are identical

    B. Those with better traits have less offspring

    C. Successive generations will possess better traits

    D. Single individuals evolve to fit their surroundings

169. **Which of the following is not a kingdom in the classification of living organisms?** *(Average) (Skill 46.1)*

    A. Plants

    B. Fungi

    C. Viruses

    D. Bacteria

170. **Which of the following describes the transformation of liquid water to ice?** *(Average) (Skill 42.2)*

    A. Chemical change

    B. Physical change

    C. Thermodynamic change

    D. Non-chemical molecular change

171. **On which of the following does the force of friction between a metal stool and a wooden floor <u>not</u> depend?** *(Rigorous) (Skill 40.8)*

    A. The speed of the chair

    B. Whether the stool has three legs or four

    C. The type of metal

    D. The smoothness of the floor

172. **Will Lithium gain or lose an electron when forming an ion? How many electrons will it gain or lose?** *(Average) (Skill 42.5)*

    A. Gain 1

    B. Gain 2

    C. Lose 1

    D. Lose 2

173. **Which of the following quantities has the units of calories per degree?** *(Easy) (Skill 46.5)*

    A. Heat capacity

    B. Specific heat

    C. Heat equivalent

    D. Heat transfer

174. Which of the following should be limited in a balanced diet?
(Easy) (Skill 46.6)

A. Carbohydrates

B. Fats and oils

C. Proteins

D. Vitamins

175. Calisthenics develops all of the following health and skill related components of fitness except:
(Average) (Skill 39.3)

A. Muscle strength

B. Body composition

C. Power

D. Agility

176. An experiment is performed to determine the effects of acid rain on plant life. Which of the following would be the variable?
(Average) (Skill 45.5)

A. The type of plant

B. The amount of light

C. The pH of the water

D. The amount of water

177. Which of the following statements about scientific knowledge best explains what scientific knowledge is?
(Average) (Skill 38.1)

A. Scientific knowledge is based on experiments

B. Science knowledge is empirical

C. Scientific knowledge is tentative

D. Scientific knowledge is based on reason

178. Which of the following describes the interaction between community members when one species feeds of another species but does not kill it immediately?
(Easy) (Skill 39.4)

A. Parasitism

B. Predation

C. Commensalism

D. Mutualism

179. **Taxonomy classifies species into genera (plural of genus) based on similarities. Species are subordinate to genera. The most general or highest taxonomical group is the kingdom. Which of the following is the correct order of the other groups from highest to lowest?**
(Easy) (Skill 39.4)

   A. Class ⇒ order⇒ family ⇒ phylum

   B. Phylum ⇒ class ⇒ family ⇒ order

   C. Phylum ⇒ class ⇒ order ⇒ family

   D. Order ⇒ phylum ⇒ class ⇒ family

180. **In which of the following eras did life appear?**
(Easy) (Skill 40.2)

   A. Paleozoic

   B. Mesozoic

   C. Cenozoic

   D. Precambrian

181. **Why is the northern winter slightly warmer than the southern winter?**
(Average) (Skill 45.7)

   A. Because the perihelion occurs in January

   B. Because of global warming

   C. Because there is more water in the southern hemisphere

   D. Because Earth rotates on an axis that is not perpendicular to the plane of rotation

182. **What are ribosomes?**
(Easy) (Skill 45.4)

   A. Contain digestive enzymes that break down food

   B. Where proteins are synthesized

   C. Make ATP

   D. Hold stored food

183. **Which term describes the relationship between barnacles and whales?**
(Rigorous) (Skill 48.5)

   A. Commensalism

   B. Parasitism

   C. Competition

   D. Mutualism

184. How many autosomes are in somatic cells of human beings?
(Easy) (Skill 46.2)

A. 22

B. 23

C. 44

D. 46

185. Which of the following laws implies that the force on an object comes from another object?
(Average) (Skill 41.4)

A. Newton's first law of motion

B. Newton's second law of motion

C. Newton's third law of motion

D. Coulomb's law

186. Which is not a characteristic of living organisms?
(Easy) (Skill 46.2)

A. Sexual reproduction

B. Ingestion

C. Synthesis

D. Respiration

187. Oogenesis is the formation of:
(Easy) (Skill 47.2)

A. Eggs

B. Sperm

C. Pollen

D. Cytoplasm

188. How does a steam radiator deliver heat energy to a room?
(Rigorous) (Skill 42.3)

A. Radiation

B. Conduction

C. Convection

D. Contact

189. Accepted procedures for preparing solutions include the use of:
(Easy) (Skill 24.2)

A. Alcohol

B. Hydrochloric acid

C. Distilled water

D. Tap water

190. Laboratory activities contribute to student performance in all of the following domains EXCEPT:
(Average) (Skill 25.1)

A. Process skills such as observing and measuring

B. Memorization skills

C. Analytical skills

D. Communication skills

191. Which is the correct order of methodology?
(Average) (Skill 25.2)

1. *Collecting data.*
2. *Planning a controlled experiment.*
3. *Drawing a conclusion.*
4. *Hypothesizing a result.*
5. *Revisiting a hypothesis to answer a question.*

A. 1, 2, 3, 4, 5

B. 4, 2, 1, 3, 5

C. 4, 5, 1, 3, 2

D. 1, 3, 4, 5, 2

192. In an experiment measuring the growth of bacteria at different temperatures, what is the independent variable?
(Rigorous) (Skill 25.5)

A. Number of bacteria

B. Growth rate of bacteria

C. Temperature

D. Size of bacteria

193. Which of the following is a misconception about the task of teaching science in elementary school?
(Average) (Skill 25.5)

A. Teach facts as a priority over teaching how to solve problems.

B. Involve as many senses as possible in the learning experience.

C. Accommodate individual differences in pupils' learning styles.

D. Consider the effect of technology on people rather than on material things.

194. An important map property is _____, or correct shapes.
(Average) (Skill 30.1)

  A. consistent scales

  B. conformal

  C. equal areas

  D. relief

195. All of the following are hormones in the human body EXCEPT:
(Average) (Skill 27.3)

  A. Cortisol

  B. Testosterone

  C. Norepinephrine

  D. Hemoglobin

196. Models are used in science in all of the following ways EXCEPT:
(Rigorous) (Skill 27.8)

  A. Models are crucial for understanding the structure and function of scientific processes

  B. Models help us visualize the organs/systems they represent

  C. Models create exact replicas of the real items they represent

  D. Models are useful for predicting and foreseeing future events such as hurricanes

197. There are a number of common misconceptions that claim to be based in science. All of the following are misconceptions EXCEPT:
(Rigorous) (Skill 28.4)

  A. Evolution is a process that does not address the origins of life

  B. The average person uses only a small fraction of his or her brain

  C. Raw sugar causes hyperactive behavior in children

  D. Seasons are caused by the Earth's elliptical orbit

198. One characteristic of electrically charged objects is that any charge is conserved. This means that:
(Rigorous) (Skill 30.1)

  A. Because of the financial cost, electricity should be conserved (saved)

  B. A neutral object has no net charge

  C. Like charges repel and opposite charges attract

  D. None of the above

199. **Which of the following describes a state of balance between opposing forces of change?**
    (Easy) (Skill 30.3)

    A. Equilibrium

    B. Homeostasis

    C. Ecological balance

    D. All of the above

200. **Which of the following describes the amount of matter in an object:**
    (Average) (Skill 31.1)

    A. Weight

    B. Mass

    C. Density

    D. Volume

ANSWER KEY

	42. D	84. A	126. B	168. C
1. A	43. D	85. B	127. C	169. C
2. C	44. A	86. C	128. D	170. B
3. C	45. C	87. C	129. A	171. B
4. A	46. A	88. D	130. C	172. C
5. D	47. D	89. B	131. A	173. A
6. A	48. C	90. D	132. C	174. B
7. B	49. D	91. D	133. A	175. C
8. A	50. B	92. B	134. A	176. C
9. D	51. A	93. C	135. B	177. B
10. D	52. A	94. C	136. A	178. A
11. B	53. B	95. B	137. D	179. C
12. C	54. A	96. A	138. C	180. D
13. D	55. B	97. B	139. C	181. A
14. D	56. A	98. C	140. B	182. B
15. B	57. B	99. C	141. A	183. A
16. D	58. D	100. C	142. A	184. C
17. B	59. D	101. A	143. C	185. C
18. D	60. D	102. D	144. B	186. A
19. B	61. C	103. B	145. A	187. A
20. A	62. C	104. C	146. A	188. C
21. C	63. A	105. D	147. D	189. C
22. B	64. A	106. C	148. A	190. B
23. A	65. B	107. D	149. B	191. B
24. D	66. D	108. C	150. B	192. C
25. A	67. B	109. B	151. B	193. A
26. C	68. A	110. A	152. D	194. B
27. C	69. C	111. A	153. C	195. D
28. A	70. A	112. C	154. A	196. C
29. B	71. B	113. D	155. C	197. A
30. D	72. A	114. C	156. A	198. B
31. B	73. B	115. A	157. D	199. D
32. A	74. D	116. C	158. B	200. B
33. D	75. D	117. A	159. A	
34. C	76. D	118. A	160. B	
35. A	77. C	119. B	161. C	
36. A	78. A	120. D	162. B	
37. D	79. C	121. B	163. B	
38. A	80. A	122. C	164. C	
39. A	81. B	123. D	165. B	
40. B	82. A	124. A	166. B	
41. D	83. A	125. A	167. D	

TExES Core Subjects 4-8 Test 2
ANSWER KEY WITH RATIONALE

LANGUAGE ARTS

1. **Which of the following is NOT a characteristic of a good reader?**
    (Average) (Skill 1.8)

    A. When faced with unfamiliar words, they skip over them unless meaning is lost

    B. They formulate questions that they predict will be answered in the text

    C. They establish a purpose before reading

    D. They go back to reread when something doesn't make sense

    Answer: A. When faced with unfamiliar words, they skip over them unless meaning is lost

    While skipping over an unknown word may not compromise the meaning of the text, a good reader will attempt to pronounce the word by using analogies to familiar words. They also formulate questions, establish a purpose, and go back to reread if meaning is lost.

2. **Phonological awareness includes all of the following skills except:**
    (Average) (Skill 1.1)

    A. Rhyming and syllabification

    B. Blending sounds into words

    C. Understanding the meaning of the root word

    D. Removing initial sounds and substituting others

    Answer: C. understanding the meaning of the root word

    Phonological awareness involves the recognition that spoken words are composed of a set of smaller units such as onsets and rhymes, syllables, and sounds.

3. **If a student's fluency rate is low, which of the following may occur:**
    (Easy) (Skill 3.2)

    A. The student's vocabulary level will be low.

    B. He or she will have difficulty with grammar skills.

    C. The student will have difficulty remembering what has been read.

    D. There will be no negative consequences stemming from a low fluency rate.

    Answer: C. The student will have difficulty remembering what has been read.
    When a student reads very slowly, the text will dissolve and chunks of information may be lost from a lack of consistency. He or she is likely to have difficulty remembering what has been read.

4. **Which of the following is NOT utilized by a reader when trying to comprehend the meaning behind the literal text?**
    (Rigorous) (Skill 4.1)

    A. Pictures and graphics in the text

    B. Background knowledge about a topic

    C. Knowledge of different types of text structure

    D. Context clues

    Answer: A. Pictures and graphics in the text
    While pictures and graphics can be helpful, good readers are trying to extract meaning from the text itself by comparing new information to background knowledge, using knowledge of a type of text to build expectations, and making use of context clues to help identify unknown words.

5. **Which is NOT a true statement concerning informational texts?**
    (Rigorous) (Skill 5.3)

    A. They contain concepts or phenomena

    B. They could explain history

    C. They are based on research

    D. They are presented in a very straightforward, choppy manner

    Answer: D. They are presented in a very straightforward, choppy manner
    Informational texts are types of books that explain concepts or phenomena like history or the idea of photosynthesis. Informational texts are usually based on research. Texts that are presented in a very straightforward or choppy manner are newspaper articles.

6. **What does the word *convoluted* mean in the sentence below?**
    (Easy) (Skill 3.4)

    Misty listened to Marty intently. But as Marty revealed more of her plan, Misty wasn't sure she wanted anything to do with it. Marty's plan was <u>convoluted</u> and twisted and, quite frankly, Misty was worried about her own safety.

    A. Strange

    B. Straight

    C. Thorough

    D. Polluted

    Answer: A. Strange
    The author gives clarification for the word *convoluted* by adding the word "twisted" to the sentence. Therefore, the reader knows that the plan is strange and twisted because *strange* is a synonym of twisted in this context.

7. **Which of the following contains a subordinating conjunction?**
   (Rigorous) (Skill 6.1)

   A. Matthew is a great student, but his handwriting is poor.

   B. As I have already stated, you may have this one or that one.

   C. Do you want pizza, or would you rather have a sub?

   D. Anthony's mom is a dentist, and Brian's mom is an attorney.

   Answer: B. As I have already stated, you may have this one or that one.
   Choice B's sentence contains a dependent clause and a subordinating conjunction. Subordinating conjunctions are used to connect a dependent clause, when one thing happened because of another. Choices A, C, and D contain coordinating conjunctions that join two independent sentence parts together.

8. **All of the following are true about an expository essay EXCEPT:**
   (Average) (Skill 7.5)

   A. Its purpose is to make an experience available through one of the five senses

   B. It is not interested in changing anyone's mind

   C. It exists to give information

   D. It is not trying to get anyone to take a certain action

   Answer: A. Its purpose is to make an experience available through one of the five senses
   The expository essay's purpose is to inform and not persuade or describe. Choice A is the purpose of a descriptive essay.

9. **All of the following are stages of the writing process EXCEPT:**
   (Average) (Skill 7.1)

   A. Prewriting

   B. Revising

   C. Organizing

   D. Presenting

   Answer: D. Presenting
   Writing is a process that can be clearly defined. First, students must prewrite to discover ideas, materials, experiences, sources, etc. Next, they must organize and determine their purpose, thesis, and supporting details. Last, they must edit and revise to polish the paper. While presenting is a nice finale to the writing process, it is not necessary for a complete and polished work.

10. **Which of the following sentences is a compound sentence?**
    (Easy)(Skill 6.2)

    A. Elizabeth took Gracie to the dog park but forgot to bring the leash.

    B. We thoroughly enjoyed our trip during Spring Break and will plan to return next year.

    C. We were given two choices: today or tomorrow.

    D. By the end of the evening, we were thoroughly exhausted; we decided to forego the moonlight walk.

    Answer: D. By the end of the evening, we were thoroughly exhausted; we decided to forego the moonlight walk.
    A compound sentence is two independent clauses joined by a coordinating conjunction or a semicolon. The sentences in choices A, B, and C have coordinating conjunctions but they do not connect two clauses. Sentences A and B have compound verb phrases. Sentence C has a compound object.

11. **Topic sentences, transition words, and appropriate vocabulary are used by writers to:** *(Easy) (Skill 6.4)*

    A. Meet various purposes

    B. Organize a multi-paragraph essay

    C. Express an attitude on a subject

    D. Explain the presentation of ideas

    Answer: B. Organize a multi-paragraph essay
    Correctly organizing an essay allows a writer to clearly communicate their ideas. To organize, a writer needs topic sentences, transition words, and appropriate vocabulary. Meeting a purpose, expressing an attitude, and explaining ideas are all done by an author in a piece of writing, but they are separate elements.

12. **When speaking on a formal platform, students should do all of the following EXCEPT:** *(Average) (Skill 1.10)*

    A. Use no contractions

    B. Have longer sentences

    C. Connect with the audience

    D. Strictly organize longer segments

    Answer: C. Connect with the audience
    When speaking formally, students should use fewer or no contractions, have longer sentences, and be more organized during longer segments of the speech. While connecting with the audience may seem beneficial, the personal antidotes or humorous pieces required to do that are not appropriate in a formal setting.

13. **Good listeners do which of the following:**
(Average) (Skill 1.3)

A. Make eye contact with the speaker

B. Avoid jumping to conclusions.

C. Ask clarifying questions only at an appropriate time.

D. All of the above.

Answer: D. All of the above.
In order to be a good listener, it is important to remain attentive using eye contact, listening completely without jumping to conclusions, and waiting until the right time to ask questions. This ensures that a learner or audience member is focused and takes in the new knowledge that is being presented.

14. **Four of Ms. Wolmark's students have lived in other countries. She is particularly pleased to be studying Sumerian proverbs with them as part of the fifth grade unit in analyzing the sayings of other cultures because:**
(Rigorous) (Skill 1.7)

A. This gives her a break from teaching, and the children can share sayings from other cultures they and their families have experienced

B. This validates the experiences and expertise of ELL learners in her classroom

C. This provides her children from the U.S. with a lens on other cultural values

D. All of the above

Answer: D. All of the above
It is recommended that all teachers of reading and particularly those who are working with ELL students use meaningful, student centered, and culturally customized activities. These activities may include: language games, word walls, and poems. Some of these activities might, if possible, be initiated in the child's first language and then reiterated in English.

15. **What does the word *pang* mean in the sentence below?**
    (Easy) (Skill 3.7)

    Standing outside of her homeroom, Lauren watched other children enter the room and overheard them sharing stories about their summer adventures. She couldn't help but feel a <u>pang</u> of loneliness as she thought of her best friend Morgan back in Colorado.

    A. Pain

    B. Hint

    C. Depression

    D. Song

    Answer: B. Hint
    The student feels a little bit lonely as she adjusts to a new school without her best friend from where she used to live.

16. **A strong topic sentence will:**
    (Average) (Skill 7.8)

    A. Be phrased as a question.

    B. Always be the first sentence in a paragraph.

    C. Both A and B

    D. Neither A nor B

    Answer: D. Neither A nor B
    A topic sentence will tell what the passage is about. A tip for finding a topic sentence is to phrase the possible topic sentence as a question and see if the other sentences answer the question, but the topic sentence doesn't need to be in question form. A topic sentence is usually the first sentence in a paragraph but could also be in any other position. Therefore neither choices A nor B are correct choices.

17. **Which of the following is true about semantics?**
(Average) (Skill 3.3)

A. Semantics will sharpen the effect and meaning of a text

B. Semantics refers to the meaning expressed when words are arranged in a specific way

C. Semantics is a vocabulary instruction technique

D. Semantics is representing spoken language through the use of symbols

Answer: B. Semantics refers to the meaning expressed when words are arranged in a specific way

Understanding semantics means understanding that meaning is imbedded in the order of words in a sentence. Changing the order of the words would change the meaning of a sentence. The other three choices do not involve finding meaning through the order of words.

18. **John Bunyan, Coleridge, Shakespeare, Homer, and Chaucer all contributed to what genre of literature?**
(Average) (Skill 4.1)

A. Children's literature

B. Preadolescent literature

C. Adolescent literature

D. Adult literature

Answer: D. Adult literature

These five authors contributed to the adult literature genre as they were authoring titles before children's and preadolescent/adolescent literature became recognized as separate genres that authors purposefully contributed towards.

19. **Which of the following is NOT true of slant rhyme?**
    (Rigorous) (Skill 5.9)

    A. This occurs when a rhyme is not exact

    B. Words are used to evoke meaning by their sounds

    C. The final consonant sounds are the same, but the vowels are different

    D. It occurs frequently in Welsh verse

    Answer: B. Words are used to evoke meaning by their sounds
    Slant rhyme occurs when a rhyme is not exact because the final consonant sounds may be the same while the vowel sounds are different. Examples include: "green" and "gone" or "that" and "hit." This type of device occurs frequently in Welsh verse as well as in Irish and Icelandic verse. Poets who use words to evoke meaning by their sounds are using onomatopoeia.

20. **Which of the following should students use to improve coherence of ideas within an argument?**
    (Rigorous) (Skill 6.6)

    A. Transitional words or phrases to show relationship of ideas

    B. Conjunctions like "and" to join ideas together

    C. Use direct quotes extensively to improve credibility

    D. Adjectives and adverbs to provide stronger detail

    Answer: A. Transitional words or phrases to show relationship of ideas
    Transitional words and phrases are two-way indicators that connect the previous idea to the following idea. Sophisticated writers use transitional devices to clarify text (for example), to show contrast (despite), to show sequence (first, next), to show cause (because).

21. **Which of the following are punctuated correctly?**
    (Rigorous) (Skill 6.5)

    I.   The teacher directed us to compare Faulkner's three symbolic novels *Absalom, Absalom*; *As I Lay Dying*; and *Light in August*.
    II. Three of Faulkner's symbolic novels are: *Absalom, Absalom*; *As I Lay Dying*; and *Light in August*.
    III. The teacher directed us to compare Faulkner's three symbolic novels: *Absalom, Absalom*; *As I Lay Dying*; and *Light in August*.
    IV. Three of Faulkner's symbolic novels are *Absalom, Absalom*; *As I Lay Dying*; and *Light in August*.

    A. I and II only

    B. II and III only

    C. III and IV only

    D. IV only

    Answer: C. III and IV only
    These sentences are focusing on the use of a colon. The rule is to place a colon at the beginning of a list of items except when the list is preceded by a verb. Sentences I and III do not have a verb before the list and therefore need a colon. Sentences II and IV have a verb before the list and therefore do not need a colon.

22. **Being competent in _____, a reader is able to understand what the writer is trying to convey to the audience.**
    (Average) (Skill 4.3)

    A. Semantics

    B. Pragmatics

    C. Morphemes

    D. Phonemes

    Answer: B. Pragmatics
    Semantics concerns the difference between the writer's meaning and the literal meaning of the sentence based on social context.

23. **Which of the following is NOT utilized by a reader when trying to comprehend the meaning behind the literal text?**
(Rigorous) (Skill 4.3)

A. Pictures and graphics in the text

B. Background knowledge about a topic

C. Knowledge of different types of text structure

D. Context clues

Answer: A. Pictures and graphics in the text
While pictures and graphics can be helpful, good readers are trying to extract meaning from the text itself by comparing new information to background knowledge, using knowledge of a type of text to build expectations, and making use of context clues to help identify unknown words.

24. **To make an inference a reader must:**
(Average) (Skill 3.15)

A. Make a logical guess as to the next event.

B. Find a line of reasoning on which to rely.

C. Make a decision based on an observation.

D. Use prior knowledge and apply it to the current situation.

Answer: D. Use prior knowledge and apply it to the current situation.
Prior knowledge applied to the situation at hand is essential in making a valid inference. Because choices A–C do not involve prior knowledge, they are not correct ways to make an inference.

25. **A second grade teacher explains the steps of the writing process to her learners. For the first step, she demonstrates the use of a Venn Diagram to compare and contrast two characters from a story the class recently read. These visual representations of content are known as:**
(Easy) (Skill 8.9)

A. Graphic Organizers

B. Running Records

C. Blogs

D. Phonemes

Answer: A. Graphic Organizers
Graphic organizers can be used to visually represent text. Examples include Venn Diagrams, flowcharts, and webs.

26. **All of the following are true about schemata EXCEPT:**
(Rigorous) (Skill 4.1)

A. Used as a basis for literary response

B. Structures that represent concepts stored in our memories

C. A generalization that is proven with facts

D. Used together with prior knowledge for effective reading comprehension

Answer: C. A generalization that is proven with facts
Schemata are structures that represent concepts stored in the memory. When used together with prior knowledge and ideas from the printed text while reading, comprehension takes place. Schemata have nothing to do with making a generalization and proving it with facts.

27. **Asking a child if what he or she has read makes sense to him or her, is prompting the child to use:**
(Average) (Skill 3.6)

A. Phonics cues

B. Syntactic cues

C. Semantic cues

D. Prior knowledge

Answer: C. Semantic cues
Children use their prior knowledge, sense of the story, and pictures to support their predicting and confirming the meaning of the text.

28. **Which of the following indicates that a student is a fluent reader?**
(Rigorous) (Skill 3.1)

A. Reads texts with expression or prosody

B. Reads word-to-word and haltingly

C. Must intentionally decode a majority of the words

D. In a writing assignment, sentences are poorly-organized, structurally

Answer: A. Reads texts with expression or prosody.
The teacher should listen to the children read aloud, but there are also clues to reading levels in their writing.

29. **To decode is to:**
    (Average) (Skill 2.2)

    A. Construct meaning

    B. Sound out a printed sequence of letters

    C. Use a special code to decipher a message

    D. None of the above

    Answer: B. Sound out a printed sequence of letters.
    To decode means to change communication signals into messages. Reading comprehension requires that the reader learn the code within which a message is written and be able to decode it to get the message.

30. **John Bunyan, Coleridge, Shakespeare, Homer, and Chaucer all contributed to what genre of literature?**
    (Average) (Skill 5.13)

    A. Children's literature

    B. Preadolescent literature

    C. Adolescent literature

    D. Adult literature

    Answer: D. Adult literature
    These five authors contributed to the adult literature genre as they were authoring titles before children's and preadolescent/adolescent literature became recognized as separate genres that authors purposefully contributed towards.

31. **All of the following are true about graphic organizers EXCEPT:**
    (Rigorous) (Skill 5.8)

    A. Solidify a visual relationship among various reading and writing ideas

    B. Organize information for an advanced reader

    C. Provide scaffolding for instruction

    D. Activate prior knowledge

    Answer: B. Organize information for an advanced reader
    A graphic organizer is a tool that students can use to help them visualize ideas in a text. They are also a helpful scaffolding tool as they help students activate their prior knowledge on the topic at hand. Choice B is incorrect because graphic organizers are relevant tools for young and/or basic readers and are not just for the advanced or independent.

32. **Identify the type of appeal used by Molly Ivins's in this excerpt from her essay "Get a Knife, Get a Dog, But Get Rid of Guns."**
    (Rigorous) (Skill 5.14)

    As a civil libertarian, I, of course, support the Second Amendment. And I believe it means exactly what it says:
    "A well regulated militia being necessary to the security of a free state, the right of the people to keep and bear arms shall not be infringed."

    A. Appeal based on writer's credibility

    B. Appeal to logic

    C. Appeal to the emotion

    D. Appeal to the reader

    Answer: A. Appeal based on writer's credibility
    By announcing that she is a civil libertarian and that she supports the Second Amendment, the author is establishing her credibility. At this point, Ivins has not provided reasons or appealed to the emotion, nor has she addressed the reader.

33. **"What is the point?" is the first question to be asked when:**
(Average) (Skill 5.12)

   A. Reading a written piece

   B. Listening to a presentation

   C. Writing a composition

   D. All of the above

Answer: D. All of the above
When reading, listening, or writing one should first ask, "What is the point?" The answer will be in the thesis. If a piece doesn't make a point, the reader/listener/viewer is likely to be confused or feel that it was not worth the effort.

34. **All of the following are true about writing an introduction EXCEPT:**
(Average) (Skill 7.11)

   A. It should be written last

   B. It should lead the audience into the discourse

   C. It is the point of the paper

   D. It can take up a large percentage of the total word count

Answer: C. It is the point of the paper
The thesis is the point of the paper not the introduction. The rest of the choices are true about an introduction.

35. **Which of the following is an important feature of vocabulary instruction, according to the National Reading Panel?**
(Average) (Skill 7.2)

   A. Repetition of vocabulary items

   B. Keeping a consistent task structure at all times

   C. Teaching vocabulary in more than one language

   D. Isolating vocabulary instruction from other subjects

   Answer: A. Repetition of vocabulary items.
   According to the National Reading Panel, repetition and multiple exposures to vocabulary items are important. Students should be given items that will be likely to appear in many contexts.

36. **Isaac is mimicking the way his father is writing. He places a piece of paper on the table and holds the pencil in his hand correctly, but he merely draws lines and makes random marks on the paper. What type of writer is he?**
(Average) (Skill 7.2)

   A. Role play writer

   B. Emergent writer

   C. Developing writer

   D. Beginning writer

   Answer: A. Role play writer.
   A role play writer uses writing-like behavior but has no phonetic association. He is aware of print but scribbles at this point.

37. **The following sentences are correct EXCEPT:**
    (Rigorous) (Skill 7.4)

    A. One of the boys was playing too rough.

    B. A man and his dog were jogging on the beach.

    C. The House of Representatives has adjourned for the holidays.

    D. Neither Don nor Joyce have missed a day of school this year.

    Answer: D. Neither Don nor Joyce have missed a day of school this year.
    A verb should always agree in number with its subject. Making them agree requires the ability to locate the subject of a sentence. In choice A the subject, one, is singular and requires a singular verb. In choice B the subject, man and dog, is plural and requires a plural verb, In choice C the subject, House of Representatives, is collectively singular and requires a singular verb. In choice D the subject, Don and Joyce, are both singular and connected by nor which requires the use of a singular verb, and "have" is plural and therefore incorrect.

38. **To determine an author's purpose a reader must:**
    (Average) (Skill 5.2)

    A. Use his or her own judgment.

    B. Verify all the facts.

    C. Link the causes to the effects.

    D. Rely on common sense.

    Answer: A. Use his or her own judgment.
    An author may have more than one purpose in writing. There are no tricks or rules to follow, and the reader must use his or her own judgment to determine the author's purpose for writing. Verifying all the facts, linking causes to effects, and relying on common sense can all help a reader in judging the author's purpose, but none are solely responsible.

39. **Which of the following skills can help students improve their listening comprehension?**
(Rigorous) (Skill 4.2)

I.   **Tap into prior knowledge.**
II. **Look for transitions between ideas.**
III. **Ask questions of the speaker.**
IV. **Discuss the topic being presented.**

A. I and II only

B. II and IV only

C. II and IV only

D. IV only

Answer: A. I and II only
Many strategies that are effective in improving reading comprehension are also effective in improving listening comprehension. Tapping into prior knowledge and looking for transitions between ideas are excellent listening and reading comprehension strategies. Asking questions of the speaker may help clarify ideas and discussing the topic may help organize the thoughts being presented, but both are difficult to do during the actual act of listening.

40. **Academically, appropriate literature primarily helps students to _____.**
(Rigorous) (Skill 5.17)

A. Become better readers

B. See how the skills they learned are applied to writing

C. Enjoy library time

D. Increase academic skills in other content areas

Answer B. see how the skills they learned are applied to writing
When students are exposed to appropriate literature selections, and are taught to select appropriate texts for themselves, they are able to observe how the reading and writing skills they learn in classroom mini-lessons are applied to published writing. Published works are an excellent place for students to see not only proper conventions of grammar, but "real-life" examples of imagery and figurative language.

41. **While standing in line at the grocery store, three-year-old Megan says to her mother in a regular tone of voice, "Mom, why is that woman so fat?" What does this indicate a lack of understanding of?**
   (Average) (Skill 1.1)

   A. Syntax

   B. Semantics

   C. Morphology

   D. Pragmatics

   Answer: D. Pragmatics
   Pragmatics is the development and understanding of social relevance to conversations and topics. It develops as children age. In this situation Megan simply does not understand, as an adult would, how that question could be viewed as offensive.

42. **Oral language development can be enhanced by which of the following?**
   (Easy) (Skill 1.4)

   A. Meaningful conversation

   B. Storytelling

   C. Alphabet songs

   D. All of the above

   Answer: D. All of the above
   Effective oral language development can be encouraged by many different activities including storytelling, rhyming books, meaningful conversation, alphabet songs, dramatic playtime, listening games, and more.

43. **Ms. Chomski is presenting a new story to her class of first graders. In the story, a family visits their grandparents, where they all gather around a record player and listen to music. Many students do not understand what a record player is, especially some children for whom English is not their first language. Which of the following would be best for Ms. Chomski to do?**
(Rigorous) (Skill 1.5)

A. Discuss what a record player is with her students

B. Compare a record player with a CD player

C. Have students look up *record player* in a dictionary

D. Show the students a picture of a record player

Answer: D. Show the students a picture of a record player
The most effective method for ensuring adequate comprehension is through direct experience. Sometimes this cannot be accomplished and therefore it is necessary to utilize pictures or other visual aids to provide students with experience in another mode besides oral language.

44. **Reading aloud correlates with all of the following EXCEPT:**
(Rigorous) (Skill 1.7)

A. Reader self-confidence

B. Better reading comprehension

C. Literacy development

D. Overall school success

Answer: A. Reader self-confidence
Reading aloud promotes language acquisition and correlates with literacy development, achieving better reading comprehension, and overall success in school. It may or may not promote reader self-confidence, depending on the reader and his or her skills and personality.

45. **Mr. Johns is using an activity that involves having students analyze the public speaking of others. All of the following would be guidelines for this activity EXCEPT: (Rigorous) (Skill 1.10)**

   A. The speeches to be evaluated are not given by other students

   B. The rubric for evaluating the speeches includes pace, pronunciation, body language, word choice, and visual aids

   C. The speeches to be evaluated are best presented live to give students a more engaging learning experience

   D. One of Mr. Johns's goals with this activity is to help students improve their own public speaking skills

   Answer: C. The speeches to be evaluated are best presented live to give students a more engaging learning experience
   Analyzing the speech of others is an excellent technique for helping students improve their own public speaking abilities. In most circumstances students cannot view themselves as they give speeches and presentations, so when they get the opportunity to critique, question, and analyze others' speeches, they begin to learn what works and what doesn't work in effective public speaking. However, an important word of warning: *do not* have students critique each other's public speaking skills. It could be very damaging to a student to have his or her peers point out what did not work in a speech. Instead, video is a great tool teachers can use. Any appropriate source of public speaking can be used in the classroom for students to analyze and critique.

46. **All of the following are true about phonological awareness EXCEPT: (Average) (Skill 2.1)**

   A. It may involve print

   B. It is a prerequisite for spelling and phonics

   C. Activities can be done by the children with their eyes closed

   D. It starts before letter recognition is taught

   Answer: A. It may involve print
   All of the options are aspects of phonological awareness except the first one, A, because phonological awareness does not involve print.

47. **Which of the following explains a significant difference between phonics and phonemic awareness?**
(Rigorous) (Skill 2.1)

A. Phonics involves print, while phonemic awareness involves language

B. Phonics is harder than phonemic awareness

C. Phonics involves sounds, while phonemic awareness involves letters

D. Phonics is the application of sounds to print, while phonemic awareness is oral

Answer: D. Phonics is the application of sounds to print, while phonemic awareness is oral
Both phonics and phonemic awareness involve sounds, but it is with phonics that the application of these sounds is applied to print. Phonemic awareness is an oral activity.

48. **Theorist Marilyn Jager Adams, who researches early reading, has outlined five basic types of phonemic awareness tasks. Which of the following is NOT one of the tasks noted by Jager Adams?**
(Average) (Skill 2.2)

A. Ability to do oddity tasks

B. Ability to orally blend words and split syllables

C. Ability to sound out words when reading aloud

D. Ability to do phonics manipulation tasks

Answer: C. Ability to sound out words when reading aloud
The tasks Jager Adams has outlined do not include the ability to sound out words when reading aloud. Her five tasks are: 1) The ability to hear rhymes and alliteration, 2) The ability to do oddity tasks (recognize the member of a set that is different, or odd, among the group, 3) The ability to orally blend words and split syllables, 4) The ability to orally segment words, and 5) The ability to do phonics manipulation tasks.

49. **Activities that parents can practice at home to improve phonological and phonemic awareness include which of the following?**
    (Average) (Skill 2.5)

    A. Play games with words that sound alike as you experience them in everyday home activities

    B. Demonstrate how sounds blend together in familiar words

    C. Play a game in which the goal is to find objects with names that begin with a certain initial sound

    D. All of the above

    Answer: D. All of the above
    Games and demonstrations that help children focus on distinguishing sounds are all useful in improving phonological and phonemic awareness.

50. **The alphabetic principle can best be described by which of the following statements?**
    (Rigorous) (Skill 3.1)

    A. Most reading skills need to be acquired through a regular teaching of the alphabet

    B. Written words are composed of patterns of letters that represent the sounds of spoken words

    C. Written words are composed of patterns that must be memorized in order to read well

    D. Spoken words (regular and irregular) lead to phonological reading

    Answer: B. Written words are composed of patterns of letters that represent the sounds of spoken words
    The alphabetic principle is sometimes called graphophonemic awareness. This multi-syllabic technical reading foundation term describes the understanding that written words are composed of patterns of letters that represent the sounds of spoken words.
    There are basically two parts to the alphabetic principle: 1) An understanding that words are made up of letters and that each letter has a specific sound, 2) The correspondence between sounds and letters leads to phonological reading. This consists of reading regular and irregular words and doing advanced analysis of words.

51. **Which of the following is NOT true about multisensory approaches to teaching the alphabetic principle?**
(Rigorous) (Skill 3.3)

A. Some children can only learn through multisensory techniques

B. Multisensory techniques give multiple cues to enhance memory and learning

C. Quilt book, rhyme time, letter path, and shape game are multisensory strategies

D. Multisensory techniques require direct teaching and ongoing engagement

Answer: A. Some children can only learn through multisensory techniques
Although some children may learn more effectively when multiple senses are involved, there is not evidence to suggest that this is the only way some students can learn. Multisensory techniques do enhance learning and memory and provide more solid grounding when students later learn to apply phonics skills to print. Such activities demand teacher engagement with students to directly teach the concepts related to the alphabetic principle.

52. **Activities that facilitate learning the alphabetic principle include:**
(Average) (Skill 3.4)

A. Read alouds, alphabet art, concept books, and name sorts

B. Read alouds, shared reading, concept books, and picture books

C. Picture books, concept books, and alphabet books

D. Alphabet art, name sorts, shared reading, and phonics

Answer: A. Read alouds, alphabet art, concept books, and name sorts
Read alouds, alphabet art, concept books, name sorts, and shared reading are all activities useful to help young children learn the alphabetic principle. Picture books and phonics develop other aspects of reading skills and literacy development.

53. **Which of the following is a convention of print that children learn during reading activities?**
(*Rigorous*) *(Skill 4.1)*

   A. The meaning of words

   B. The left-to-right motion

   C. The purpose of print

   D. The identification of letters

Answer: B. The left-to-right motion
During reading activities, children learn conventions of print. Children learn the way to hold a book, where to begin to read, the left-to-right motion, and how to continue from one line to another.

54. **Alphabet books are classified as:**
(*Average*) *(Skill 4.6)*

   A. Concept books

   B. Easy-to-read books

   C. Board books

   D. Picture books

Answer: A. Concept books
Concept books combine language and pictures to show concrete examples of abstract concepts. One category of concept books is alphabet books, which are popular with children from preschool through grade 2.

55. **To draw inferences and make conclusions, an**
(Average) (Skill 4.10)

A. Author's Purpose

B. Author's Tone

C. Main Idea

D. Inference

Answer: B. Author's Tone
A reader can determine the overall tone of a statement or passage through author's word choice.

56. **The process in which one takes different things and makes them one whole thing:**
(Average) (Skill 4.10)

A. synthesis

B. evaluation

C. analysis

D. context

Answer: A. Synthesis
Synthesis occurs when one examines different objects and draws a global conclusion. It is often thought of as the opposite of analysis.

57. **Contextual redefinition is a strategy that encourages children to use the context more effectively by presenting them with sufficient vocabulary _____ the reading of a text.**
(Rigorous) (Skill 5.2)

A. After

B. Before

C. During

D. None of the above

Answer: B. Before
Contextual redefinition is a strategy that encourages children to use the context more effectively by presenting them with sufficient context *before* they begin reading. To apply this strategy, the teacher should first select unfamiliar words for teaching. No more than two or three words should be selected for direct teaching.

58. **What is the best place for students to find appropriate synonyms, antonyms, and other related words to enhance their writing?**
(Average) (Skill 5.6)

A. Dictionary

B. Spell check

C. Encyclopedia

D. Thesaurus

Answer: D. Thesaurus
Students need plenty of exposure to new words. A thesaurus is an excellent resource to use when writing. Students can use a thesaurus to find appropriate synonyms, antonyms, and other related words to enhance their writing.

59. **An _____ is a story in verse or prose with characters representing virtues and vices.**
    (Average) (Skill 5.9)

    A. epistle

    B. epic

    C. essay

    D. allegory

    Answer: D. Allegory
    A story in verse or prose with characters representing virtues and vices. There are two meanings, symbolic and literal.

60. **Which of the following reading strategies is NOT associated with fluent reading abilities?**
    (Average) (Skill 6.1)

    A. Pronouncing unfamiliar words by finding similarities with familiar words

    B. Establishing a purpose for reading

    C. Formulating questions about the text while reading

    D. Reading sentences word by word

    Answer: D. Reading sentences word by word
    Pronouncing unfamiliar words by finding similarities with familiar words, establishing a purpose for reading, and formulating questions about the text while reading are all strategies fluent readers use to enhance their comprehension of a text. Reading sentences word by word is a trait of a nonfluent reader. It inhibits comprehension, as the reader focuses on each word separately rather than the meaning of the whole sentence and how it fits into the text.

61. **Automaticity refers to all of the following EXCEPT:**
(Rigorous) (Skill 6.2)

   A. Automatic whole-word identification

   B. Automatic recognition of syllable types

   C. Automatic reactions to the content of a paragraph

   D. Automatic identification of graphemes as they relate to four basic word types

Answer: C. Automatic reactions to the content of a paragraph
Automaticity is the ability to automatically recognize words, graphemes, word types, and syllables. This ability progresses through various stages and facilitates reading fluency and prosody. Automaticity is not related to the content of a paragraph or the student's reactions to the content.

62. **Which of the following activities are likely to improve fluency?**
(Easy) (Skill 6.4)

   A. Partner reading and a reading theater

   B. Phrased reading

   C. Both A and B

   D. None of the above

Answer: C. Both A and B
Partner reading, tutors, a reading theater, modeling fluent reading, and opportunities for phrased reading are all strategies designed to enhance fluency.

63. **Students are about to read a text that contains words that will need to be understood for the students to understand the text. When should the vocabulary be introduced to students?**
(Average) (Skill 7.2)

A. Before reading

B. During reading

C. After reading

D. It should not be introduced

Answer: A. Before reading
Vocabulary should be introduced before reading if there are words in the text that are necessary for reading comprehension.

64. **Which of the following is an important feature of vocabulary instruction, according to the National Reading Panel?**
(Average) (Skill 7.2)

A. Repetition of vocabulary items

B. Keeping a consistent task structure at all times

C. Teaching vocabulary in more than one language

D. Isolating vocabulary instruction from other subjects

Answer: A. Repetition of vocabulary items
According to the National Reading Panel, repetition and multiple exposures to vocabulary items are important. Students should be given items that will be likely to appear in many contexts.

65. **The book *The Giver* by Lois Lowry is a great book. The characters are interesting and they are unique. Everyone who reads *The Giver* will enjoy it and not be able to put it down.**

    Is this a valid or invalid argument?
    (Average) (Skill 5.1)

    A. Valid

    B. Invalid

    Answer: B. Invalid
    The author does not support their opinions with any evidence or facts from the story.

66. **Which of the following is not a strategy of teaching reading comprehension?**
    (Rigorous) (Skill 7.7)

    A. Asking questions

    B. Utilizing graphic organizers

    C. Focusing on mental images

    D. Manipulating sounds

    Answer: D. Manipulating sounds
    Comprehension simply means that the reader can ascribe meaning to text. Teachers can use many strategies to teach comprehension, including questioning, asking students to paraphrase or summarize, utilizing graphic organizers, and focusing on mental images.

67. **The children's literature genre came into its own in the:**
    (Easy) (Skill 7.11)

    A. Seventeenth century

    B. Eighteenth century

    C. Nineteenth century

    D. Twentieth century

    Answer: B. Eighteenth century
    Children's literature is a genre of its own that emerged as a distinct and independent form in the second half of the eighteenth century. *The Visible World in Pictures,* by John Amos Comenius, a Czech educator, was one of the first printed works and the first picture book.

68. **When evaluating reference sources, students should do all of the following EXCEPT:**
    (Rigorous) (Skill 8.1)

    A. Look for self-published books by the author as evidence of expert status

    B. Examine the level of detail provided by the source

    C. Review the references at the end of the book or article

    D. See if the author presents both sides of an argument or viewpoint

    Answer: A. Look for self-published books by the author as evidence of expert status
    Anyone can self-publish a book or pamphlet. Experience and background in the subject area have not been reviewed by anyone in many cases. Therefore, more research needs to be done to determine whether a source document is based on reliable, expert information when it has been published by the author.

69. **Graphic organizers:**
    (Average) (Skill 8.2)

    A. are used primarily in grades K-3

    B. work better with poetry than other forms of writing

    C. help readers think critically by pulling out the main idea and supporting details

    D. generally aren't helpful to ELL students

    Answer: C. help readers think critically by pulling out the main idea and supporting details
    Graphic organizers help readers think critically about an idea, concept, or story by pulling out the main idea and supporting details. These pieces of information can then be depicted graphically through the use of connected geometric shapes. Readers who develop this skill can use it to increase their reading comprehension. Graphic organizers are useful for all ages and types of students, and for many forms for literature and writing.

70. **Which of the following helps students in a way that is similar to using a glossary?**
    (Average) (Skill 8.4)

    A. Information in the text such as charts, graphs, maps, diagrams, captions, and photos

    B. Prewriting

    C. Classroom discussion of the main idea

    D. Paired reading

    Answer: A. Information in the text such as charts, graphs, maps, diagrams, captions, and photos
    Charts, graphs, maps, diagrams, captions, and photos in text can work in the same way as looking up unknown words in the glossary. They can provide more insight into and clarification of concepts and ideas the author is conveying. Students may need to develop these skills to interpret the information accurately, which makes a natural cross-subject opportunity.

71. **Which of these describes the best way to teach spelling?**
    (Rigorous) (Skill 9.4)

    A. At the same time that grammar and sentence structure are taught

    B. Within the context of meaningful language experiences

    C. Independently so that students can concentrate on spelling

    D. In short lessons, as students pick up spelling almost immediately

    Answer: B. Within the context of meaningful language experiences
    Spelling should be taught within the context of meaningful language experiences. Giving a child a list of words to learn to spell and then testing the child on the words every Friday will not aid in the development of spelling. The child must be able to use the words in context and they must have some meaning for the child. The assessment of how well a child can spell or where there are problems also has to be done within a meaningful environment.

72. **Which of the following sentences contains an error in agreement?**
    (Rigorous) (Skill 9.8)

    A. Jennifer is one of the women who writes for the magazine.

    B. Each one of their sons plays a different sport.

    C. This band has performed at the Odeum many times.

    D. The data are available online at the listed Web site.

    Answer: A. Jennifer is one of the women who writes for the magazine.
    Women is the plural subject of the verb. The verb should be *write*.

73. **All of the following are correctly punctuated EXCEPT:**
    (Rigorous) (Skill 9.8)

    A. "The airplane crashed on the runway during takeoff."

    B. I was embarrassed when Ms. White said, "Your slip is showing!"

    C. "The middle school readers were unprepared to understand Bryant's poem 'Thanatopsis.'"

    D. The hall monitor yelled, "Fire! Fire!"

    Answer: B. I was embarrassed when Ms. White said, "Your slip is showing!"
    B is incorrectly punctuated because in exclamatory sentences, the exclamation point should be positioned outside the closing quotation marks if the quote itself is a statement, command, or cited title. The exclamation point is correctly positioned in choice D because the sentence is declarative but the quotation is an exclamation.

74. **Which of the following is not a technique of prewriting?**
    (Average) (Skill 10.4)

    A. Clustering

    B. Listing

    C. Brainstorming

    D. Proofreading

    Answer: D. Proofreading
    Proofreading cannot be a method of prewriting because it is done only on texts that have already been written.

MATHEMATICS

75. **Which of the following statements best characterizes the meaning of "absolute value of *x*"?**
(Average) (Skill 15.1)

    A. The square root of *x*

    B. The square of *x*

    C. The distance on a number line between *x* and –*x*

    D. The distance on a number line between 0 and *x*

    Answer: D. The distance on a number line between 0 and *x*
    The absolute value of a number *x* is best described as the distance on a number line between 0 and *x*, regardless of whether *x* is positive or negative. Note that the following expression is valid for $x \geq 0$:

    $$|x| = |-x|$$

76. **Which of the following terms most accurately describes the set of numbers below?**
(Average) (Skill 10.2)

    $$\{3, \sqrt{16}, \pi^0, 6, \frac{28}{4}\}$$

    A. Rationals

    B. Irrationals

    C. Complex

    D. Whole numbers

    Answer: D. Whole numbers
    Let's simplify the set of numbers as follows.

    $$\{3, 4, 1, 6, 7\}$$

    Note that this set of numbers can be described as real numbers, rationals, integers, and whole numbers, but they are *best* described as whole numbers.

77. **Calculate the value of the following expression.**
(Average) (Skill 11.3)

$$\left(\frac{6}{3}+1\cdot 5\right)^2 \cdot \left(\frac{1}{7}\right) + (3\cdot 2 - 1)$$

A. 6

B. 10

C. 12

D. 294

Answer: C. 12
Apply the correct order of operations to get the correct result: first, calculate all terms in parentheses, followed by exponents, division and multiplication, and addition and subtraction (in that order).

$$(2+5)^2 \cdot \left(\frac{1}{7}\right) + (6-1) = 7^2 \cdot \frac{1}{7} + 5 = 49 \cdot \frac{1}{7} + 5 = 7 + 5 = 12$$

78. **What is the GCF of 12, 30, 56, and 144?**
(Rigorous) (Skill 11.1)

A. 2

B. 3

C. 5

D. 7

Answer: A. 2
One way to determine the greatest common factor (GCF) is to list the factors for each number. Although this can be tedious, it is a relatively sure method of determining the GCF. Note that you need not determine any factors larger than the smallest number in the list (12, in this case)—12 doesn't have any factors greater than 12.

12:	2, 3, 4, 6, 12
30:	2, 3, 5, 6, 10
56:	2, 4, 7, 8
144:	2, 3, 4, 6, 8, 9, 12

By inspection of these lists, we see that 2 is the greatest common factor.

79. **What is the value of the following expression?** *(Rigorous) (Skill 11.2)*

$$\frac{25-2(6-2\bullet3)}{^-5(2+2\bullet4)}$$

A. 0.5

B. 5.0

C. -0.5

D. 3.4

Answer: C. –0.5
The fraction line is equivalent to parentheses and indicates that the numerator is to be simplified first. Then use the standard order of operations.

$$\frac{25-2(6-2\bullet3)}{^-5(2+2\bullet4)}=\frac{25-2(6-6)}{-5(2+8)}=\frac{25-0}{-5(10)}=\frac{25}{-50}=-0.5$$

80. **The final cost of an item (with sales tax) is $8.35. If the sales tax is 7%, what was the pre-tax price of the item?**
(Average,) (Skill 12.5)

A. $7.80

B. $8.00

C. $8.28

D. $8.93

Answer: A. $7.80
We can solve this problem by constructing a proportionality expression. Let's call the pre-tax price of the item x; then, if we add 7% of x to this price, we get a final cost of $8.35.

$x + 0.07x = \$8.35$
$1.07x = \$8.35$
$x = \frac{\$8.35}{1.07} = \$7.80$

Thus, the initial price of the item was $7.80 (answer A). You can also determine this answer by multiplying each option by 1.07; the correct answer is the one that yields a product of $8.35.

81. **Which expression best characterizes the shaded area in the graph below?**

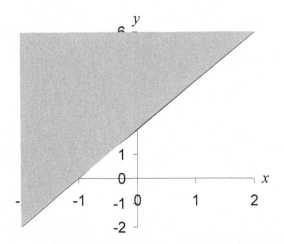

(Rigorous) (Skill 14.1)

A. $y \leq -x + 2$

B. $y \geq 2x + 2$

C. $y = 2x + 2$

D. $y \geq 2x - 1$

Answer: B. $y \geq 2x + 2$
The shaded region includes all the points above the line. Thus, we need only find the equation for the line and then choose the correct symbol for the inequality. Note that the line has a slope of 2 (it increases by two units in the y direction for every one unit of increase in the x direction) and a y-intercept of 2. Thus, the equation for the line is

$y = 2x + 2$

Note that the shaded region is above the line; the best choice is then answer B, or $y \geq 2x + 2$.

82. **Solve for L:**

$$R = r + \frac{400(W - L)}{N}$$

(Rigorous) (Skill 10.4)

A. $L = W - \frac{N}{400}(R - r)$

B. $L = W + \frac{N}{400}(R - r)$

C. $L = W - \frac{400}{N}(R - r)$

D. $L = \frac{NR}{r} - 400W$

Answer: A. $L = W - \frac{N}{400}(R - r)$

$$R = r + \frac{400(W - L)}{N}; \Rightarrow R - r = \frac{400(W - L)}{N}; \Rightarrow \frac{N}{400}(R - r) = W - L; \Rightarrow L = W - \frac{N}{400}(R - r)$$

83. **A burning candle loses ½ inch in height every hour. If the original height of the candle was 6 inches, which of the following equations describes the relationship between the height h of the candle and the number of hours t since it was lit?**
(Average) (Skill 13.4)

A. $2h + t = 12$

B. $2h - t = 12$

C. $h = 6 - t$

D. $h = 0.5t + 6$

Answer: A. $2h + t = 12$
Since the height of the candle is falling, the slope = -1/2. Thus, the equation in the slope-intercept form is h = - (1/2) t + 6 since h = 6 for t = 0. Multiplying both sides of the equation by 2, we get 2h = -t + 12 or 2h + t = 12.

84. **Which set cannot be considered "dense"?**
(Rigorous) (Skill 11.5)

   A. Integers

   B. Rationals

   C. Irrationals

   D. Reals

Answer: A. Integers
A set of numbers is considered dense if between any two arbitrary values from the set, there exists another value from the set that lies between these two values. For instance, between 1 and 3 is the number 2. For integers, however, there is no integer between 1 and 2, for example (or between any two consecutive integers). Thus, the correct answer is choice A. For the other sets (rationals, irrationals, and reals), there is always a value between any two arbitrary values from those sets.

85. **Which of the following expressions are equivalent to 28 – 4 • 6 +12?**

   I. $(28 – 4) • 6 +12$
   II. $28 – (4 • 6) +12$
   III. $(28 – 4) • (6 +12)$
   IV. $(28 + 12) – (4 • 6)$
   V. $28 – 4 • 12 + 6$

   (Average) (Skill 14.2)

   A. I and V

   B. II and IV

   C. III and V

   D. IV and V

Answer: B. II and IV
The parentheses in expression II indicate that the multiplication is to be done first. Using the standard order of operations: multiply and divide from left to right, then add and subtract from left to right.

86. A recipe makes 6 servings and calls for $1\frac{1}{2}$ cups of rice. How much rice is needed to make 10 servings?
(Average) (Skill 10.5)

A. 2 cups

B. $2\frac{1}{4}$ cups

C. $2\frac{1}{2}$ cups

D. $2\frac{3}{4}$ cups

Answer: C. $2\frac{1}{2}$ **cups**

Write and solve a proportion.

$$\frac{1.5}{6} = \frac{x}{10}$$

$$1.5(10) = 6x$$
$$x = 25$$

When writing a proportion, check that the ratios are equivalent:

$$\frac{\text{cups of rice}}{\text{servings}} = \frac{\text{cups of rice}}{\text{servings}}$$

87. **The following represents the net of a**
(Average) (Skill 18.3)

A. Cube

B. Tetrahedron

C. Octahedron

D. Dodecahedron

Answer: C. Octahedron
The eight equilateral triangles make up the eight faces of an octahedron.

88. **Ginny and Nick head back to their respective colleges after being home for the weekend. They leave their house at the same time and drive for 4 hours. Ginny drives due south at the average rate of 60 miles per hour and Nick drives due east at the average rate of 60 miles per hour. What is the straight-line distance between them, in miles, at the end of the 4 hours?** *(Rigorous)* *(Skill 15.8)*

   A. 169.7 miles

   B. 240 miles

   C. 288 miles

   D. 339.4 miles

Answer: D. 339.4 miles
Ginny and Nick each drive a distance of 4 × 60, or 240 miles. Draw a diagram.

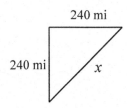

240 mi

240 mi

x

Then apply the Pythagorean Theorem: $c^2 = a^2 + b^2$.

$$x^2 = 240^2 + 240^2$$
$$= 115,200$$
$$x = \sqrt{115,200}$$
$$x \approx 339.4$$

So x is about 339.4 miles. Be sure to use the standard order of operations when solving for x.

89. **A school band has 200 members. Looking at the pie chart below, determine which statement is true about the band.**
(Average) (Skill 21.1)

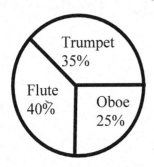

A. There are more trumpet players than flute players

B. There are fifty oboe players in the band

C. There are forty flute players in the band

D. One-third of all band members play the trumpet

Answer: B. There are fifty oboe players in the band
There are fifty oboe players in the band since 25% of 200 is 50.

90. **A restaurant offers the following menu choices.**

Green Vegetable	Yellow Vegetable
Asparagus	Carrots
Broccoli	Corn
Peas	Squash
Spinach	

If a customer chooses a green vegetable and a yellow vegetable at random, what is the probability that the customer will order neither asparagus nor corn? *(Rigorous)* *(Skill 21.3)*

A. $\frac{1}{12}$

B. $\frac{1}{6}$

C. $\frac{1}{3}$

D. $\frac{1}{2}$

Answer: D. $\frac{1}{2}$

There are 4 × 3, or 12 possible combinations of choices. Of those, 6 include either asparagus or corn or both (1 asparagus and corn, 2 asparagus and not corn, and 3 corn but not asparagus). Since 6 out of the 12 choices are favorable, the probability is $\frac{6}{12}$, or $\frac{1}{2}$. Be careful not to count any choice (asparagus and corn) more than once.

91. **A music store owner wants to change the window display every week. Only 4 out of 6 instruments can be displayed in the window at the same time. How many weeks will it be before the owner must repeat the same arrangement (in the same order) of instruments in the window display?**
(Rigorous) (Skill 21.3)

A. 24 weeks

B. 36 weeks

C. 120 weeks

D. 360 weeks

Answer: D. 360 weeks
There are 6 choices for the first position. For each of those choices, there are 5 choices for the second position and 6×5 choices for the first two positions. For each of those there are 3 choices for the third position and 2 for the fourth position: $6 \times 5 \times 4 \times 3 = 360$.

92. **Half the students in a class scored 80% on an exam; one student scored 10%; and the rest of the class scored 85%. Which would be the best measure of central tendency for the test scores?**
(Rigorous) (Skill 21.4)

A. Mean

B. Median

C. Mode

D. Either the median or the mode because they are equal

Answer: B. Median
The median is the least sensitive to extreme values. The mode reports only one score and is not a reflection of the entire data set. The mean will be skewed by the outlier of 10%.

93. **Which of the following is an example of a multiplicative inverse?**
(Average) (Skill 15.2)

A. $x^2 - x^2 = 0$

B. $(y - 3)^0 = 1$

C. $\dfrac{1}{e^{3z}} e^{3z} = 1$

D. $f^2 = \dfrac{1}{g}$

Answer: C. $\dfrac{1}{e^{3z}} e^{3z} = 1$

A multiplicative inverse has the form:

$$a \cdot \frac{1}{a} = 1$$

Thus, answer C best fits this definition.

94. **Based upon the following examples, can you conclude that the sum of two prime numbers is also a prime number? Why or why not?**

$$2 + 3 = 5$$
$$2 + 5 = 7$$
$$11 + 2 = 13$$

(Rigorous) (Skill 15.4)

A. Yes; there is a pattern

B. Yes; there are many more examples, such as $17 + 2 = 19$ and $29 + 2 = 31$

C. No; there are many counterexamples

D. No; the sums are not prime numbers

Answer: C. No; there are many counterexamples
Only one counterexample is needed to disprove a statement. For example, in $3 + 5 = 8$ the sum is a composite number. Care must be taken not to generalize a perceived pattern based upon too few examples. Additional examples are not sufficient to establish a pattern. In choice D, 5, 7, and 13 are prime numbers.

95. **Two farmers are buying feed for animals. One farmer buys eight bags of grain and six bales of hay for $105, and the other farmer buys three bags of grain and nine bales of hay for $69.75. How much is a bag of grain?**
     (Rigorous) (Skill 12.2)

     A. $4.50

     B. $9.75

     C. $14.25

     D. $28.50

Answer: B. $9.75
Let x be the price of a bag of grain, and let y be the price of a bale of hay. We can then write two equations based on the information provided in the problem.

Farmer 1: $8x + 6y = \$105$
Farmer 2: $3x + 9y = \$69.75$

We want to find x, the price of a bag of grain. One approach to solving this problem is to solve either the first or second equation for y and then substitute the result into the other equation and solve for x. Another approach involves subtraction. Let's multiply both sides of the second equation by 2/3.

$$\frac{2}{3}(3x + 9y = \$69.75)$$
$2x + 6y = \$46.50$

Now, subtract this from the first equation.

$$\begin{array}{r} 8x + 6y = \$105 \\ -\quad 2x + 6y = \$46.50 \\ \hline 6x \quad\ = \$58.5 \end{array}$$

Solving for x yields the solution.

$x = \$9.75$

96. **Which of the following is correct?**
    (Easy) (Skill 11.7)

    A. $2365 > 2340$

    B. $0.75 > 1.25$

    C. $3/4 < 1/16$

    D. $-5 < -6$

    Answer: A. 2365 > 2340

97. **For which of the following is the additive inverse equal to the multiplicative inverse?**
    (Rigorous) (Skill 12.1)

    A. $\dfrac{2}{3} + \dfrac{3}{2}$

    B. $\sqrt{-1}$

    C. $\dfrac{1-\sqrt{2}}{1+\sqrt{2}}$

    D. $(a+b)/(b-a)$

    Answer: B. $\sqrt{-1}$
    Let the number for which the additive inverse is equal to the multiplicative inverse be x.
    Then $-x = \dfrac{1}{x}; \Rightarrow x^2 = -1; x = \sqrt{-1}$

98. **Which of the statements below explain the error(s), if any, in the following calculation?** *(Rigorous)* *(Skill 12.3)*

$$\frac{18}{18} + 23 = 23$$

I.   A number divided by itself is 1, not 0.
II. The sum of 1 and 23 is 24, not 23.
III. The 18s are "cancelled" and replaced by 0.

A. I and II

B. II and III

C. I, II, and III

D. There is no error.

Answer: C. I, II, and III

$\dfrac{18}{18} = 1$ and $1 + 23 = 24$

99. **What is the length of the shortest side of a right isosceles triangle if the longest side is 5 centimeters?** *(Rigorous) (Skill 19.1)*

    A. 2.24 centimeters

    B. 2.5 centimeters

    C. 3.54 centimeters

    D. Not enough information

    Answer: C. 3.54 centimeters
    If a triangle is isosceles, then two of its sides are congruent, as are two of its angles. The longest side of such a triangle must be the hypotenuse; the other two sides, the legs, must be of equal length (this is because the congruent angles must be less than 90° each). Let's call the length of a leg x. Then, using the Pythagorean Theorem,

    $$x^2 + x^2 = 2x^2 = 5^2 = 25$$
    $$x^2 = \frac{25}{2} = 12.5$$

    $$x = \sqrt{12.5} \approx 3.54$$

    Thus, the shortest side (the legs are congruent) of the triangle described in the problem is 3.54 centimeters.

100. **What is the sample space for the sum of the outcomes for two rolls of a six-sided die?** *(Easy) (Skill 23.1)*

    A. {1, 2, 3, 4, 5, 6}

    B. {1, 2, 3, 4, 5, 6, 7, 8, 9, 10, 11, 12}

    C. {2, 3, 4, 5, 6, 7, 8, 9, 10, 11, 12}

    D. {7, 8, 9, 10, 11, 12}

    Answer: C. {2, 3, 4, 5, 6, 7, 8, 9, 10, 11, 12}
    A six-sided die can turn up any number between one and six, inclusive. The smallest sum that could be obtained from two rolls is for the case where both rolls turn up a one—the sum would then be two. The maximum sum would be the case where both rolls turn up a six—the sum would then be 12. Thus, the sample space for this experiment is 2 through 12, inclusive.

101. What is the GCF of 12, 30, 56, and 144?
(Rigorous) (Skill 11.4)

A. 2

B. 3

C. 5

D. 7

Answer: A. 2
One way to determine the greatest common factor (GCF) is to list the factors for each number. Although this can be tedious, it is a relatively sure method of determining the GCF. Note that you need not determine any factors larger than the smallest number in the list (12, in this case)—12 doesn't have any factors greater than 12.

12:	2, 3, 4, 6, 12
30:	2, 3, 5, 6, 10
56:	2, 4, 7, 8
144:	2, 3, 4, 6, 8, 9, 12

By inspection of these lists, we see that 2 is the greatest common factor.

102. **A traveler uses a ruler and finds the distance between two cities to be 3.5 inches. If the legend indicates that 100 miles is the same as an inch, what is the distance in miles between the cities?**
(Average) (Skill 17.2)

A. 29 miles

B. 35 miles

C. 100 miles

D. 350 miles

Answer: D. 350 miles
Construct a proportion relating inches to miles. Let the unknown distance in miles be *d*.

$$\frac{100 \text{ miles}}{1 \text{ inch}} = \frac{d}{3.5 \text{ inches}}$$

Cross multiply to find the value of *d*.

$$d = 3.5 \text{ inches} \frac{100 \text{ miles}}{1 \text{ inch}} = 350 \text{ miles}$$

103. What is the area of the shaded region below, where the circle has a radius *r*?

(Average) (Skill 18.4)

A. r^2

B. $(4-\pi)r^2$

C. $(2-\pi)r^2$

D. $4\pi r^2$

Answer: B. $(4-\pi)r^2$

Notice that the figure is a circle of radius *r* inscribed in a quadrilateral—this quadrilateral must therefore be a square. Thus, the sides of the square each have a length twice that of the radius, as shown below.

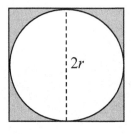 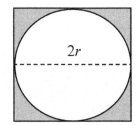

To find the area of the shaded region, subtract the area of the circle (πr^2) from the area of the square ($4r^2$).

$$A_{shaded} = 4r^2 - \pi r^2 = (4-\pi)r^2$$

104. **Students in Mr. Anderson's class want to know which train car will hold more plastic apples: the long, thin car, or the square car. First, they fill the long, thin car with apples and record their answer. Then they fill the square car with apples and record their answer. Which math principles does this activity demonstrate?** *(Rigorous) (Skill 26.1)*

    A. Problem solving, subtraction

    B. Subtraction, meaningful counting

    C. Problem solving, number sense

    D. Addition, problem solving

    Answer C: Problem solving, number sense
    The students are using problem solving skills by experimenting to see which train car can hold more plastic apples. They demonstrate number sense as they count both sets of apples to determine which set has more.

105. **Which of the following is a true statement regarding manipulatives in mathematics instruction?** *(Average) (Skill 13.4)*

    A. Manipulatives are materials that students can physically handle

    B. Manipulatives help students make concrete concepts abstract

    C. Manipulatives include fingers, tiles, paper folding, and ice cream sticks

    D. Manipulatives help students make abstract concepts concrete

    Answer: D. Manipulatives help students make abstract concepts concrete
    Manipulatives are materials that students can physically handle and move, such as fingers and tiles. Manipulatives allow students to understand mathematic concepts by allowing them to see concrete examples of abstract processes. Manipulatives are attractive to students because they appeal to their visual and tactile senses.

106. All of the following are tools that can strengthen students' mathematical understanding EXCEPT: *(Easy) (Skill 13.6)*

A. Rulers, scales, and protractors

B. Calculators, counters, and measuring containers

C. Software and hardware

D. Money and software

Answer: C. Software and hardware
Students' understanding of mathematical concepts is strengthened when they use tools to help make the abstract concepts become concrete realities. Teachers have a wide variety of tools available to help students learn mathematics. These include all of the above except for hardware. Hardware technically is not a tool but part of the infrastructure of the classroom.

107. Which of the following is not a good example of helping students make connections between the real world and mathematics? *(Average) (Skill 13.9)*

A. Studying a presidential election from the perspective of the math involved

B. Using weather concepts to teach math

C. Having student helpers take attendance

D. Reviewing major mathematical theorems on a regular basis

Answer: D. Reviewing major mathematical theorems on a regular basis
Theorems are abstract math concepts, and reviews, while valuable, are not an example of using everyday events to teach math. Teachers can increase student interest in math by relating mathematical concepts to familiar events in their lives and using real-world examples and data whenever possible. Instead of presenting only abstract concepts and examples, teachers should relate concepts to everyday situations to shift the emphasis from memorization and abstract application to understanding and applied problem solving. This will not only improve students' grasp of math ideas and keep them engaged, it will also help answer the perennial question, "Why do we have to learn math?"

108. Which of the following is an example of the associative property?
(Rigorous) (Skill 14.1)

A. $a(b+c) = ab + bc$

B. $a + 0 = a$

C. $(a+b) + c = a + (b+c)$

D. $a + b = b + a$

Answer: C. $(a+b) + c = a + (b+c)$
The associative property is when the parentheses of a problem are switched.

109. Simplify:

$$\frac{5^{-2} \times 5^3}{5^5 \times 5^{-7}}$$

(Average) (Skill 11.6)

A. 5^5

B. 125

C. $\dfrac{1}{125}$

D. 25

Answer: B. 125

$$\frac{5^{-2} \times 5^3}{5^5 \times 5^{-7}} = \frac{5^{-2+3}}{5^{5-7}} = \frac{5}{5^{-2}} = 5^{1+2} = 5^3 = 125$$

110. **Mathematical operations are done in the following order:**
(Rigorous) (Skill 14.4)

   A. Simplify inside grouping characters such as parentheses, brackets, square roots, fraction bars, etc.; multiply out expressions with exponents; do multiplication or division, from left to right; do addition or subtraction, from left to right

   B. Do multiplication or division, from left to right; simplify inside grouping characters such as parentheses, brackets, square roots, fraction bars, etc.; multiply out expressions with exponents; do addition or subtraction, from left to right

   C. Simplify inside grouping characters such as parentheses, brackets, square roots, fraction bars, etc.; do addition or subtraction, from left to right; multiply out expressions with exponents; do multiplication or division, from left to right

   D. None of the above

Answer: A. Simplify inside grouping characters such as parentheses, brackets, square roots, fraction bars, etc.; multiply out expressions with exponents; do multiplication or division, from left to right; do addition or subtraction, from left to right
When facing a mathematical problem that requires all mathematical properties to be performed first, you do the math within the parentheses, brackets, square roots, or fraction bars. Then you multiply out expressions with exponents. Next, you do multiplication or division. Finally, you do addition or subtraction.

111. **Which of the following is an irrational number?**
(Rigorous) (Skill 14.5)

   A. .36262626262…

   B. 4

   C. 8.2

   D. -5

Answer: A. .362626262626…
Irrational numbers are numbers that cannot be made into a fraction. This number cannot be made into a fraction.

112. **The number "0" is a member of all of the following groups of numbers EXCEPT:**
     (Rigorous) (Skill 14.5)

   A. Whole numbers

   B. Real numbers

   C. Natural numbers

   D. Integers

   Answer: C. Natural numbers
   The number zero is a whole number, real number, and an integer, but the natural numbers (also known as the counting numbers) start with the number one, not zero.

113. **4,087,361: What number represents the ten thousands' place?**
     (Easy) (Skill 14.9)

   A. 4

   B. 6

   C. 0

   D. 8

   Answer: D. 8
   The ten thousands' place is the number 8 in this problem.

114. Two mathematics classes have a total of 410 students. The 8:00 a.m. class has 40 more students than the 10:00 a.m. class. How many students are in the 10:00 a.m. class? *(Average) (Skill 15.3)*

A. 123.3

B. 370

C. 185

D. 330

Answer: C. 185
Let x = the number of students in the 8:00 a.m. class and $x - 40$ = the number of students in the 10:00 a.m. class. So there are 225 students in the 8:00 a.m. class, and $225 - 40 = 185$ in the 10:00 a.m. class, which is answer C.

115. Three-dimensional figures in geometry are called: *(Easy) (Skill 16.1)*

A. Solids

B. Cubes

C. Polygons

D. Blocks

Answer: A. Solids
Three-dimensional figures are referred to as solids.

116. The volume is:
(Easy) (Skill 16.2)

A. Area of the faces excluding the bases

B. Total area of all the faces, including the bases

C. The number of cubic units in a solid

D. The measure around the object

Answer: C. The number of cubic units in a solid
Volume refers to how much "stuff" can be placed in a solid. Cubic units are one of many things that can be placed in a solid to measure its volume.

SOCIAL STUDIES

117. The state of Louisiana is divided into parishes. What type of region do the parishes represent? *(Rigorous) (Skill 30.1)*

A. Formal region

B. Functional region

C. Vernacular region

D. Human region

Answer: A. Formal region
There are three main types of regions. Formal regions are areas defined by actual political boundaries, such as a city, county, or state. Functional regions are defined by a common function, such as the area covered by a telephone service. Vernacular regions are less formally defined areas that are formed by people's perception (e.g., "the Middle East" or "the South").

118. **Which continent is only one country?**
(Easy) (Skill 30.2)

    A. Australia

    B. New Zealand

    C. The Arctic

    D. Antarctica

Answer: A. Australia
Of the seven continents, Australia is the only one that contains just one country. It is also the only island continent. Antarctica is the southernmost continent. It surrounds the South Pole. New Zealand is made up of two large islands, but it is not a continent. The Arctic is a region that includes parts of several continents, but is not in and of itself a continent. In fact, much of the Arctic is ice-covered ocean.

119. **Anthropology is:**
(Easy) (Skill 33.11)

    A. The profession that made the Leakey family famous

    B. The scientific study of human culture and humanity

    C. Not related to geography at all

    D. Margaret Mead's study of the Samoans

Answer: B. The scientific study of human culture and humanity
Anthropology did make the Leakeys famous (choice A) but that does not define anthropology. The text states that anthropology is related to geography (choice C). Margaret Mead's study of the Samoans (choice D) is only one part of anthropology.

120. In the 1920s, Margaret Mead wrote *Coming of Age in Samoa,* **relating her observations about this group's way of life. What of these types of geographical study best describes her method?**
(Rigorous) (Skill 30.3)

A. Regional

B. Topical

C. Physical

D. Human

Answer: D. Human
Mead studied the Samoans' human activity patterns and how they related to the environment including political, cultural, historical, urban, and social geographical fields of study. Regional study is limited to the elements and characteristics of a place or region. In a topical, a research would focus on an earth feature or one human activity occurring throughout the entire world. In a physical study, the researcher would focus on the earth's physical features and what creates and changes them, how they relate to each other and to human activities.

121. Which civilization laid the foundations of geometry?
(Average) (Skill 30.10)

A. Egyptian

B. Greek

C. Roman

D. Chinese

Answer: B. Greek
In the field of mathematics, Pythagoras and Euclid laid the foundation of geometry and Archimedes calculated the value of *pi* during the Ancient Greek civilization. Egypt made numerous significant contributions, including the invention of the method of counting in groups of 1–10 (the decimal system). The contributions and accomplishments of the Romans are numerous, but their greatest included language, engineering, building, law, government, roads, trade, and the "Pax Romana," the long period of peace enabling free travel and trade, spreading people, cultures, goods, and ideas all over a vast area of the known world. The Chinese studied nature and weather; stressed the importance of education, family, and a strong central government; followed the religions of Buddhism, Confucianism, and Taoism; and invented such things as gunpowder, paper, printing, and the magnetic compass.

122. **Consumers are, in effect, voting for the goods and services that they want with dollars, or what is called:**
(Average) (Skill 31.4)

   A. Economics

   B. Scarcity

   C. Dollar Voting

   D. Profitability Voting

Answer: C. Dollar Voting
Consumers are, in effect, voting for the goods and services that they want with dollars, or what is called dollar voting. A good that society wants acquires enough dollar votes for the producer to make a profit.

123. **Which of the following are two agricultural innovations that began in China?**
(Average) (Skill 31.3)

   A. Using pesticides and fertilizer

   B. Irrigation and cuneiform

   C. Improving the silk industry and inventing gunpowder

   D. Terrace farming and crop rotation

Answer: D. Terrace farming and crop rotation
Pesticides and fertilizer (choice A) are modern innovations. It was the Sumerians who introduced irrigation and cuneiform (choice B), not the Chinese. The Chinese did improve the silk industry and invent gunpowder (choice C), but these are not agricultural innovations.

124. English and Spanish colonists took what from Native Americans?
(Easy) (Skill 29.2)

A. Land

B. Water rights

C. Money

D. Religious beliefs

Answer: A. Land
The settlers took a lot of land from the Native Americans. Water rights (choice B), money (choice C), and religious beliefs (choice D) are not mentioned as areas of contention between the European settlers and the Native Americans.

125. In the events leading up to the American Revolution, which of these methods was effective in dealing with the British taxes? *(Rigorous) (Skill 31.6)*

A. Boycotts

B. Strikes

C. Armed conflicts

D. Resolutions

Answer: A. Boycotts
In several instances, boycotts were effective in convincing the British to repeat taxes. For example in 1765, merchants boycotted imported English goods, and the Stamp Act was repealed three months later. In 1767, boycotts led to the repeal of the Townshend Acts. Strikes were not a factor. Armed conflicts tended to strengthen British resolve and resolutions had no weight. Boycotts affected the British economy and achieved greater success for the colonies.

126. How did the labor force change after 1830?
(Easy) (Skill 31.2)

A. Employers began using children

B. Employers began hiring immigrants

C. Employers began hiring women

D. Employers began hiring non-immigrant men

Answer: B. Employers began hiring immigrants
Employers began hiring immigrants who were arriving in large numbers. Children (choice A) and women (choice C) began entering the labor force prior to 1830. Employers had always used non-immigrant men (choice D).

127. Which of these was not a result of World War I in the United States?
(Easy) (Skill 29.14)

A. Establishment of new labor laws.

B. Prosperous industrial growth.

C. Formation of the United Nations

D. Growth of the stock market.

Answer: C. Formation of the United Nations
The United Nations was formed after World War II. After World War I, the League of Nations formed and established the United States in a central position in international relations that would increase in importance through the century.

128. **Among civilized people:**
(Easy) (Skill 32.1)

A. Strong government is not necessary

B. Systems of control are rudimentary at best

C. Government has no sympathy for individuals or for individual happiness

D. Governments began to assume more institutional forms

Answer: D. Governments began to assume more institutional forms
Absence of strong government (choice A) is harmful. Systems of government that are rudimentary at best (choice B) are not suitable for civilized people. It is not true that government among civilized people has no sympathy for individuals or for individual happiness (choice C).

129. **Which of the following was not a source of conflict in writing the U.S. Constitution?**
(Average) (Skill 32.3)

A. Establishing a monarchy

B. Equalizing power between the small states and the large states

C. Dealing with slavery

D. Electing a president

Answer: A. Establishing a monarchy
Although the British system of government was the basis of the U.S. Constitution, the delegates to the Constitutional Convention were divided on the way power would be held. Some wanted a strong, centralized, individual authority. Others feared autocracy or the growth of monarchy. The compromise was to give the president broad powers but to limit the amount of time, through term of office, that any individual could exercise that power.

130. Upon arrest, a person is read a "Miranda warning" which reads, in part, "You have the right to remain silent. Anything you say can and will be used against you in a court of law." Under what amendment in the Bill of Rights is this covered? *(Rigorous) (Skill 32.11)*

A. The right against unreasonable search and seizures

B. The right to trial by jury and right to legal council

C. The right against self-incrimination

D. The right to jury trial for civil actions

Answer: C. The right against self-incrimination
According to the Fifth Amendment, a citizen has the privilege to prevent self-incrimination. Law enforcement officials advise a suspect in custody of his/her right to remain silent. While the right to council is also part of the Miranda warning, it is not part of the question as written here.

131. **The equilibrium price:**
(Rigorous) (Skill 31.5)

A. Is the price that clears the markets

B. Is the price in the middle

C. Identifies a shortage or a surplus

D. Is an agricultural price support

Answer: A. Is the price that clears the markets.
The price in the middle (choice B) is related to the principle of equilibrium, but it is not the equilibrium price. The equilibrium price has no direct connection to shortages and surpluses (choice C). It is also not an agricultural price support (choice D).

132. Capital is:
(Average) (Skill 31.2)

A. Anyone who sells his or her ability to produce goods and services

B. The ability of an individual to combine the three inputs with his or her own talents to produce a viable good or service

C. Anything that is manufactured to be used in the production process

D. The land itself and everything occurring naturally on it

Answer: C. Anything that is manufactured to be used in the production process
Anyone who sells his or her ability to produce goods and services (choice A) is labor, not capital. Combining three inputs with one's own talents to produce a viable good or service (choice B) is related to entrepreneurship. The land (choice D) and what is on it pertains to land.

133. Which of the following countries has historically operated in a market economy?
(Rigorous) (Skill 31.13)

A. Great Britain

B. Cuba

C. Yugoslavia

D. India

Answer: A. Great Britain
A market economy is based on supply and demand and the use of markets. While Great Britain may have socialized medicine, it operates a market economy. Cuba, with its ties to Communism, has a centrally planned economy. Historically, China has had a centrally planned economy but is now moving towards a market economy. Yugoslavia was a market socialist economy, but the country no longer exists; it has been split into Montenegro and Serbia.

134. **For their research paper on the use of technology in the classroom, students have gathered data that shows a sharp increase in the number of online summer classes over the past five years. What would be the best way for them to depict this information visually?** *(Average) (Skill 34.15)*

A. A line chart

B. A table

C. A pie chart

D. A flow chart

Answer: A. A line chart
A line chart is used to show trends over time and will emphasize the sharp increase. A table is appropriate to show the exact numbers but does not have the same impact as a line chart. Not appropriate are a pie chart that shows the parts of a whole or a flow chart that details processes or procedures.

135. **An example of something that is not a primary source is:** *(Easy) (Skill 34.5)*

A. The published correspondence between Winston Churchill and Franklin D. Roosevelt during World War II

B. Martin Gilbert's biography of Winston Churchill

C. The diary of Field Marshal Sir Alan Brooke, the head of the British Army during World War II

D. Franklin D. Roosevelt's handwritten notes from the World War II era

Answer: B. Martin Gilbert's biography of Winston Churchill
Martin Gilbert's biography of Winston Churchill is a secondary source because it was not written by Churchill himself. The Churchill-Roosevelt correspondence, Brooke's diary, and FDR's handwritten notes are all primary source documents written by actual historical figures.

136. Mr. Phillips is creating a unit to study *To Kill a Mockingbird* and wants to familiarize his high school freshmen with the attitudes and issues of the historical period. Which activity would familiarize students with the attitudes and issues of the Depression-era South? *(Rigorous) (Skill 35.9)*

    A. Create a detailed timeline of 15–20 social, cultural, and political events that focus on race relations in the 1930s

    B. Research and report on the life of its author Harper Lee; compare her background with the events in the book

    C. Watch the movie version and note language and dress

    D. Write a research report on the stock market crash of 1929 and its effects

Answer: A. Create a detailed timeline of 15–20 social, cultural, and political events that focus on race relations in the 1930s
By identifying the social, cultural, and political events of the 1930s, students will better understand the attitudes and values of America during the time of the novel. While researching the author's life could add depth to their understanding of the novel, it is unnecessary to the appreciation of the novel by itself. The movie version is an accurate depiction of the novel's setting, but it focuses on the events in the novel, not the external factors that fostered the conflict. The stock market crash and the subsequent Great Depression would be important to note on the timeline but students would be distracted from themes of the book by narrowing their focus to only these two events.

137. Which of the following are non-renewable resources? *(Easy)(Skill 31.9)*

    A. Fish, coffee, and forests

    B. Fruit, water, and solar energy

    C. Wind power, alcohol, and sugar

    D. Coal, natural gas, and oil

Answer: D. Coal, natural gas, and oil
Coal, natural gas, and oil are fossil fuels, which cannot be renewed. Nonrenewable resources are natural resources that cannot be remade or regenerated in the same proportion that they are used. Renewable resources are generally living resources (fish, coffee, and forests, for example), which can restock (renew) themselves if they are not over harvested. Renewable resources can restock themselves and be used indefinitely if they are sustained.

138. What people perfected the preservation of dead bodies?
(Average) (Skill 33.2)

A. Sumerians

B. Phoenicians

C. Egyptians

D. Assyrians

Answer: C. Egyptians
The Sumerians (choice A), Phoenicians (choice B), and Assyrians (choice D) all made contributions to ancient civilization but preserving dead bodies was not among their respective contributions.

139. Which major economic activity of the Southern colonies led to the growth of slavery?
(Rigorous)(Skill 32.4)

A. Manufacturing

B. Fishing

C. Farming

D. Coal mining

Answer: C. Farming
The major economic activity in this region was farming. Here the soil was very fertile, and the climate was very mild with an even longer growing season than farther north. The large plantations, eventually requiring large numbers of slaves, were found in the coastal or tidewater areas. Although the wealthy slave-owning planters set the pattern of life in this region, most of the people lived inland away from coastal areas. They were small farmers and very few, if any, owned slaves.

140. **In the fictional country of Nacirema, the government controls the means of production and directs resources. It alone decides what will be produced; as a result, there is an abundance of capital and military goods but a scarcity of consumer goods. What type of economy is this?** *(Rigorous) (Skill 31.7)*

   A. Market economy

   B. Centrally planned economy

   C. Market socialism

   D. Capitalism

   Answer: B. Centrally planned economy
   In a planned economy, the means of production are publicly owned, with little, if any private ownership. Instead of the "three questions" being solved by markets, there is a planning authority that makes the decisions. The planning authority decides what will be produced and how. Since most planned economies direct resources into the production of capital and military goods, there is little remaining for consumer goods; the result is often chronic shortages.

141. **Which of the following are secondary research materials?** *(Average)(Skill 34.7)*

   A. The conclusions and inferences of other historians

   B. Literature and nonverbal materials, novels, stories, poetry, and essays from the period, as well as coins, archaeological artifacts, and art produced during the period

   C. Interviews and surveys conducted by the researcher

   D. Statistics gathered as the result of the research's experiments

   Answer: A. The conclusions and inferences of other historians
   Secondary sources are works written significantly after the period being studied and based upon primary sources. In this case, historians have studied artifacts of the time and drawn their conclusion and inferences. Primary sources are the basic materials that provide raw data and information. Students or researchers may use literature and other data they have collected to draw their own conclusions or inferences.

142. **In December, Ms. Griffin asks her students to talk about their holiday traditions. Rebecca explains about lighting the nine candles during Chanukkah, Josh explains about the lighting of the seven candles during Kwanzaa, and Bernard explains about lighting the four candles during Advent. This is an example of:** *(Rigorous) (Skill 33.9)*

    A. Cross-cultural exchanges

    B. Cultural diffusion

    C. Cultural identity

    D. Cosmopolitanism

    Answer: A. Cross-cultural exchanges
    Cross-cultural exchanges involved the discovery of shared values and needs as well as an appreciation of differences. Cultural diffusion is the movement of cultural ideas or materials between populations independent of the movement of those populations. Cultural identity is the identification of individuals or groups as they are influenced by their belonging to a particular group or culture. Cosmopolitanism blurs cultural differences in the creation of a shared new culture.

143. **Socialism is:**
    (Rigorous) (Skill 32.5)

    A. A system of government with a legislature

    B. A system where the government is subject to a vote of "no confidence"

    C. A political belief and system in which the state takes a guiding role in the national economy

    D. A system of government with three distinct branches

    Answer: C. A political belief and system in which the state takes a guiding role in the national economy
    Socialism does not involve a legislature (choice A). A vote of "no confidence" (choice B) is associated with a parliamentary system, not with socialism. The U.S. government has three branches (choice D). This is not socialism.

144. The U.S. House of Representatives has:
(Average) (Skill 32.6)

A. 100 members

B. 435 members

C. Three branches

D. A president and a vice president

Answer: B. 435 members
The U.S. Senate has 100 members (choice A). The U.S. government as a whole has three branches (choice C). The executive branch of the U.S. government has a president and a vice-president (choice D).

145. Which of the following was not a source of conflict in writing the U.S. Constitution?
(Average) (Skill 32.7)

A. Establishing a monarchy

B. Equalizing power between the small states and the large states

C. Dealing with slavery

D. Electing a president

Answer: A. Establishing a monarchy
Although the British system of government was the basis of the U.S. Constitution, the delegates to the Constitutional Convention were divided on the way power would be held. Some wanted a strong, centralized, individual authority. Others feared autocracy or the growth of monarchy. The compromise was to give the president broad powers but to limit the amount of time, through term of office, that any individual could exercise that power.

146. The existence of economics is based on:
(Average) (Skill 31.10)

   A. The scarcity of resources

   B. The abundance of resources

   C. Little or nothing that is related to resources

   D. Entrepreneurship

Answer: A. The scarcity of resources
If resources were always abundant (choice B), economics would be unnecessary. Economics is closely, not loosely (choice C) related to resources. Entrepreneurship (choice D) is part of economics, but is not the primary basis of economics.

147. Using graphics can enhance the presentation of social science information because:
(Average) (Skill 19.3)

   A. They can explain complex relationships among various data points

   B. Charts and graphs summarize information well

   C. Maps can describe geographic distribution of historical information

   D. All of the above

Answer: D. All of the above
Social science reporting can be interesting and exciting without graphics, however, visual presentations can aid in bringing the data to life. Any idea presented visually in some manner is easier to understand than simply getting an idea across verbally, by hearing it or reading it.

148. **All of the following are key elements in planning a child-centered curriculum EXCEPT:** *(Rigorous) (Skill 19.5)*

    A. Referring students who need special tutoring

    B. Identifying students' prior knowledge and skills

    C. Sequencing learning activities

    D. Specifying behavioral objectives

    Answer: A. Referring students who need special tutoring
    Although the referral of students who need specialized services is an ongoing task, it is not a central element of the overall planning and organization of a curriculum. Well-thought-out planning includes specifying behavioral objectives, identifying students' entry behavior (knowledge and skills), selecting and sequencing learning activities to move students from entry behavior to objective, and evaluating the outcomes of instruction in order to improve planning.

149. **The Texas Assessment of Knowledge and Skills (TAKS) test is an example of:** *(Average) (Skill 19.11)*

    A. Criterion-referenced assessment

    B. Norm-referenced assessment

    C. Performance-based assessment

    D. Other type of assessment

    Answer: B. Norm-referenced assessment
    Norm-referenced tests (NRTs) are used to classify student learners for homogenous groupings based on ability levels or basic skills. In many school communities, NRTs are used to classify students into AP (Advanced Placement), honors, regular, or remedial classes that can significantly affect the student's future educational opportunities or success.

    TAKS measures statewide curriculum in reading for grades 3-9; writing for grades 4 and 7; English language arts for grades 10 and 11; mathematics for grades 3-11; science for grades 5, 10, and 11, and social studies for grades 8, 10, and 11. The Spanish TAKS is given to grades 3-6. Satisfactory performance on the TAKS at grade 11 is prerequisite for a high-school diploma.

150. **Ms. Gomez has a number of ESL students in her class. In order to meet their specific needs as second-language learners, which of the following would NOT be an appropriate approach?** *(Easy) (Skill 19.11)*

    A. Pair students of different ability levels for English practice

    B. Focus most of her instruction on teaching English rather than content

    C. Provide accommodations during testing and with assignments

    D. Use visual aids to help students make word links with familiar objects

    Answer: B. Focus most of her instruction on teaching English rather than content
    In working with ESOL students, different approaches should be used to ensure that students (a) Get multiple opportunities to learn and practice English, and (b) Still learn content. Content should not be given short shrift or be "dumbed down" for ESOL students.

151. **Which one of the following is NOT a reason why Europeans came to the New World?** *(Rigorous) (Skill 20.1)*

    A. To find resources in order to increase wealth

    B. To establish trade

    C. To increase a ruler's power and importance

    D. To spread Christianity

    Answer: B. To establish trade
    The Europeans came to the New World for a number of reasons; they often came to find new natural resources to extract for manufacturing. The Portuguese, Spanish, and English were sent over to increase the monarch's power and to spread influences such as religion (Christianity) and culture. Therefore, the only reason given that Europeans didn't come to the New World was to establish trade.

152. Which of the following were results of the Age of Exploration?
(Easy) (Skill 20.1)

A. More complete and accurate maps and charts

B. New and more accurate navigational instruments

C. Proof that the Earth is round

D. All of the above

Answer: D. All of the above
The importance of the Age of Exploration was not only the discovery and colonization of the New World, but also better maps and charts; new accurate navigational instruments; increased knowledge; great wealth; new and different foods and items not known in Europe; a new hemisphere as a refuge from poverty and persecution, and as a place to start a new and better life; and proof that Asia could be reached by sea and that the Earth was round; ships and sailors would not sail off the edge of a flat Earth and disappear forever into nothingness.

153. This is used to show the relationship between a unit of measurement on the map versus the real world measure on the Earth:
(Average) (Skill 30.2)

A. legend

B. grid

C. scale

D. title

Answer: C. scale
This is used to show the relationship between a unit of measurement on the map versus the real world measure on the Earth. Maps are drawn to many different scales. Some maps show a lot of detail for a small area. Others show a greater span of distance. One should always be aware of what scale is being used.

154. Nationalism can be defined as the division of land and resources according to which of the following? *(Rigorous) (Skill 20.1)*

A. Religion, race, or political ideology

B. Religion, race, or gender

C. Historical boundaries, religion, or race

D. Race, gender, or political ideology

Answer: A. Religion, race, or political ideology
Religion, race, and political ideology are some of the characteristics that determine national entity. Tribal membership, language, ethnic affiliation, and even treaty demarcations can dictate national boundaries. Historical boundaries may contribute to conflicts among people but they are generally secondary to another affiliation. To date, gender has not been a determining factor, although the treatment of women, for example, may be a contributing factor in some nationalistic conflicts.

155. The study of the social behavior of minority groups would be in the area of: *(Average) (Skill 20.8)*

A. Anthropology

B. Psychology

C. Sociology

D. Cultural geography

Answer: C. Sociology
The study of social behavior in minority groups would be primarily in the area of sociology, as it is the discipline most concerned with social interaction. However, it could be argued that anthropology, psychology, and cultural geography would have some interest in the study of social behavior as well.

156. **"Participant observation" is a method of study most closely associated with and used in:** *(Rigorous) (Skill 20.8)*

    A. Anthropology

    B. Archaeology

    C. Sociology

    D. Political science

    Answer: A. Anthropology
    "Participant observation" is a method of study most closely associated with and used in anthropology, the study of human cultures. Archaeologists typically study the remains of people, animals, or other physical things. Sociology is the study of human society and usually involves surveys, controlled experiments, and field studies. Political science is the study of political life, including justice, freedom, power, and equality, using a variety of methods.

157. **For the historian studying ancient Egypt, which of the following would be least useful?** *(Rigorous) (Skill 20.11)*

    A. The record of an ancient Greek historian on Greek-Egyptian interaction

    B. Letters from an Egyptian ruler to his/her regional governors

    C. Inscriptions on stele of the fourteenth Egyptian dynasty

    D. Letters from a nineteenth-century Egyptologist to his wife

    Answer: D. Letters from a nineteenth-century Egyptologist to his wife
    Historians use primary sources from the actual time they are studying whenever possible. Ancient Greek records of interaction with Egypt, letters from an Egyptian ruler to regional governors, and inscriptions from the fourteenth Egyptian dynasty are all primary sources created at or near the actual time being studied. Letters from a nineteenth-century Egyptologist would not be considered primary sources, as they were created thousands of years after the time period being studied and may not even be about the subject being studied.

158. The term *sectionalism* refers to:
(Easy) (Skill 20.20)

A. Different regions of the continent

B. Issues between the North and South

C. Different regions of the country

D. Different groups of countries

Answer: B. Issues between the North and South
The term *sectionalism* referred to slavery and related issues before the Civil War. The Southern economy was agricultural and used slave labor. The North was antislavery and industrial.

SCIENCE

159. Which is the correct order for the layers of Earth's atmosphere?
(Easy) (Skill 42.6)

A. Troposphere, stratosphere, mesosphere, and thermosphere

B. Mesosphere, stratosphere, troposphere, and thermosphere

C. Troposphere, stratosphere, thermosphere, and mesosphere

D. Thermosphere, troposphere, stratosphere, mesosphere

Answer: A. Troposphere, stratosphere, mesosphere, and thermosphere
All weather occurs in the troposphere. There are few clouds in the stratosphere, but weather balloons can float in this region. Air temperatures start to drop in the mesosphere. The coldest spot on Earth is where the mesosphere meets the thermosphere. The thermosphere extends into outer space.

160. What type of rock can be classified by the size of the crystals in the rock? *(Easy) (Skill 46.1)*

A. Metamorphic

B. Igneous

C. Minerals

D. Sedimentary

Answer: B. Igneous
Igneous rock is formed when molten rock material cools. It is characterized by its grain size and mineral content. Metamorphic rocks are formed from other rocks as a result of heat and pressure. Sedimentary rocks come from weathering and erosion of preexisting rocks.

161. What are solids with a definite chemical composition and a tendency to split along planes of weakness?
(Easy) (Skill 40.1)

A. Ores

B. Rocks

C. Minerals

D. Salts

Answer: C. Minerals
Rocks are made up of minerals, and ores are rocks than can be processed for a commercial use. Salts are ionic compounds formed from acids and bases.

162. **Which of the following objects in the universe is the largest?**
(Average)(Skill 40.5)

    A. Pulsars

    B. Quasars

    C. Black holes

    D. Nebulas

    Answer: B. Quasars
    Pulsars are neutron stars. Black holes are stars that have become so dense that light can't escape from the surface. Quasars appear to be stars but are distant galaxies. Nebulas are clouds of dust and gas that give rise to stars under the force of gravity.

163. **Why is the winter in the southern hemisphere colder than winter in the northern hemisphere?** *(Average)(Skill 40.3)*

    A. Earth's axis of 24-hour rotation tilts at an angle of 23°

    B. The elliptical orbit of Earth around the Sun changes the distance of the Sun from Earth

    C. The southern hemisphere has more water than the northern hemisphere

    D. The greenhouse effect is greater for the northern hemisphere

    Answer: B. The elliptical orbit of Earth around the Sun changes the distance of the Sun from Earth
    The tilt of Earth's axis causes the seasons. The Earth is close to the Sun during winter in the northern hemisphere. Winter in the southern hemisphere occurs six months later when Earth is farther from the Sun. The presence of water explains why winters are harsher inland than by the coast.

164. Which of the following processes and packages macromolecules?
(Easy)(Skill 43.1)

A. Lysosomes

B. Cytosol

C. Golgi apparatus

D. Plastids

Answer: C. Golgi apparatus
Lysosomes contain digestive enzymes. Cytosol is the liquid inside cells. Plastids manufacture chemicals used in plant cells.

165. Which of the following is not a property that eukaryotes have and prokaryotes do not have?
(Average) (Skill 43.1)

A. Nucleus

B. Ribosomes

C. Chromosomes

D. Mitochondria

Answer: B. Ribosomes
Prokaryotes do not have a nuclear membrane, and the DNA is not packed into chromosomes. Mitochondria are organelles that produce power are not in the smaller, simpler cell. Ribosomes are the sites where cells assemble proteins.

166. **What is the purpose of sexual reproduction?**
(Rigorous)(Skill 46.3)

A. Produce more organisms

B. Produce organisms that are genetically diverse

C. Give organisms the protection of male and female parents

D. Increase social cooperation between organisms

Answer: B. Produce organisms that are genetically diverse
Single-celled organisms reproduce by cell division and somatic cells in a multicellular organism reproduce the same way (mitosis). The purpose of sex is to produce diverse offspring so that the offspring have a better chance of surviving. In meiosis, the chromosome number is half the number in the parent cell, so that there is genetic diversity when the sex cells recombine.

167. **In mitotic cell division, at what stage do the chromosomes line up in the cell?**
(Average)(Skill 46.2)

A. Interphase

B. Anaphase

C. Prophase

D. Metaphase

Answer: D. Metaphase
The interphase is the period before mitosis begins. In the anaphase, the chromosomes are pulled apart. In the prophase, the chromatin condenses to become visible chromosomes.

168. According to natural selection:
(Easy)(Skill 48.1)

A. Individuals within a population are identical

B. Those with better traits have less offspring

C. Successive generations will possess better traits

D. Single individuals evolve to fit their surroundings

Answer: C. Successive generations will possess better traits
Organisms that possess better traits in order for survival tend to have greater numbers of offspring. These traits get passed down from generation to generation, causing later generations to possess the better traits.

169. Which of the following is not a kingdom in the classification of living organisms?
(Average)(Skill 46.1)

A. Plants

B. Fungi

C. Viruses

D. Bacteria

Answer: C. Viruses
Viruses do not obtain nutrients from their environment and produce new materials. The other kingdoms are animals and protists. Protists are single-celled organisms with nuclei, and bacteria do not have nuclei.

170. **Which of the following describes the transformation of liquid water to ice?**
(Average)(Skill 42.2)

   A. Chemical change

   B. Physical change

   C. Thermodynamic change

   D. Non-chemical molecular change

Answer: B. Physical change
Since heat is taken away, it could be called a thermodynamic change. However, a change in state or phase is considered a physical change. It is more closely related to changing wood into saw dust then burning wood.

171. **On which of the following does the force of friction between a metal stool and a wooden floor <u>not</u> depend?**
(Rigorous)(Skill 40.8)

   A. The speed of the chair

   B. Whether the stool has three legs or four

   C. The type of metal

   D. The smoothness of the floor

Answer: B. Whether the stool has three legs or four
The frictional force depends only on the force between the two surfaces and the nature of the two surfaces. Choice A is wrong because static friction is greater than moving friction. The number of legs determines the area of contact.

172. **Will Lithium gain or lose an electron when forming an ion? How many electrons will it gain or lose?**
    (Average)(Skill 42.5)

    A. Gain 1

    B. Gain 2

    C. Lose 1

    D. Lose 2

    Answer: C. Lose 1
    Lithium will lose 1 electron to form an ion. Lithium has a lone electron in its outer shell. Atoms want to be stable by having their outer shells full. It is easier for lithium to lose 1 electron, thereby knocking off an entire shell, then to gain 7 more electrons to fill its outer shell.

173. **Which of the following quantities has the units of calories per degree?**
    (Easy)(Skill 46.5)

    A. Heat capacity

    B. Specific heat

    C. Heat equivalent

    D. Heat transfer

    Answer: A. Heat capacity
    Heat capacity is how much the temperature of an object will increase when a quantity of heat is added to the object. The specific heat is the heat capacity divided by the mass.

174. **Which of the following should be limited in a balanced diet?**
(Easy)(Skill 46.6)

A. Carbohydrates

B. Fats and oils

C. Proteins

D. Vitamins

Answer: B. Fats and oils
Fats and oils should be used in moderation. Saturated fats can lead to heart disease and high cholesterol.

175. **Calisthenics develops all of the following health and skill related components of fitness except:**
(Average) (Skill 39.3)

A. Muscle strength

B. Body composition

C. Power

D. Agility

Answer: C. Power
Calisthenics is a sport that actually helps to keep a body fit in by combining gymnastic and aerobic activities. Calisthenics develop muscle strength and agility and improves body composition. However, calisthenics do not develop power because they do not involve resistance training or explosiveness.

176. **An experiment is performed to determine the effects of acid rain on plant life. Which of the following would be the variable?**
(Average)(Skill 45.5)

A. The type of plant

B. The amount of light

C. The pH of the water

D. The amount of water

Answer: C. The pH of the water
The variable is the value that is manipulated during the experiment. In order to determine proper cause and effect, the plant type, light, and amount of water should be kept the same for various plants, and the pH of the water should change.

177. **Which of the following statements about scientific knowledge best explains what scientific knowledge is?**
(Average)(Skill 38.1)

A. Scientific knowledge is based on experiments

B. Science knowledge is empirical

C. Scientific knowledge is tentative

D. Scientific knowledge is based on reason

Answer: B. Science knowledge is empirical
Experiments involve observing two quantities to determine the relationship between them. Observing means gaining knowledge from one of the five senses, which is another word for *empirical knowledge.* Scientific knowledge in some areas is tentative because new and different observations are always possible. Science is based on reason, but so are other types of knowledge.

178. Which of the following describes the interaction between community members when one species feeds of another species but does not kill it immediately?
(Easy)(Skill 39.4)

A. Parasitism

B. Predation

C. Commensalism

D. Mutualism

Answer: A. Parasitism
Predation occurs when one species kills another species. In mutualism, both species benefit. In commensalisms, one species benefits without the other being harmed.

179. Taxonomy classifies species into genera (plural of genus) based on similarities. Species are subordinate to genera. The most general or highest taxonomical group is the kingdom. Which of the following is the correct order of the other groups from highest to lowest?
(Easy) (Skill 39.4)

A. Class $\Rightarrow$ order$\Rightarrow$ family $\Rightarrow$ phylum

B. Phylum $\Rightarrow$ class $\Rightarrow$ family $\Rightarrow$ order

C. Phylum $\Rightarrow$ class $\Rightarrow$ order $\Rightarrow$ family

D. Order $\Rightarrow$ phylum $\Rightarrow$ class $\Rightarrow$ family

Answer: C. Phylum $\Rightarrow$ class $\Rightarrow$ order $\Rightarrow$ family
In the case of the domestic dog, the genus (Canis) includes wolves, the family (Canidae) includes jackals and coyotes, the order (Carnivore) includes lions, the class (Mammals) includes mice, and the phylum (Chordata) includes fish.

180. In which of the following eras did life appear?
(Easy)(Skill 40.2)

A. Paleozoic

B. Mesozoic

C. Cenozoic

D. Precambrian

Answer: D. Precambrian
The Cambrian explosion, the rapid appearance of most groups of complex organisms, took place in the Cambrian period, which is part of the Paleozoic era. Humans evolved in the Cenozoic era, dinosaurs in the Mesozoic era, and fish in the Paleozoic era.

181. Why is the northern winter slightly warmer than the southern winter?
(Average)(Skill 45.7)

A. Because the perihelion occurs in January

B. Because of global warming

C. Because there is more water in the southern hemisphere

D. Because Earth rotates on an axis that is not perpendicular to the plane of rotation

Answer: A. Because the perihelion occurs in January
Choice D explains why there are seasons; that is, why in the northern hemisphere January is colder than July and in the southern hemisphere July is colder than January. However, Earth travels in an elliptical path. It is closer to the sun in January than in July.

182. **What are ribosomes?**
(Easy)(Skill 45.4)

A. Contain digestive enzymes that break down food

B. Where proteins are synthesized

C. Make ATP

D. Hold stored food

Answer: B. where proteins are synthesized
Vacuoles store food and pigments and are large in plants. Mitochondria are the organelles that produce ATP for energy. Lysosomes contain digestive enzymes and are found mainly in animals.

183. **Which term describes the relationship between barnacles and whales?**
(Rigorous)(Skill 48.5)

A. Commensalism

B. Parasitism

C. Competition

D. Mutualism

Answer: A. Commensalism
Barnacles need to attach themselves to a hard surface to survive. They benefit from being attached to whales. If the whales benefited too, the relationship would be mutualism. If the whales were harmed, the barnacles would be parasites. If they ate the same food, there would be competition.

184. How many autosomes are in somatic cells of human beings?
(Easy) (Skill 46.2)

A. 22

B. 23

C. 44

D. 46

Answer: C. 44
The total number of chromosomes is 46, but two of them are the sex chromosomes. Autosomes refer to the chromosomes that are not X or Y chromosomes.

185. Which of the following laws implies that the force on an object comes from another object?
(Average) (Skill 41.4)

A. Newton's first law of motion

B. Newton's second law of motion

C. Newton's third law of motion

D. Coulomb's law

Answer: C. Newton's third law of motion
Newton's second law states the connection between force and acceleration. Newton's first law says if there is no force there will be no acceleration. Coulomb's law and the law of gravity says what the force between two objects will be. Newton's third law says forces come in pairs, which implies that the force comes from another object.

186. Which is not a characteristic of living organisms?
(Easy) (Skill 46.2)

A. Sexual reproduction

B. Ingestion

C. Synthesis

D. Respiration

Answer: A. Sexual reproduction
Only certain organisms reproduce sexually, that is by mixing DNA. Single-celled organisms generally reproduce by cell division. Ingestion means taking nutrients from outside the cell wall. Synthesis means creating new cellular material. Respiration means generating energy by combining oxygen or some other gas with material in the cell.

187. Oogenesis is the formation of:
(Easy) (Skill 47.2)

A. Eggs

B. Sperm

C. Pollen

D. Cytoplasm

Answer: A. Eggs
Oogenesis is the formation of eggs. Spermatogenesis is the formation of sperm.

188. **How does a steam radiator deliver heat energy to a room?**
(Rigorous) (Skill 42.3)

   A. Radiation

   B. Conduction

   C. Convection

   D. Contact

Answer: C. Convection
While the radiator gets hot from the steam the amount of infrared radiation it emits into the room is small. Contact is the same as conduction. There is very little conduction of heat because air is a good insulator. Air very close to the radiator will get hot, but nearby air will not. The air near the radiator expands and rises. New cooler air replaces the hot rising air. As a result, the room reaches a higher temperature.

189. **Accepted procedures for preparing solutions include the use of:**
(Easy) (Skill 24.2)

   A. Alcohol

   B. Hydrochloric acid

   C. Distilled water

   D. Tap water

Answer: C. Distilled water
Alcohol and hydrochloric acid should never be used to make solutions unless one is instructed to do so. All solutions should be made with distilled water because tap water contains dissolved particles that can affect the results of an experiment.

190. Laboratory activities contribute to student performance in all of the following domains EXCEPT: *(Average)(Skill 25.1)*

A. Process skills such as observing and measuring

B. Memorization skills

C. Analytical skills

D. Communication skills

Answer: B. Memorization skills
Laboratory activities develop a wide variety of investigative, organizational, creative, and communicative skills. The laboratory provides an optimal setting for motivating students while they experience what science is. Such learning opportunities are not focused on memorization but on critical thinking and doing. Laboratory activities enhance student performance in the following domains:

- Process skills: observing, measuring, and manipulating physical objects
- Analytical skills: reasoning, deduction, and critical thinking
- Communication skills: organizing information and writing
- Conceptualization of scientific phenomena

191. Which is the correct order of methodology?
(Average)(Skill 25.2)

1. *Collecting data.*
2. *Planning a controlled experiment.*
3. *Drawing a conclusion.*
4. *Hypothesizing a result.*
5. *Revisiting a hypothesis to answer a question.*

A. 1, 2, 3, 4, 5

B. 4, 2, 1, 3, 5

C. 4, 5, 1, 3, 2

D. 1, 3, 4, 5, 2

Answer: B. 4, 2, 1, 3, 5
The correct methodology for the scientific method is first to make a meaningful hypothesis (educated guess) and then to plan and execute a controlled experiment to test that hypothesis. Using the data collected in the experiment, the scientist then draws conclusions and attempts to answer the original question related to the hypothesis.

192. **In an experiment measuring the growth of bacteria at different temperatures, what is the independent variable?**
(Rigorous)(Skill 25.5)

    A. Number of bacteria

    B. Growth rate of bacteria

    C. Temperature

    D. Size of bacteria

Answer: C. Temperature
To answer this question, recall that the independent variable in an experiment is the entity that the scientist changes in order to observe the effects, or the dependent variable(s). In this experiment, temperature is changed in order to measure growth of bacteria, so (C) is the answer. Note that choice (A) is the dependent variable, and neither (B) nor (D) is directly relevant to the question.

193. **Which of the following is a misconception about the task of teaching science in elementary school?**
(Average)(Skill 25.5)

    A. Teach facts as a priority over teaching how to solve problems.

    B. Involve as many senses as possible in the learning experience.

    C. Accommodate individual differences in pupils' learning styles.

    D. Consider the effect of technology on people rather than on material things.

Answer: A. Teach facts as a priority over teaching how to solve problems.
Prioritizing facts over problem solving is a common misconception in elementary schools. Often, teachers focus on requiring students to learn and recall facts and information alone, rather than teaching them how to apply the learned facts in solving real scientific problems. In fact, problem solving is a vital skill that students need to learn and utilize in all classroom settings, as well as in the real world. Choices B, C, and D all describe effective teaching strategies that exceptional teachers use in their science classrooms.

194. An important map property is _____, or correct shapes.
(Average) (Skill 30.1)

A. consistent scales

B. conformal

C. equal areas

D. relief

Answer: B. conformal
An important map property is conformal, or correct shapes. There are no maps that can show very large areas of the Earth in their exact shapes. Only globes can do that; however, conformal maps are as close as possible to true shapes.

195. All of the following are hormones in the human body EXCEPT:
(Average)(Skill 27.3)

A. Cortisol

B. Testosterone

C. Norepinephrine

D. Hemoglobin

Answer: D. Hemoglobin
Hemoglobin refers to red blood cells. Cortisol and norepinephrine are stress-related hormones. Testosterone is a sex-related hormone.

196. **Models are used in science in all of the following ways EXCEPT:**
     (Rigorous)(Skill 27.8)

     A. Models are crucial for understanding the structure and function of scientific processes

     B. Models help us visualize the organs/systems they represent

     C. Models create exact replicas of the real items they represent

     D. Models are useful for predicting and foreseeing future events such as hurricanes

     Answer: C. Models create exact replicas of the real items they represent.
     One of the limitations of models is that they *cannot* be exact replicas of real objects or processes. However, they are very useful for conceptualization, visualization, and prediction.

197. **There are a number of common misconceptions that claim to be based in science. All of the following are misconceptions EXCEPT:**
     (Rigorous) (Skill 28.4)

     A. Evolution is a process that does not address the origins of life

     B. The average person uses only a small fraction of his or her brain

     C. Raw sugar causes hyperactive behavior in children

     D. Seasons are caused by the Earth's elliptical orbit

     Answer: A. Evolution is a process that does not address the origins of life
     The theory of evolution presupposes existing life, but does not explain the *origins* of life. This is a good example of a truth that can easily be misconstrued. Most people holding misconceptions are not aware that their beliefs are erroneous. It is critical that instructors understand common misconceptions in science so that they can not only avoid them but also correct them. Some of the most common misconceptions are derived from imprecise language—students often do not understand scientific terminology very well and words with precise scientific meaning are sometimes interpreted in a nonscientific, more general way. Also, media reporting on scientific subjects (particularly politically sensitive issues or popular science topics) is sometimes inaccurate or speculative. Finally, widely held public opinions of scientific topics are often incorrect or only partially correct.

198. **One characteristic of electrically charged objects is that any charge is conserved. This means that:**
(Rigorous) (Skill 30.1)

A. Because of the financial cost, electricity should be conserved (saved)

B. A neutral object has no net charge

C. Like charges repel and opposite charges attract

D. None of the above

Answer: B. A neutral object has no net charge
A plastic rod that is rubbed with fur will become electrically charged and will attract small pieces of paper. The charge on the plastic rod rubbed with fur is negative. If the plastic rod and fur are initially neutral, when the fur charges the rod a negative charge is transferred from the fur to the rod. The net negative charge on the rod is equal to the net positive charge on the fur. This is an example of the charge being conserved.

199. **Which of the following describes a state of balance between opposing forces of change?**
(Easy) (Skill 30.3)

A. Equilibrium

B. Homeostasis

C. Ecological balance

D. All of the above

Answer: D. All of the above
Homeostasis and ecological balance are specific examples of equilibrium, a state of balance between opposing forces of change.

200. Which of the following describes the amount of matter in an object:
(Average) (Skill 31.1)

A. Weight

B. Mass

C. Density

D. Volume

Answer: B. Mass
Mass is a measure of the amount of matter in an object. Two objects of equal mass will balance each other on a simple balance scale, no matter where the scale is located. For instance, two rocks with the same mass that are in balance on Earth will also be in balance on the Moon. They will feel heavier on Earth than on the Moon because of the gravitational pull of the Earth. So, although the two rocks have the same mass, they will have different weight. Weight is the measure of the Earth's pull of gravity on an object. It can also be defined as the pull of gravity between other bodies. Volume is the amount of cubic space an object occupies, and density is the mass of a substance per unit of volume.

TExES Core Subjects 4-8
SAMPLE TEST 3

LANGUAGE ARTS

1. **Oral language development can be enhanced by which of the following?**
(Easy) (Skill 1.1)

   A. Meaningful conversation

   B. Storytelling

   C. Alphabet songs

   D. All of the above

2. **Mr. Johns is using an activity that involves having students analyze the public speaking of others. All of the following would be guidelines for this activity EXCEPT:**
(Rigorous) (Skill 1.6)

   A. The speeches to be evaluated are not given by other students

   B. The rubric for evaluating the speeches includes pace, pronunciation, body language, word choice, and visual aids

   C. The speeches to be evaluated are best presented live to give students a more engaging learning experience

   D. One of Mr. Johns's goals with this activity is to help students improve their own public speaking skills

3. **Contextual redefinition is a strategy that encourages children to use the context more effectively by presenting them with sufficient vocabulary _____the reading of a text.**
(Rigorous) (Skill 3.7)

   A. after

   B. before

   C. during

   D. none of the above

4. **A _____ is the longest form of fictional prose containing a variety of characterizations, settings, and regionalism.**
(Average) (Skill 4.10)

   A. legend

   B. novel

   C. myth

   D. fable

5. A _____ can be divided into a subgenre which include fixed types of literature such as the sonnet, elegy, ode, pastoral, and villanelle. *(Average) (Skill 4.10)*

   A. poem

   B. romance

   C. drama

   D. short story

6. **When evaluating reference sources, students should do all of the following EXCEPT:** *(Rigorous) (Skill 9.4)*

   A. Look for self-published books by the author as evidence of expert status

   B. Examine the level of detail provided by the source

   C. Review the references at the end of the book or article

   D. See if the author presents both sides of an argument or viewpoint

7. **Middle-level learners are composing this type of story in English class. It is typically a terse narrative, with less developmental background about characters than a novel. It may include description, author's point of view, and tone, and is known as a:** *(Average) (Skill 4.10)*

   A. Poem

   B. Romance

   C. Drama

   D. short story

8. _____ refers to an object or action that can be observed with the senses and that suggests other things. *(Easy) (Skill 5.1)*

   A. Alliteration

   B. Allusion

   C. Symbol

   D. Illusion

9. **Which of these describes the best way to teach spelling? (Rigorous) (Skill 6.8)**

   A. At the same time that grammar and sentence structure are taught

   B. Within the context of meaningful language experiences

   C. Independently so that students can concentrate on spelling

   D. In short lessons, as students pick up spelling almost immediately

10. **A student has written a paper with the following characteristics: written in first person; characters, setting, and plot; some dialogue; events organized in chronological sequence with some flashbacks. In what genre has the student written? (Easy)(Skill 7.12)**

    A. Expository writing

    B. Narrative writing

    C. Persuasive writing

    D. Technical writing

11. **Which of the following messages provides the most accessibility to the most learners? (Average) (Skill 8.4)**

    A. Print message

    B. Audiovisual message

    C. Graphic message

    D. Audio message

12. **Which of the following advertising techniques is based on appealing to our desire to think for ourselves? (Easy) (Skill 8.9)**

    A. Celebrity endorsement

    B. Intelligence

    C. Independence

    D. Lifestyle

13. **Which of the following is NOT useful in creating visual media for the classroom? (Average) (Skill 8.8)**

    A. Limit your graph to just one idea or concept and keep the content simple

    B. Balance substance and visual appeal

    C. Match the information to the format that will fit it best

    D. Make sure to cite all references to copyrighted material

14. **All of the following are examples of ongoing informal assessment techniques used to observe student progress EXCEPT:** *(Rigorous) (Skill 7.6)*

   A. Analysis of student work product

   B. Collection of data from assessment tests

   C. Effective questioning

   D. Observation of students

15. **Read the following sentences:**

   It was a bright, sunny day in dallas, texas. mr. perez could feel the sun's rays on his shoulders as he walked down columbus st.

   Which words should be capitalized? *(Easy) (Skill 6.6)*

   A. Texas, Perez, St.

   B. Texas, Mr., Perez, St.

   C. Dallas, Texas, Mr., Perez, Sun's, Columbus

   D. Dallas, Texas, Mr., Perez, Columbus, St.

16. **Which of the following is NOT considered a reading level?** *(Easy) (Skill 2.8)*

   A. Independent

   B. Instructional

   C. Intentional

   D. Frustrational

17. **Which of the following are good choices for supporting a thesis?** *(Rigorous) (Skill 7.13)*

   A. Reasons

   B. Examples

   C. Answer to the question, "why?"

   D. All of the above

18. **Proofread the following sentence and locate any error in capitalization:**

   My teacher, mrs. grimsley, told us about the mighty kingdoms and empires that existed for hundreds of years in africa. *(Easy) (Skill 6.6)*

   A. mrs. Grimsley; hundreds

   B. Mrs. Grimsley; my teacher

   C. Mrs. grimsley; Africa

   D. Mrs. Grimsley; Africa

19. **Spelling instruction should include:** *(Average) (Skill 6.7)*

    A. Breaking down sentences

    B. Developing a sense of correct and incorrect spellings

    C. Identifying every word in a given text

    D. Spelling words the way that they sound

20. **Answering questions, monitoring comprehension, and interacting with a text are common methods of:** *(Average) (Skill 4.2)*

    A. Whole-class instruction

    B. Comprehension instruction

    C. Research-based instruction

    D. Evidence-based instruction

21. **Which of the following is NOT characteristic of a folktale?** *(Average) (Skill 5.10)*

    A. Considered true among various societies

    B. A hero on a quest

    C. Good versus evil

    D. Adventures of animals

22. **Which of the following did NOT contribute to a separate literature genre for adolescents?** *(Rigorous) (Skill 5.9)*

    A. The social changes of post–World War II

    B. The Civil Rights movement

    C. An interest in fantasy and science fiction

    D. Issues surrounding teen pregnancy

23. **Which of the following is important in understanding fiction?** *(Rigorous) (Skill 5.11)*

    I. **Realizing the artistry in telling a story to convey a point.**
    II. **Knowing fiction is imaginary.**
    III. **Seeing what is truth and what is perspective.**
    IV. **Acknowledging the difference between opinion and truth.**

    A. I and II only

    B. II and IV only

    C. III and IV only

    D. IV only

24. **Assonance is a poetic device where:** *(Average) (Skill 7.3)*

    A. The vowel sound in a word matches the same sound in a nearby word, but the surrounding consonant sounds are different

    B. The initial sounds of a word, beginning either with a consonant or a vowel, are repeated in close succession

    C. The words used evoke meaning by their sounds

    D. The final consonant sounds are the same, but the vowels are different

25. **"Reading maketh a full man, conference a ready man, and writing an exact man" is an example of which type of figurative language?** *(Average) (Skill 4.13)*

    A. Euphemism

    B. Bathos

    C. Parallelism

    D. Irony

26. **Which of the following is NOT a strategy of teaching reading comprehension?** *(Rigorous) (Skill 4.1)*

    A. Summarization

    B. Utilizing graphic organizers

    C. Manipulating sounds

    D. Having students generate questions

27. **Which of the following sentences contains a subject-verb agreement error?** *(Average) (Skill 6.5)*

    A. Both mother and her two sisters were married in a triple ceremony

    B. Neither the hen nor the rooster is likely to be served for dinner

    C. My boss, as well as the company's two personnel directors, have been to Spain

    D. Amanda and the twins are late again

28. **The repetition of consonant sounds in two or more neighboring words or syllables is called:** *(Easy) (Skill 4.10)*

    A. Irony

    B. Alliteration

    C. Onomatopoeia

    D. Malapropism

29. **All of the following are true about verb tense EXCEPT: (Rigorous) (Skill 6.6)**

    A. Present perfect tense is used to express action or a condition that started in the past and is continued to or completed in the present

    B. Future tense is used to express a condition of future time

    C. Past perfect tense expresses action or a condition that occurred as a precedent to some other action or condition

    D. Future participial tense expresses action that started in the past or present and will conclude at some time in the future

30. **All of the following are true about a descriptive essay EXCEPT: (Average) (Skill 7.9)**

    A. Its purpose is to make an experience available through one of the five senses

    B. Its words make it possible for the reader to see with their mind's eye

    C. Its language will move people because of the emotion involved

    D. It is not trying to get anyone to take a certain action

31. **_____ is discourse that is arranged chronologically. (Easy) (Skill 5.2)**

    A. Description

    B. Narration

    C. Exposition

    D. Persuasion

32. **After completing a unit on verbs, Ms. Allen assesses her students to gauge their understanding of the desired objectives. This type of assessment, _____, means to measure student progress or achievement. (Average) (Skill 1.4)**

    A. Formative

    B. Summative

    C. Both A and B

    D. Neither A, nor B

33. **_____ are assessments that are self-appraisal instruments completed by the students or observation-based instruments completed by the teacher. (Average) (Skill 1.4)**

    A. Anecdotal Records

    B. Rating Scales

    C. Informal Reading Inventories

    D. None of the above

34. **The main idea of a paragraph or story:** *(Average) (Skill 4.3)*

    A. Is what the paragraph or story is about

    B. Indicates what the passage is about

    C. Gives more information about the topic

    D. States the important ideas that the author wants the reader to know about a topic

35. **Which of the following is a great way to keep a natural atmosphere when speaking publicly?** *(Average) (Skill 1.3)*

    A. Speak slowly

    B. Maintain a straight, but not stiff, posture

    C. Use friendly gestures

    D. Take a step to the side every once in a while

36. **An interpretative response is one that:** *(Average) (Skill 5.15)*

    A. Makes value judgments about the quality of a piece of literature.

    B. Allows the reader to identify with the characters and situations.

    C. Encourages the reader to reflect on the social and ethical morals of society

    D. Analyzes style elements including metaphors, similes, and tone.

37. **Which of the following are important skills to evaluate when determining readiness and language competency?** *(Average) (Skill 1.2)*

    A. Knowledge of the standard rules of conversation.

    B. The size and range of a student's vocabulary and syntax skills.

    C. The ability to invent and entertain.

    D. All of the above.

38. A traditional narrative popularly regarded as historically factual, but actually a combination of both fact and fiction is:*(Average) (Skill 5.9)*

    A. A fable

    B. A legend

    C. An epistle

    D. An epic

39. The unique way a writer uses language is referred to as: *(Easy) (Skill 7.3)*

    A. Tone

    B. Style

    C. Theme

    D. personification

40. Identifying the main points of a text and restating them in their own words is what a learner does to: *(Easy) (2.3)*

    A. summarize

    B. instruct

    C. differentiate

    D. influence

41. Which of the following is NOT a prewriting strategy? *(Average) (Skill 10.4)*

    A. Analyzing sentences for variety

    B. Keeping an idea book

    C. Writing in a daily journal

    D. Writing down whatever comes to mind

42. _____ attempt to identify topics areas in which students may need extra motivational activities. *(Rigorous) (Skill 1.4)*

    A. Diagnostic Assessments

    B. Readiness Assessments

    C. Interest Assessments

    D. Evaluation Assessments

43. Exposition occurs within a story: *(Rigorous) (Skill 10.6)*

    A. After the rising action

    B. After the denouement

    C. Before the rising action

    D. Before the setting

44. **A running record is one way to evaluate:** *(Easy) (Skill 1.4)*

    A. Fluency

    B. Vocabulary

    C. phonics skills

    D. pragmatics

45. **The systematic exploration of a concept, event, term, piece of writing, element of media, or any other complex item is known as _____.** *(Average) (Skill 1.10)*

    A. synthesis

    B. evaluation

    C. analysis

    D. context

46. **An _____ is a long poem usually of book length reflecting values inherent in the generative society.** *(Average) (Skill 2.1)*

    A. epistle

    B. epic

    C. essay

    D. allegory

47. **An _____ is a letter that is not always originally intended for public distribution, but due to the fame of the sender and/or recipient, becomes public.** *(Average) (Skill 5.12)*

    A. epistle

    B. epic

    C. essay

    D. allegory

48. **Stories that are more or less universally shared within a culture to explain its history and traditions are known as:** *(Average) (Skill 5.12)*

    A. legend

    B. novel

    C. myth

    D. fable

49. **A highly imaginative tale set in a fantastical realm dealing with the conflicts between heroes, villains and/or monsters is known as a:** *(Average) (Skill 5.12)*

    A. poem

    B. romance

    C. drama

    D. short story

50. In these type stories, the hero is usually on a quest and is aided by other-worldly helpers. More often than not, the story focuses on good and evil and reward and punishment. *(Average) (Skill 5.12)*

    A. Myths

    B. Tall tales

    C. Fairy Tales

    D. Fables

51. Presented in a historically-accurate setting, these stories are known as: *(Easy) (Skill 5.12)*

    A. Modern Fantasy

    B. Science Fiction

    C. Modern Realistic Fiction

    D. Historical Fiction

52. Attributing human characteristics to an inanimate object, an abstract quality, or an animal is known as: *(Easy) (Skill 4.14)*

    A. Simile

    B. Metaphor

    C. Personification

    D. Hyperbole

53. A deliberate exaggeration for effect or comedic effect is known as: *(Easy) (Skill 4.14)*

    A. Simile

    B. Metaphor

    C. Personification

    D. Hyperbole

54. Mr. Michaela's students are writing essays using the writing process. Which of the following is not a technique they will use to prewrite? *(Average) (Skill 7.1)*

    A. Clustering

    B. Listing

    C. Brainstorming

    D. Proofreading

55. Miguel completes an organizer for a writing project. His teacher reviews his work and conferences with him. Miguel is ready to begin writing his ideas down in sentence and paragraph for. This next step after the prewriting stage of the writing process is known as: *(Easy) (Skill 7.3)*

    A. Drafting

    B. Prewriting

    C. Revising and Editing

    D. Proofreading

56. In this step of the writing process, students examine their work and make changes in wording, details, and ideas. *(Easy) (Skill 7.3)*

    A. Drafting

    B. Prewriting

    C. Revising and Editing

    D. Proofreading

57. During this final step known as _____, students may have their work displayed on a bulletin board, read aloud in class, or printed in a literary magazine or school anthology. *(Easy) (Skill 7.3)*

    A. Drafting

    B. Prewriting

    C. Publishing

    D. Proofreading

58. _____ is discourse that is informative in nature. *(Easy) (Skill 5.2)*

    A. Description

    B. Narration

    C. Exposition

    D. Persuasion

59. Read the following sentences.

    Gabe looks sleepy this morning. Why is he so tired? He had forgotten that he had a big report to write for his Social Studies class. The report is due today, and Gabe had wanted to give his best effort to the assignment. With his deadline approaching, he had burned the midnight oil.

    Based upon these sentences, the idiom "burned the midnight oil" means: *(Average) (Skill 5.1)*

    A. Rested too little

    B. Worked too late at night

    C. Wasted a lot of energy

    D. Stressed out over his assignment

60. Mrs. Amalent meets with her students individually as they complete a book report project. She is careful to focus on specific aspects of their work in progress that is done well, and she makes suggestions for improvements. This type of evaluation provides feedback to help these students learn: *(Average) (Skill 4.4)*

    A. Formative

    B. Summative

    C. Both A and B

    D. Neither A, nor B

61. **Which of the following strategies encourages print awareness in classrooms?** *(Easy) (Skill 2.1)*

    A. Word walls

    B. Using big books to read to students

    C. Using highlighters to locate upper-case letters

    D. All of the above

62. **_____ assessments are generally program- or teacher-focused.** *(Rigorous) (Skill 4.4)*

    A. Diagnostic Assessments

    B. Readiness Assessments

    C. Interest Assessments

    D. Evaluation Assessments

63. **_____ defined as focusing attention on one thing only.** *(Rigorous) (Skill 1.8)*

    A. Association

    B. Visualization

    C. Concentration

    D. Repetition

64. **Teaching students how to interpret _____ involves evaluating a text's headings, subheadings, bolded words, and side notes.** *(Easy) (Skill 5.1)*

    A. graphic organizers

    B. text structure

    C. textual marking

    D. summaries

65. **Identify the sentence type:**

    Madison went to Paris during the winter vacation, but her best friend stayed home because she had made other plans with some friends. *(Average) (Skill 6.6)*

    A. simple

    B. compound

    C. complex

    D. compound-complex

66. The teacher states, "We will work on the first page of vocabulary words. On the second page we will work on the structure and meaning of the words. We will go over these together and then you will write out the answers to the exercises on your own. I will be circulating to give help if needed." What is this an example of? *(Rigorous) (Skill 4.14)*

    A. Evaluation of instructional activity

    B. Analysis of instructional activity

    C. Identification of expected outcomes

    D. Pacing of instructional activity

67. Spelling instruction should include: *(Average) (Skill 2.2)*

    A. Breaking down sentences

    B. Developing a sense of correct and incorrect spellings

    C. Identifying every word in a given text

    D. Spelling words the way that they sound

68. Children typically learn the majority of their words and phrases from: *(Easy) (Skill 3.9)*

    A. School

    B. Reading

    C. Peers

    D. Other

69. In the _____ stage of writing, students write in scribbles and can assign meaning to the markings. *(Rigorous) (Skill 6.1)*

    A. role-play writing

    B. experimental writing

    C. early writing

    D. conventional writing

70. Children are taught phonological awareness when they are taught all but which concept? *(Average) (Skill 1.1)*

    A. The sounds made by the letters

    B. The correct spelling of words

    C. The sounds made by various combinations of letters

    D. The ability to recognize individual sounds in words

71. Answering questions, monitoring comprehension, and interacting with a text are common methods of: *(Average) (Skill 4.4)*

    A. Whole-class instruction

    B. Comprehension instruction

    C. Research-based instruction

    D. Evidence-based instruction

72. Which of the following is NOT characteristic of a folktale? *(Average) (Skill 5.14)*

    A. Considered true among various societies

    B. A hero on a quest

    C. Good versus evil

    D. Adventures of animals

73. A(n) _____ can be used to estimate a student's reading level and also to assess a student's ability to use word identification strategies. *(Average) (Skill 4.4)*

    A. Anecdotal Record

    B. Rating Scale

    C. Informal Reading Inventory

    D. None of the above

74. Which of the following is important in understanding fiction? *(Rigorous) (Skill 4.1)*

    I. Realizing the artistry in telling a story to convey a point.
    II. Knowing fiction is imaginary.
    III. Seeing what is truth and what is perspective.
    IV. Acknowledging the difference between opinion and truth.

    A. I and II only

    B. II and IV only

    C. III and IV only

    D. IV only

MATHEMATICS

75. Which of the following is a true statement regarding manipulatives in mathematics instruction? *(Average) (Skill 26.4)*

    A. Manipulatives are materials that students can physically handle

    B. Manipulatives help students make concrete concepts abstract

    C. Manipulatives include fingers, tiles, paper folding, and ice cream sticks

    D. Manipulatives help students make abstract concepts concrete

76. **All of the following are tools that can strengthen students' mathematical understanding EXCEPT:** *(Easy) (Skill 26.3)*

    A. Rulers, scales, and protractors

    B. Calculators, counters, and measuring containers

    C. Software and hardware

    D. Money and software

77. **Which of the following is not a good example of helping students make connections between the real world and mathematics?** *(Average) (Skill 26.2)*

    A. Studying a presidential election from the perspective of the math involved

    B. Using weather concepts to teach math

    C. Having student helpers take attendance

    D. Reviewing major mathematical theorems on a regular basis

78. **Which of the following is an example of the associative property?** *(Rigorous) (Skill 11.2)*

    A. $a(b+c) = ab + bc$

    B. $a + 0 = a$

    C. $(a+b) + c = a + (b+c)$

    D. $a + b = b + a$

79. **Jen, Tim and Anna are members of the same family. Tim is 5 years older than Jen. Anna is 6 years older than Tim. The sum of their three ages is 31 years. What is the age of each family member?** *(Easy)(Skill 13.7)*

    A. 12,500

    B. 15,000

    C. 11,800

    D. 10,500

80. **Mathematical operations are done in the following order:** *(Rigorous) (Skill 11.4)*

    A. Simplify inside grouping characters such as parentheses, brackets, square roots, fraction bars, etc.; multiply out expressions with exponents; do multiplication or division, from left to right; do addition or subtraction, from left to right

    B. Do multiplication or division, from left to right; simplify inside grouping characters such as parentheses, brackets, square roots, fraction bars, etc.; multiply out expressions with exponents; do addition or subtraction, from left to right

    C. Simplify inside grouping characters such as parentheses, brackets, square roots, fraction bars, etc.; do addition or subtraction, from left to right; multiply out expressions with exponents; do multiplication or division, from left to right

    D. None of the above

81. _____ **lines or planes form a 90-degree angle to each other.** *(Easy)(Skill 18.1)*

    A. Parallel

    B. Complimentary

    C. Supplementary

    D. Perpendicular

82. **The least common multiple of a group of numbers is the _____ number that all of the given numbers will divide into. The LCM will always be the _____ of the given numbers or a multiple of the _____ number.** *(Rigorous)(Skill 12.1)*

    A. largest; largest; smallest

    B. smallest; smallest; largest

    C. largest; smallest; smallest

    D. smallest; largest; largest

83. **Numbers that can only be factored into 1 and the number itself:** *(Average) (Skill 12.1)*

    A. Prime numbers

    B. Composite numbers

    C. Whole numbers

    D. Round numbers

84. **A number is divisible by 5 if:** *(Rigorous)(Skill 12.1)*

    A. it is an even number.

    B. It is divisible by 3.

    C. the number formed by its last two digits is evenly divisible by 4.

    D. the number ends in either a 5 or a 0.

85. **These lines share a common point, and intersecting planes share a common set of points, or line:** *(Average) (Skill 18.1)*

   A. Parallel

   B. Perpendicular

   C. Intersecting

   D. Skew

86. **These angles have sides that form two pairs of opposite rays:** *(Rigorous) (Skill 18.1)*

   A. Alternate interior

   B. Alternate exterior

   C. Corresponding

   D. Vertical

87. **If a right triangle has legs with the measurements of 3 cm and 4 cm, what is the measure of the hypotenuse?** *(Average) (Skill 18.3)*

   A. 6 cm

   B. 1 cm

   C. 7 cm

   D. 5 cm

88. **If the radius of a right circular cylinder is doubled, how does its volume change?** *(Rigorous) (Skill 19.2)*

   A. No change

   B. Also is doubled

   C. Four times the original

   D. Pi times the original

89. **Find the area of a rectangle if you know that the base is 8 cm and the diagonal of the rectangle is 8.5 cm:** *(Rigorous) (Skill 19.3)*

   A. 24 cm²

   B. 30 cm²

   C. 18.9 cm²

   D. 24 cm

90. **An item that sells for $375.00 is put on sale at $120.00. What is the percentage of decrease?** *(Average) (Skill 12.2)*

   A. 25%

   B. 28%

   C. 68%

   D. 34%

91. **What is a translation?**
    (Rigorous) (Skill 20.2)

    A. To turn a figure around a fixed point

    B. When the object has the same shape and same size, but figures face in different directions

    C. To "slide" an object a fixed distance in a given direction

    D. The transformation that "shrinks" or "makes it bigger"

92. **What measures could be used to report the distance traveled in walking around a track? *(Easy) (Skill 17.2)***

    A. Degrees

    B. Square meters

    C. Kilometers

    D. Cubic feet

93. **Corporate salaries are listed for several employees. Which would be the best measure of central tendency? *(Average) (Skill 21.4)***

$24,000	$24,000
$26,000	$28,000
$30,000	$120,000

    A. Mean

    B. Median

    C. Mode

    D. No difference

94. **Given a drawer with 5 black socks, 3 blue socks, and 2 red socks, what is the probability that you will draw two black socks in two draws in a dark room? *(Rigorous) (Skill 22.5)***

    A. 2/9

    B. 1/4

    C. 17/18

    D. 1/18

95. **Suppose you have a bag of marbles that contains 2 red marbles, 5 blue marbles, and 3 green marbles. If you replace the first marble chosen, what is the probability you will choose 2 green marbles in a row? *(Average) (Skill 22.3)***

    A. 2/5

    B. 9/100

    C. 9/10

    D. 3/5

96. **In probability, the sample space represents: *(Average) (Skill 22.1)***

    A. An outcome of an experiment

    B. A list of all possible outcomes of an experiment

    C. The number of times you must flip a coin

    D. The amount of room needed to conduct an experiment

97. **Deduction is:**
(Average) (Skill 13.1)

A. Logical reasoning

B. The process of arriving at a conclusion based on other statements that are known to be true

C. Both A and B

D. Neither A nor B

98. **Find the inverse of the following statement: If I like dogs, then I do not like cats.**
(Rigorous) (Skill 24.1)

A. If I like dogs, then I do like cats.

B. If I like cats, then I like dogs.

C. If I like cats, then I do not like dogs.

D. If I do not like dogs, then I like cats.

99. **Find the converse of the following statement: If I like math, then I do not like science.**
(Average) (Skill 24.2)

A. If I do not like science, then I like math.

B. If I like math, then I do not like science.

C. If I do not like math, then I do not like science.

D. If I like math, then I do not like science.

100. **Which of the following is the basic language of mathematics?**
(Easy) (Skill 24.5)

A. Symbolic representation

B. Number lines

C. Arithmetic operations

D. Deductive thinking

101. **The mass of a cookie is closest to:**
(Easy) (Skill 17.1)

A. 0.5 kg

B. 0.5 grams

C. 15 grams

D. 1.5 grams

102. **A car is rented in Quebec. The outside temperature shown on the dashboard reads 17°C. What is the temperature in degrees Fahrenheit? (Use the formula $F = \dfrac{9}{5}C + 32$.)**
(Average) (Skill 17.3)

A. 27.2°F

B. 41.4°F

C. 62.6°F

D. 88.2°F

103. The two solutions of the quadratic equation $ax^2 + bx + c = 0$ are given by the formula $x = \dfrac{-b \pm \sqrt{b^2 - 4ac}}{2a}$.

What are the solutions of the equation $x^2 - 18x + 32$? *(Rigorous) (Skill 12.4)*

A. ‾5 and 23

B. 2 and 16

C. $9 \pm \sqrt{113}$

D. $9 \pm 2\sqrt{113}$

104. Which of the following is not equivalent to 3 km? *(Average) (Skill 17.3)*

I. 3.0×10^3 m
II. 3.0×10^4 cm
III. 3.0×10^6 mm

A. I

B. II

C. III

D. None of the above

105. A right angle is: *(Easy) (Skill 18.1)*

A. greater than 90 and less than 180 degrees

B. greater than 0 and less than 90 degrees

C. exactly 90 degrees

D. exactly 180 degrees

106. A simple closed surface formed from planar polygonal regions is known as a: *(Easy) (Skill 19.4)*

A. vertex

B. polyhedron

C. edge

D. face

Use the data below to answer questions 107-110.

The following are the amounts of groups of seeds counted during preparation for a science experiment:

70	80	86
90	91	90
87	70	98
54	63	62
98	76	70

107. Find the median of the given test scores: *(Average) (Skill 12.1)*

A. 84

B. 79

C. 80

D. 83

108. Find the mean of the given test scores: *(Average) (Skill 12.1)*

A. 79

B. 83

C. 84

D. None of the above

109. Find the mode of the given test scores: *(Average) (Skill 12.1)*

A. 84

B. 79

C. 80

D. 70

110. Find the range of the given test scores: *(Average) (Skill 12.1)*

A. 46

B. 44

C. 64

D. 34

111. Which two fractions are equivalent? *(Easy)(Skill 12.5)*

A. 5/2 and 2/5

B. 4/3 and 8/6

C. 1/4 and 2/4

D. 1/4 and 2/4

112. 5 2/3 - 3 1/2 = *(Easy)(Skill 12.5)*

A. 2 2/3

B. 2 1/6

C. 2 ½

D. 1 3/8

113. 2/5 × 3/7 = *(Easy)(Skill 12.5)*

A. 6/35

B. 7/35

C. 10/21

D. 14/15

114. Lilian works 15 hours a week (Monday to Friday). Last week she worked 3 1/2 hours on Monday, 4 hours on Tuesday, 2 1/6 hours on Wednesday and 1 1/2 on Thursday. How many hours did she work on Friday? *(Easy)(Skill 12.5)*

A. 3 5/6

B. 4 1/2

C. 3 1/6

D. 2 1/6

115. **James read 2 books. He read the first one in one week with 25 pages everyday. He read the second book in 12 days with 23 pages everyday. What is the total number of pages that James read?** *(Easy)(Skill 12.5)*

    A. 276 pages

    B. 451 pages

    C. 175 pages

    D. 476 pages

116. **It takes John 25 minutes to walk to the car park and 45 to drive to work. At what time should he get out of the house in order to get to work at 9:00 a.m.?** *(Easy)(Skill 12.5)*

    A. 7:45 a.m.

    B. 7:30 a.m.

    C. 7:50 a.m.

    D. 8:10 a.m.

HISTORY AND SOCIAL SCIENCE

117. **The study of behavior of individual players in an economy, such as individuals, families and businesses is called:** (Easy) (Skill 31.5)

    A. Economics

    B. Microeconomics

    C. Macroeconomics

    D. Normative Economics

118. **Ms. Gomez has a number of ESL students in her class. In order to meet their specific needs as second-language learners, which of the following would NOT be an appropriate approach?** *(Easy) (Skill 30.7)*

    A. Pair students of different ability levels for English practice

    B. Focus most of her instruction on teaching English rather than content

    C. Provide accommodations during testing and with assignments

    D. Use visual aids to help students make word links with familiar objects

119. **Which one of the following is NOT a reason why Europeans came to the New World?** *(Rigorous) (Skill 29.9)*

    A. To find resources in order to increase wealth

    B. To establish trade

    C. To increase a ruler's power and importance

    D. To spread Christianity

120. Which of the following were results of the Age of Exploration? *(Easy) (Skill 29.6)*

A. More complete and accurate maps and charts

B. New and more accurate navigational instruments

C. Proof that the Earth is round

D. All of the above

121. The ancient civilization of the _____ invented the wheel. *(Rigorous) (Skill 29.4)*

A. Sumerians

B. Assyrians

C. Egyptians

D. Phoenicians

122. In order to put the Earth's spherical features on a flat map, they must be stretched in some way. This stretching is called _____. *(Average) (Skill 30.2)*

A. Distortion

B. Cartography

C. Projection

D. Illustrating

123. The _____ tells you what information is found on the map. *(Easy) (Skill 30.2)*

A. Legend

B. Grid

C. Scale

D. Title

124. An important map property is _____, or correct shapes. *(Easy) (Skill 30.2)*

A. consistent scales

B. conformal

C. equal areas

D. relief

125. The quantity of a good or service that a producer is willing and able to sell at different prices during a given period of time: *(Average) (Skill 31.2)*

A. demand

B. supply

C. market

D. economy

126. The _____ is the basis for the existence of economics.
(Rigorous) (Skill 31.2)

A. law of supply and demand

B. value of the dollar

C. scarcity of resources

D. means of production

127. Which political group pushed the Reconstruction measures through Congress after Lincoln's death? *(Rigorous) (Skill 29.12)*

A. The Radical Republicans

B. The Radical Democrats

C. The Whigs

D. The Independents

128. As a result of the Missouri Compromise:
(Average) (Skill 29.15)

A. Slavery was not allowed in the Louisiana Purchase

B. The Louisiana Purchase was nullified

C. Louisiana separated from the Union

D. The Embargo Act was repealed

129. Which country was a cold war foe of the United States?
(Easy) (Skill 29.13)

A. Soviet Union

B. Brazil

C. Canada

D. Argentina

130. A newspaper article has the following title:

"Hawaii is expensive, challenging place to run small business"

Which of the following ideas are likely to be found in this article: *(Rigorous) (Skill 8.1)*

A. Hawaii is the place where the sport of surfing originated, and famous international surfing championships are held there every year.

B. Hawaii is in the middle of the Pacific Ocean, far away from the U.S. mainland and other large land-masses, so everything that can't be produced locally in-state has to be shipped or flown there over great distances.

C. Pure Hawaiian Kona coffee is some of the most prized and expensive coffee in the world.

D. None of the above

131. **What is the most significant environmental change in Texas over the last century?** *(Rigorous) (Skill 30.5)*

    A. The number of square miles devoted to living space

    B. Continued exploration for oil and gas

    C. Development along the Gulf Coast

    D. Changes in agricultural practices

132. **The end to hunting, gathering, and fishing of prehistoric people was due to:** *(Average) (Skill 30.4)*

    A. Domestication of animals

    B. Building crude huts and houses

    C. Development of agriculture

    D. Organized government in villages

133. **Which of the following is most useful in showing differences in variables at a specific point in time?** *(Average) (Skill 34.11)*

    A. Histogram

    B. Scatter plots

    C. Pie chart

    D. Bar graph

134. **The New Deal was designed to get America back on its feet during:** *(Average) (Skill 29.5)*

    A. World War I

    B. The Pandemic Flu

    C. The Great Depression

    D. The Spanish American War

135. **During the 1920s, the United States almost completely stopped all immigration. One of the reasons was:** *(Rigorous) (Skill 31.3)*

    A. Plentiful, cheap unskilled labor was no longer needed by industrialists

    B. War debts from World War I made it difficult to render financial assistance

    C. European nations were reluctant to allow people to leave since there was a need to rebuild populations and economic stability

    D. The United States did not become a member of the League of Nations

136. In the 1800s, the era of industrialization and growth was characterized by: *(Average) (Skill 31.2)*

    A. Small firms

    B. Public ownership

    C. Worker-owned enterprises

    D. Monopolies and trusts

137. Which one of the following would NOT be considered a result of World War II? *(Rigorous) (Skill 31.4)*

    A. Economic depressions and slow resumption of trade and financial aid

    B. Western Europe was no longer the center of world power

    C. The beginnings of new power struggles, not only in Europe but in Asia as well

    D. Territorial and boundary changes for many nations, especially in Europe

138. The New Deal was: *(Average) (Skill 31.6)*

    A. A trade deal with England

    B. A series of programs to provide relief during the Great Depression

    C. A new exchange rate regime

    D. A plan for tax relief

139. Which of the following is an example of a direct democracy? *(Average) (Skill 32.2)*

    A. Elected representatives

    B. Greek city-states

    C. The Constitution

    D. The Confederate states

140. Many governments in Europe today have which of the following type of government? *(Average) (Skill 32.6)*

    A. Absolute monarchies

    B. Constitutional governments

    C. Constitutional monarchies

    D. Another form of government

141. Which of these is NOT a true statement about the Roman civilization? *(Rigorous) (Skill 29.16)*

A. Its period of Pax Romana provided long periods of peace during which travel and trade increased, enabling the spread of culture, goods, and ideas over the known world

B. It borrowed the concept of democracy from the Greeks and developed it into a complex representative government

C. It flourished in the arts with realistic approach to art and a dramatic use of architecture

D. It developed agricultural innovations such as crop rotation and terrace farming

142. The identification of individuals or groups as they are influenced by their own group or culture is called: *(Average) (Skill 29.3)*

A. Cross-cultural exchanges

B. Cultural diffusion

C. Cultural identity

D. Cosmopolitanism

143. Which of the following is not a right declared by the U.S. Constitution? *(Average) (Skill 32.3)*

A. The right to speak out in public

B. The right to use cruel and unusual punishment

C. The right to a speedy trial

D. The right not to be forced to testify against yourself

144. The cold weather froze orange crops in Florida and the price of orange juice increased. This is an example of what economic concept? *(Rigorous) (Skill 31.9)*

A. Output market

B. Input market

C. Supply and demand

D. Entrepreneurship

145. John C. Fremont, Zebulon Pike, and Kit Carson are all well-known: *(Rigorous) (Skill 29.2)*

A. Ministers

B. Doctors

C. Writers

D. Explorers

146. **Which if the following tribes did not inhabit the region that is now Texas?** *(Average) (Skill 29.2)*

   A. Iroquois

   B. Cherokee

   C. Wichita

   D. Apache

147. **An input into the production process:** *(Rigorous) (Skill 31.7)*

   A. Capital

   B. Market

   C. Need

   D. Resource

148. **An individual who has the ability to combine the land, labor, and capital to produce a good or service:**
   (Average) (Skill 31.7)

   A. market analyst

   B. stockbroker

   C. entrepreneur

   D. CEO

149. **The _____ River begins in Minnesota and flows to the Gulf of Mexico draining 31 states.** *(Average) (Skill 8.2)*

   A. Amazon

   B. Nile

   C. Mississippi

   D. Maumee

150. **The United States and Canada share:** *(Average) (Skill 8.2)*

   A. Manitoba

   B. Idaho

   C. Mississippi River

   D. The Great Lakes

151. **Although many religions are represented in both countries, the main religion in the United States and Canada is:** *(Easy) (Skill 33.1)*

   A. Christianity

   B. Islam

   C. Free Market

   D. Buddhism

152. **A term that economists use to describe and measure personal and collective wellbeing is known as:** *(Easy) (Skill 33.1)*

    A. Quality of Life

    B. Term of Endearment

    C. Personal Objective

    D. Collective Action

153. **A connection among people by blood, marriage or adoption is called:** *(Easy) (Skill 33.2)*

    A. Clan

    B. Kinship

    C. Society

    D. Culture

154. **Which of the Following is NOT an example of capitalism?** *(Average) (Skill 31.4)*

    A. free market and supply and demand

    B. competition

    C. government control of production and property

    D. unequal distribution of wealth

155. **A person who believes in the Social Darwinist theory of survival of the fittest would agree that:** *(Rigorous) (Skill 31.7)*

    A. poor people should get help from the government

    B. rich nations should give aid to poor nations

    C. individuals should succeed through their own efforts

    D. government should tax the rich to help the poor

156. **Made a fortune in steel; founded U.S. Steel; philanthropist who advocated giving away wealth:** *(Rigorous) (Skill 31.13)*

    A. J.P Morgan

    B. Andrew Carnegie

    C. Henry Ford

    D. Cornelius Vanderbilt

157. **The Federal Reserve System directly influences the United States economy by causing changes in:** *(Rigorous) (Skill 31.11)*

    A. the amount of income taxes collected

    B. the size of the federal budget

    C. the supply of money in circulation and credit rates

    D. wages and prices

158. During the Kennedy Administration a nuclear test ban treaty followed this event that brought the world closer to nuclear war than any other event since World War II:
(Rigorous) (Skill 29.19)

A. Bay of Pigs invasion

B. building of the Berlin Wall

C. Vietnam War

D. Cuban Missile Crisis

SCIENCE

159. Laboratory activities contribute to student performance in all of the following domains EXCEPT:
(Average) (Skill 38.1)

A. Process skills such as observing and measuring

B. Memorization skills

C. Analytical skills

D. Communication skills

160. _____ are single-celled prokaryotic life forms.
(Average) (Skill 46.2)

A. Bacteria

B. Archaea

C. Viruses

D. Fungi

161. In photosynthesis, _____ is a waste product.
(Average) (Skill 46.2)

A. Oxygen

B. Sunlight

C. Carbon Dioxide

D. ATP

162. What impact did television have on politics and society in the 1950's and 1960's?
(Average) (Skill 29.5)

A. created a larger gap between the rich and poor

B. rock and roll emerged to the forefront

C. eroded regional cultural differences and gave a larger spotlight to candidates

D. workers became less efficient as they spent more time watching television

163. The largest group in the plant kingdom:
(Average) (Skill 46.1)

A. Trophists

B. Chloroplasts

C. Fungi

D. Angiosperms

164. The term given to the response of plants to grow toward or away from a stimulus in the environment:
(Average) (Skill 46.1)

A. Tropism

B. Competition

C. Cellular Respiration

D. Photosynthesis

165. Spaces between neurons:
(Average) (Skill 46.3)

A. Synapses

B. Axons

C. Dendrites

D. myelin sheaths

166. Students in Mrs. Smith's class are learning about various types of rocks. She has set up stations for them to observe various samples. Three of them are: sandstone, amber, and limestone. These are samples of:
(Average) (Skill 52.1)

A. Sedimentary rocks

B. Metamorphic rocks

C. Igneous rocks

D. None of the above

167. The function of the _____ is to carry oxygenated blood and nutrients to all cells of the body and return carbon dioxide waste to be expelled from the lungs.
(Average) (Skill 46.3)

A. Respiratory System

B. Digestive System

C. Circulatory System

D. Nervous System

168. These lead blood away from the heart: *(Easy) (Skill 46.3)*

A. Veins

B. Arterioles

C. Capillaries

D. Arteries

169. Sound waves are produced by:
(Easy) (Skill 45.3)

A. Pitch

B. Noise

C. Vibrations

D. Sonar

170. **The Doppler Effect is associated most closely with which property of waves?** *(Average) (Skill 45.5)*

   A. Amplitude

   B. Wavelength

   C. Frequency

   D. Intensity

171. **The energy of electromagnetic waves is:** *(Rigorous) (Skill 45.1)*

   A. Radiant energy

   B. Acoustical energy

   C. Thermal energy

   D. Chemical energy

172. **Photosynthesis is the process by which plants make carbohydrates using:** *(Average) (Skill 45.2)*

   A. The Sun, carbon dioxide, and oxygen

   B. The Sun, oxygen, and water

   C. Oxygen, water, and carbon dioxide

   D. The Sun, carbon dioxide, and water

173. **Which of the following is not an example of a physical change?** *(Easy) (Skill 42.1)*

   A. Burning

   B. Cutting

   C. Freezing

   D. bending

174. **What cell organelle contains the cell's stored food?** *(Rigorous) (Skill 46.2)*

   A. Vacuoles

   B. Golgi apparatus

   C. Ribosomes

   D. Lysosomes

175. **Enzymes speed up reactions by:** *(Rigorous) (Skill 46.6)*

   A. Utilizing ATP

   B. Lowering pH, allowing reaction speed to increase

   C. Increasing volume of substrate

   D. Lowering energy of activation

176. **Blood cells are known as:** *(Rigorous) (Skill 46.3)*

   A. Plasma

   B. Erythrocytes

   C. Leukocytes

   D. Platelets

177. _____ make up _____, which make up tissues. *(Rigorous) (Skill 46.2)*

    A. Cells; DNA

    B. Cells; Organelles

    C. Organisms; Organelles

    D. Organelles; Cells

178. **What is the most accurate description of the water cycle?** *(Rigorous) (Skill 45.2)*

    A. Rain comes from clouds, filling the ocean. The water then evaporates and becomes clouds again.

    B. Water circulates from rivers into groundwater and back, while water vapor circulates in the atmosphere.

    C. Water is conserved except for chemical or nuclear reactions, and any drop of water could circulate through clouds, rain, groundwater, and surface water.

    D. Weather systems cause chemical reactions to break water into its atoms.

179. **Which of the following astronomical entities is not part of the galaxy the Sun is located in?** *(Easy) (Skill 40.5)*

    A. Nebulae

    B. Quasars

    C. Pulsars

    D. Neutron stars

180. _____ maintain a fluid environment for _____ exchange in mammals. *(Average) (Skill 46.4)*

    A. Lungs; gas

    B. Blood vessels; blood

    C. Carbon dioxide molecules; air

    D. None of the above

181. **Internal energy that is created by the vibration and movement of atoms and molecules is classified as: _____.** *(Rigorous) (Skill 45.6)*

    A. Mechanical energy

    B. Acoustical energy

    C. Radiant energy

    D. Thermal energy

182. **A teacher explains to the class that energy is neither created nor destroyed. Therefore, this means that _____.** *(Average) (Skill 41.1)*

   A. Matter never changes form

   B. Matter must change form

   C. Matter changes form only if it is a liquid

   D. None of the above

183. **Resistance of motion of surfaces that touch each other is considered _____** *(Average) (Skill 44.1)*

   A. Friction

   B. Inertia

   C. Gravity

   D. Force

184. **This type of ecosystem is located close to the poles, both north and south of the poles.** *(Average) (Skill 52.5)*

   A. Tundra

   B. Savanna

   C. Taiga

   D. Temperate Deciduous Forest

185. **A _____ would be a good choice when graphing the percent of time students spend on various after-school activities.** *(Average) (Skill 37.2)*

   A. line graph

   B. pie chart

   C. histogram

   D. bar graph

186. **This view of the ancient Greeks which affects scientific thinking states that moral and political obligations of an individual are dependent upon an agreement between people to form society.** *(Rigorous) (Skill 36.3)*

   A. Scientific Political Ethics Principal

   B. Utilitarianism

   C. Kantianism

   D. Social Contract Theory

187. **Destructive land-use practices can induce _____ when not properly planned.** *(Easy) (Skill 39.6)*

   A. global warming

   B. Avalanches

   C. Hurricanes

   D. volcanic eruptions

188. These types of volcanoes have been built from lava flows, as well as cinders and ash: *(Rigorous) (Skill 40.2)*

    A. Cinder cone volcanoes

    B. Shield volcanoes

    C. Warped volcanoes

    D. Composite

189. _____ cells are found in protists, fungi, plants, and animals. *(Rigorous) (Skill 46.2)*

    A. Prokaryotic

    B. Eukaryotic

    C. Chromosomal

    D. DNA

190. These assist in blood clotting: *(Easy) (Skill 46.3)*

    A. Plasma

    B. Erythrocytes

    C. Leukocytes

    D. Platelets

191. The brain of the cell: *(Easy) (Skill 46.2)*

    A. Nucleus

    B. Ribosomes

    C. Golgi Apparatus

    D. Mitochondria

192. _____ is the division of somatic cells. *(Easy) (Skill 46.2)*

    A. Mitosis

    B. Meiosis

    C. Reproduction

    D. Respiration

193. This geological process can change granite (igneous rock) into gneiss (metamorphic rock)? *(Easy) (Skill 52.1)*

    A. Heat and pressure

    B. Cooling

    D. Compacting and cementing

    C. Melting

194. _____ theorized that all individual organisms, even those of the same species, are different, and those individuals that happen to possess traits favorable for survival would produce more offspring. *(Rigorous) (Skill 48.2)*

    A. Louis Pasteur

    B. Antony van Leeuwenhoek

    C. Jean Baptiste Lamarck

    D. Charles Darwin

195. _____ refers to the chance deviation in the frequency of alleles (traits) resulting from the randomness of zygote formation and selection.
(Average) (Skill 48.2)

A. Genetic Drift

B. Consolidation

C. Recombination

D. Isolation

196. The theory of seafloor spreading explains: *(Rigorous) (Skill 38.1)*

A. The shapes of the continents

B. How continents collide

C. How continents move apart

D. How continents sink to become part of the ocean floor

197. Weather occurs in which layer of the atmosphere?
(Average) (Skill 38.3)

A. Troposphere

B. Stratosphere

C. Mesosphere

D. Thermosphere

198. Which of the following types of rock are made from magma?
(Average) (Skill 39.1)

A. Fossils

B. Sedimentary

C. Metamorphic

D. Igneous

199. _____ occurs when one species benefits from the other without causing it harm.
(Average) (Skill 48.4)

A. Competition

B. Commensalism

C. Mutualism

D. Parasitism

200. Which of the following is the best definition of *meteorite*?
(Easy) (Skill 41.3)

A. A meteorite is a mineral composed of mica and feldspar

B. A meteorite is material from outer space that has struck the Earth's surface

C. A meteorite is an element that has properties of both metals and nonmetals

D. A meteorite is a very small unit of length measurement

ANSWER KEY

1.	D	45.	C	89.	A	133.	D	177.	D
2.	C	46.	B	90.	C	134.	C	178.	C
3.	B	47.	A	91.	C	135.	A	179.	B
4.	B	48.	C	92.	C	136.	D	180.	A
5.	D	49.	B	93.	B	137.	A	181.	D
6.	A	50.	C	94.	A	138.	B	182.	B
7.	D	51.	D	95.	B	139.	B	183.	A
8.	C	52.	C	96.	B	140.	C	184.	C
9.	B	53.	D	97.	C	141.	D	185.	B
10.	B	54.	D	98.	D	142.	C	186.	D
11.	B	55.	A	99	A	143.	B	187.	B
12.	C	56.	C	100.	A	144.	C	188.	D
13.	D	57.	C	101.	C	145.	D	189.	B
14.	B	58.	C	102.	C	146.	A	190.	D
15.	D	59.	B	103.	B	147.	D	191.	A
16.	C	60.	A	104.	B	148.	C	192.	A
17.	D	61.	D	105.	C	149.	C	193.	A
18.	D	62.	D	106.	B	150.	D	194.	D
19.	B	63.	C	107.	C	151.	A	195.	A
20.	B	64.	B	108.	A	152.	A	196.	C
21.	A	65.	D	109.	D	153.	B	197.	A
22.	C	66.	B	110.	B	154.	C	198.	D
23.	A	67.	B	111.	B	155.	C	199.	B
24.	A	68.	B	112.	B	156.	B	200.	B
25.	C	69.	A	113.	A	157.	C		
26.	C	70.	B	114.	A	158.	D		
27.	C	71.	B	115.	B	159.	B		
28.	B	72.	A	116.	C	160.	B		
29.	D	73.	C	117.	B	161.	A		
30.	D	74.	A	118.	B	162.	C		
31.	B	75.	D	119.	B	163.	D		
32.	B	76.	C	120.	D	164.	A		
33.	B	77.	D	121.	A	165.	A		
34.	D	78.	C	122.	A	166.	A		
35.	C	79.	C	123.	D	167.	C		
36.	D	80.	A	124.	A	168.	D		
37.	D	81.	D	125.	B	169.	C		
38.	B	82.	D	126.	C	170.	C		
39.	B	83.	A	127.	A	171.	A		
40.	A	84.	D	128.	A	172.	D		
41.	A	85.	C	129.	A	173.	A		
42.	C	86.	D	130.	B	174.	A		
43.	C	87.	D	131.	A	175.	D		
44.	A	88.	C	132.	C	176.	B		

TExES Core Subjects 4-8 Test 3
QUESTIONS WITH RATIONALE

1. **Oral language development can be enhanced by which of the following?**
    (Easy) (Skill 1.1)

    A. Meaningful conversation

    B. Storytelling

    C. Alphabet songs

    D. All of the above

    Answer: D. All of the above
    Effective oral language development can be encouraged by many different activities including storytelling, rhyming books, meaningful conversation, alphabet songs, dramatic playtime, listening games, and more.

2. **Mr. Johns is using an activity that involves having students analyze the public speaking of others. All of the following would be guidelines for this activity EXCEPT: *(Rigorous) (Skill 1.6)***

    A. The speeches to be evaluated are not given by other students

    B. The rubric for evaluating the speeches includes pace, pronunciation, body language, word choice, and visual aids

    C. The speeches to be evaluated are best presented live to give students a more engaging learning experience

    D. One of Mr. Johns's goals with this activity is to help students improve their own public speaking skills

    Answer: C. The speeches to be evaluated are best presented live to give students a more engaging learning experience
    Analyzing the speech of others is an excellent technique for helping students improve their own public speaking abilities. In most circumstances students cannot view themselves as they give speeches and presentations, so when they get the opportunity to critique, question, and analyze others' speeches, they begin to learn what works and what doesn't work in effective public speaking. However, an important word of warning: *do not* have students critique each other's public speaking skills. It could be very damaging to a student to have his or her peers point out what did not work in a speech. Instead, video is a great tool teachers can use. Any appropriate source of public speaking can be used in the classroom for students to analyze and critique.

3. **Contextual redefinition is a strategy that encourages children to use the context more effectively by presenting them with sufficient vocabulary _____ the reading of a text. *(Rigorous) (Skill 3.7)***

    A. after

    B. before

    C. during

    D. none of the above

    Answer: B. before
    Contextual redefinition is a strategy that encourages children to use the context more effectively by presenting them with sufficient context *before* they begin reading. To apply this strategy, the teacher should first select unfamiliar words for teaching. No more than two or three words should be selected for direct teaching.

4.   A _____ is the longest form of fictional prose containing a variety of characterizations, settings, and regionalism. *(Average) (Skill 4.10)*

    A. legend

    B. Novel

    C. Myth

    D. Fable

Answer: B. Novel
The longest form of fictional prose containing a variety of characterizations, settings, and regionalism. Most have complex plots, expanded description, and attention to detail. Some of the great novelists include Austin, the Brontes, Twain, Tolstoy, Hugo, Hardy, Dickens, Hawthorne, Forster, and Flaubert.

5.   A _____ can be divided into a subgenre which include fixed types of literature such as the sonnet, elegy, ode, pastoral, and villanelle.
(Average) (Skill 4.10)

    A. Poem

    B. Romance

    C. Drama

    D. short story

Answer: D. short story
The only requirement of a poem is rhythm. Subgenres include fixed types of literature such as the sonnet, elegy, ode, pastoral, and villanelle. Unfixed types of literature include blank verse and dramatic monologue.

6. **When evaluating reference sources, students should do all of the following EXCEPT:** *(Rigorous) (Skill 9.4)*

    A. Look for self-published books by the author as evidence of expert status

    B. Examine the level of detail provided by the source

    C. Review the references at the end of the book or article

    D. See if the author presents both sides of an argument or viewpoint

    Answer: A. Look for self-published books by the author as evidence of expert status
    Anyone can self-publish a book or pamphlet. Experience and background in the subject area have not been reviewed by anyone in many cases. Therefore, more research needs to be done to determine whether a source document is based on reliable, expert information when it has been published by the author.

7. **Middle-level learners are composing this type of story in English class. It is typically a terse narrative, with less developmental background about characters than a novel. It may include description, author's point of view, and tone, and is known as a:** *(Average) (Skill 4.10)*

    A. Poem

    B. Romance

    C. Drama

    D. short story

    Answer: D. Short story
    Typically a terse narrative, with less developmental background about characters than a novel. Short stories may include description, author's point of view, and tone.

8.   _____ refers to an object or action that can be observed with the senses and that suggests other things. *(Easy) (Skill 5.1)*

   A. Alliteration

   B. Allusion

   C. Symbol

   D. Illusion

Answer: C. Symbol
Symbol refers to an object or action that can be observed with the senses and that suggests other things. A symbol can certainly have more than one meaning, and the meaning may be as personal as the memories and experiences of the particular reader.

9.   **Which of these describes the best way to teach spelling?**
(Rigorous) (Skill 6.8)

   A. At the same time that grammar and sentence structure are taught

   B. Within the context of meaningful language experiences

   C. Independently so that students can concentrate on spelling

   D. In short lessons, as students pick up spelling almost immediately

Answer: B. Within the context of meaningful language experiences
Spelling should be taught within the context of meaningful language experiences. Giving a child a list of words to learn to spell and then testing the child on the words every Friday will not aid in the development of spelling. The child must be able to use the words in context and they must have some meaning for the child. The assessment of how well a child can spell or where there are problems also has to be done within a meaningful environment.

10. **A student has written a paper with the following characteristics: written in first person; characters, setting, and plot; some dialogue; events organized in chronological sequence with some flashbacks. In what genre has the student written? (Easy) (Skill 7.12)**

    A. Expository writing

    B. Narrative writing

    C. Persuasive writing

    D. Technical writing

    Answer: B. Narrative writing
    These are all characteristics of narrative writing. Expository writing is intended to give information such as an explanation or directions, and the information is logically organized. Persuasive writing gives an opinion in an attempt to convince the reader that a point of view is valid, or tries to persuade the reader to take a specific action. The goal of technical writing is to clearly communicate particular information to a targeted reader or group of readers.

11. **Which of the following messages provides the most accessibility to the most learners? (Average) (Skill 8.4)**

    A. Print message

    B. Audiovisual message

    C. Graphic message

    D. Audio message

    Answer: B. Audiovisual message
    An audiovisual message is the most accessible for learners. It has the advantages of both mediums, the graphic and the audio. Learners' eyes and ears are engaged. Nonreaders get significant access to content. On the other hand, viewing an audiovisual presentation is an even more passive activity than listening to an audio message because information is coming to learners effortlessly through two senses.

12. **Which of the following advertising techniques is based on appealing to our desire to think for ourselves?** *(Easy) (Skill 8.9)*

    A. Celebrity endorsement

    B. Intelligence

    C. Independence

    D. Lifestyle

    Answer: C. Independence
    Celebrity endorsements associate product use with a well-known person. Intelligence techniques are based on making consumers feel smart and as if they cannot be fooled. Lifestyle approaches are designed to make us feel we are part of a particular way of living.

13. **Which of the following is NOT useful in creating visual media for the classroom?** *(Average) (Skill 8.8)*

    A. Limit your graph to just one idea or concept and keep the content simple

    B. Balance substance and visual appeal

    C. Match the information to the format that will fit it best

    D. Make sure to cite all references to copyrighted material

    Answer: D. Make sure to cite all references to copyrighted material
    Although it may be important to acknowledge copyright and intellectual property ownership of some materials used in visual media, this factor is not a guideline for creating useful visual media for the classroom.

14. **All of the following are examples of ongoing informal assessment techniques used to observe student progress EXCEPT:** *(Rigorous) (Skill 7.6)*

   A. Analysis of student work product

   B. Collection of data from assessment tests

   C. Effective questioning

   D. Observation of students

   Answer: B. Collection of data from assessment tests
   Assessment tests are formal progress-monitoring measures.

15. **Read the following sentences:**

   It was a bright, sunny day in dallas, texas. mr. perez could feel the sun's rays on his shoulders as he walked down columbus st.

   Which words should be capitalized? *(Easy) (Skill 6.6)*

   A. Texas, Perez, St.

   B. Texas, Mr., Perez, St.

   C. Dallas, Texas, Mr., Perez, Sun's, Columbus

   D. Dallas, Texas, Mr., Perez, Columbus, St.

   Answer: D. Dallas, Texas, Mr., Perez, Columbus, St.
   Choice D is correct because those are all proper nouns and need to be capitalized.

16. **Which of the following is NOT considered a reading level?**
(Easy) (Skill 2.8)

  A. Independent

  B. Instructional

  C. Intentional

  D. Frustrational

Answer: C. Intentional
Intentional is not a reading level. Reading levels for the purpose of assessment and planning instruction are as follows:

- *Independent.* This is the level at which the child can read text totally on his or her own. When reading books at the independent level, students will be able to decode between 95 and 100 percent of the words and comprehend the text with 90 percent or better accuracy.
- *Instructional.* This is the level at which the student should be taught because it provides enough difficulty to increase his or her reading skills without providing so much that it becomes too cumbersome to finish the selection. Typically, the acceptable range of accuracy is between 85 and 94 percent, with 75 percent or greater comprehension.
- *Frustrational.* Books at a student's frustrational level are too difficult for the child and should not be used. The frustrational level is any text with less than 85 percent word accuracy and/or less than 75 percent comprehension.

17. **Which of the following are good choices for supporting a thesis?**
(Rigorous) (Skill 7.13)

  A. Reasons

  B. Examples

  C. Answer to the question, "why?"

  D. All of the above

Answer: D. All of the above
The correct answer is D. When answering the question "why?" you are giving reasons, but those reasons need to be supported with examples.

18. **Proofread the following sentence and locate any error in capitalization:**

    My teacher, mrs. grimsley, told us about the mighty kingdoms and empires that existed for hundreds of years in africa.
    (Easy) (Skill 6.6)

    A. mrs. Grimsley; hundreds

    B. Mrs. Grimsley; my teacher

    D. Mrs. grimsley; Africa

    D. Mrs. Grimsley; Africa

    Answer: D. Mrs. Grimsley; Africa
    Mrs. Grimsley and Africa are proper nouns and need to be capitalized.

19. **Spelling instruction should include:**
    (Average) (Skill 6.7)

    A. Breaking down sentences

    B. Developing a sense of correct and incorrect spellings

    C. Identifying every word in a given text

    D. Spelling words the way that they sound

    Answer: B. Developing a sense of correct and incorrect spellings
    Developing a sense of correct and incorrect spellings is part of the developmental stages of spelling and is a phase that is typically entered later in elementary school. Breaking down sentences involves paragraph analysis, identifying every word in a given text is not necessary to construct meaning from that text, and spelling words the way that they sound is not an effective way to teach spelling.

20. **Answering questions, monitoring comprehension, and interacting with a text are common methods of:** *(Average) (Skill 4.2)*

   A. Whole-class instruction

   B. Comprehension instruction

   C. Research-based instruction

   D. Evidence-based instruction

   Answer: B. Comprehension instruction
   Comprehension instruction helps students learn strategies that they can use independently with any text. Answering questions, monitoring comprehension, and interacting with a text are a few strategies that teachers can teach to their students to help increase their comprehension. Research-based, evidence-based, and whole-class instruction relate to specific reading programs available.

21. **Which of the following is NOT characteristic of a folktale?** *(Average) (Skill 5.10)*

   A. Considered true among various societies

   B. A hero on a quest

   C. Good versus evil

   D. Adventures of animals

   Answer: A. Considered true among various societies
   There are few societies that would consider folktales to be true as folktale is another name for fairy tale, and elements such as heroes on a quest, good versus evil, and adventures of animals are popular, fictional, themes in fairy tales.

22. **Which of the following did NOT contribute to a separate literature genre for adolescents?** *(Rigorous) (Skill 5.9)*

    A. The social changes of post–World War II

    B. The Civil Rights movement

    C. An interest in fantasy and science fiction

    D. Issues surrounding teen pregnancy

    Answer: C. An interest in fantasy and science fiction
    Social changes after World War II, the Civil Rights movement, and personal issues like teen pregnancy all contributed to authors writing a new breed of contemporary fiction to help adolescents understand and cope with the world they live in. Adolescents may be interested in fantasy and science fiction topics but that interest did not cause the creation of an entire genre.

23. **Which of the following is important in understanding fiction?** *(Rigorous) (Skill 5.11)*

    I.   **Realizing the artistry in telling a story to convey a point.**
    II. **Knowing fiction is imaginary.**
    III. **Seeing what is truth and what is perspective.**
    IV. **Acknowledging the difference between opinion and truth.**

    A. I and II only

    B. II and IV only

    C. III and IV only

    D. IV only

    Answer: A. I and II only
    In order to understand a piece of fiction, it is important that readers realize that an author's choice in a work of fiction is for the sole purpose of conveying a viewpoint. It is also important to understand that fiction is imaginary. Seeing what is truth and what is perspective and acknowledging the difference between opinion and truth are important in understanding nonfiction.

24. **Assonance is a poetic device where:**
    (Average) (Skill 7.3)

    A. The vowel sound in a word matches the same sound in a nearby word, but the surrounding consonant sounds are different

    B. The initial sounds of a word, beginning either with a consonant or a vowel, are repeated in close succession

    C. The words used evoke meaning by their sounds

    D. The final consonant sounds are the same, but the vowels are different

    Answer: A. The vowel sound in a word matches the same sound in a nearby word, but the surrounding consonant sounds are different
    Assonance takes the middle territory of rhyming so that the vowel sounds are similar, but the consonant sounds are different: "tune" and "food" are assonant. Repeating words in close succession that have the same initial sound ("puppies who pant pathetically") is alliteration. Using the sounds of words to evoke meaning ("zip, pow, pop") is onomatopoeia. When final consonant sounds are the same and the vowels are different, and author has used a different kind of alliteration.

25. **"Reading maketh a full man, conference a ready man, and writing an exact man" is an example of which type of figurative language?** *(Average) (Skill 4.13)*

    A. Euphemism

    B. Bathos

    C. Parallelism

    D. Irony

    Answer: C. Parallelism
    Parallelism is the arrangement of ideas into phrases, sentences, and paragraphs that balance one element with another of equal importance and similar wording. In the example given, reading, conference, and writing are balanced in importance and wording. A euphemism substitutes an agreeable term for one that might offend. Bathos is a ludicrous attempt to evoke pity, sympathy, or sorrow. Irony is using an expression that is the opposite to the literal meaning.

26. **Which of the following is NOT a strategy of teaching reading comprehension?** *(Rigorous) (Skill 4.1)*

    A. Summarization

    B. Utilizing graphic organizers

    C. Manipulating sounds

    D. Having students generate questions

    Answer: C. Manipulating sounds
    Comprehension simply means that the reader can ascribe meaning to text. Teachers can use many strategies to teach comprehension, including questioning, asking students to paraphrase or summarize, utilizing graphic organizers, and focusing on mental images.

27. **Which of the following sentences contains a subject-verb agreement error?** *(Average) (Skill 6.5)*

    A. Both mother and her two sisters were married in a triple ceremony

    B. Neither the hen nor the rooster is likely to be served for dinner

    C. My boss, as well as the company's two personnel directors, have been to Spain

    D. Amanda and the twins are late again

    Answer: C. My boss, as well as the company's two personnel directors, have been to Spain
    In choice C, the true subject of the verb is "My boss," not "two personnel directors." Because the subject is singular, the verb form must be singular, "has." In choices A and D, the compound subjects are joined by "and" and take the plural form of the verb. In choice B, the compound subject is joined by "nor" so the verb must agree with the subject closer to the verb. "Rooster" is singular so the correct verb is "is."

28. **The repetition of consonant sounds in two or more neighboring words or syllables is called:** *(Easy) (Skill 4.10)*

A. Irony

B. Alliteration

C. Onomatopoeia

D. Malapropism

Answer: B. Alliteration
The repetition of consonant sounds in two or more neighboring words or syllables is known as alliteration.

29. **All of the following are true about verb tense EXCEPT:**
(Rigorous) (Skill 6.6)

A. Present perfect tense is used to express action or a condition that started in the past and is continued to or completed in the present

B. Future tense is used to express a condition of future time

C. Past perfect tense expresses action or a condition that occurred as a precedent to some other action or condition

D. Future participial tense expresses action that started in the past or present and will conclude at some time in the future

Answer: D. Future participial tense expresses action that started in the past or present and will conclude at some time in the future
Choices A–C are correct statements about each type of verb tense. D is incorrect because there is no such thing as future participial tense.

30. **All of the following are true about a descriptive essay EXCEPT:** *(Average) (Skill 7.9)*

    A. Its purpose is to make an experience available through one of the five senses

    B. Its words make it possible for the reader to see with their mind's eye

    C. Its language will move people because of the emotion involved

    D. It is not trying to get anyone to take a certain action

Answer: D. It is not trying to get anyone to take a certain action
The descriptive essay uses language to make an experience available to readers. It uses descriptive words so the reader can see with their mind's eye, smell with their mind's nose, etc. Descriptive writing will involve the emotions of both the reader and writer. Poems are excellent examples of descriptive writing. An exposition is the type of essay that is not interested in getting anyone to take a certain action.

31. _____ **is discourse that is arranged chronologically.** *(Easy) (Skill 5.2)*

    A. Description

    B. Narration

    C. Exposition

    D. Persuasion

Answer: B. Narration
Narration is discourse that is arranged chronologically: Something happened, and then something else happened, and then something else happened.

32. **After completing a unit on verbs, Ms. Allen assesses her students to gauge their understanding of the desired objectives. This type of assessment, _____, means to measure student progress or achievement.** *(Average) (Skill 1.4)*

    A. Formative

    B. Summative

    C. Both A and B

    D. Neither A, nor B

    Answer: B. Summative
    Evaluation of student progress has two primary purposes: summative, to measure student progress or achievement, and formative, to provide feedback to students to help them learn.

33. **_____ are assessments that are self-appraisal instruments completed by the students or observation-based instruments completed by the teacher.** *(Average) (Skill 1.4)*

    A. Anecdotal Records

    B. Rating Scales

    C. Informal Reading Inventories

    D. None of the above

    Answer: B. Rating Scales
    Rating Scales are assessments that are self-appraisal instruments completed by the students or observation-based instruments completed by the teacher. The focus of these is frequently on behavior or effective areas such as interest and motivation.

34. **The main idea of a paragraph or story:**
(Average) (Skill 4.3)

   A. Is what the paragraph or story is about

   B. Indicates what the passage is about

   C. Gives more information about the topic

   D. States the important ideas that the author wants the reader to know about a topic

   Answer: D. States the important ideas that the author wants the reader to know about a topic

   The main idea of a paragraph or story states the important ideas that the author wants the reader to know about his/her topic. The main idea can be directly stated or simply implied. The topic is what the paragraph or story is about. A topic sentence will indicate what a specific passage is about. And supporting details will give more information about a topic.

35. **Which of the following is a great way to keep a natural atmosphere when speaking publicly?** *(Average) (Skill 1.3)*

   A. Speak slowly

   B. Maintain a straight, but not stiff, posture

   C. Use friendly gestures

   D. Take a step to the side every once in a while

   Answer: C. Use friendly gestures

   Gestures are a great way to keep a natural atmosphere when speaking publicly. Gestures that are common in friendly conversation will make the audience feel at ease. Gestures that are exaggerated, stiff, or awkward will only distract from a speech. Speaking slowly, monitoring posture, and taking a step to the side are great speaking skills but not skills that will create a natural atmosphere.

36. **An interpretative response is one that:**
(Average)(Skill 5.15)

A. Makes value judgments about the quality of a piece of literature

B. Allows the reader to identify with the characters and situations

C. Encourages the reader to reflect on the social and ethical morals of society

D. Analyzes style elements including metaphors, similes, and tone

Answer: D. Analyzes style elements including metaphors, similes, and tone.
Interpretive responses are ones that result in inferences and analysis of the text. These responses can be made both verbally or in writing.

37. **Which of the following are important skills to evaluate when determining readiness and language competency?** *(Average) (Skill 1.2)*

A. Knowledge of the standard rules of conversation

B. The size and range of a student's vocabulary and syntax skills

C. The ability to invent and entertain

D. All of the above

Answer: D. All of the above
Choices A, B, and C are all equally important in determining a student's readiness and language competency. There are a variety of assessments and observation tools that can be utilized to measure and quantify how a student is progressing with his or her language development.

38. **A traditional narrative popularly regarded as historically factual, but actually a combination of both fact and fiction is:** *(Average) (Skill 5.9)*

    A. A fable

    B. A legend

    C. An epistle

    D. An epic

    Answer: B. A legend
    A legend is a traditional narrative (or collection of narratives). It is a mixture of both fact and fiction, but people often think that it is solely factual.

39. **The unique way a writer uses language is referred to as:** *(Easy) (Skill 7.3)*

    A. tone

    B. style

    C. theme

    D. personification

    Answer: B. style
    The unique way a writer uses language is his or her style. Understanding a writer's strengths and weaknesses will help him or her to become more successful and able to use continuity in writing.

40. **Identifying the main points of a text and restating them in their own words is what a learner does to:** *(Easy) (2.3)*

   A. summarize

   B. instruct

   C. differentiate

   D. influence

   Answer: A. summarize
   Reading information, choosing the main points, and then placing them into your own words is the technique of summarizing.

41. **Which of the following is NOT a prewriting strategy?**
   (Average) (Skill 10.4)

   A. Analyzing sentences for variety

   B. Keeping an idea book

   C. Writing in a daily journal

   D. Writing down whatever comes to mind

   Answer: A. Analyzing sentences for variety
   Prewriting strategies assist students in a variety of ways. Common prewriting strategies include keeping an idea book for jotting down ideas, writing in a daily journal, and writing down whatever comes to mind, which is also called "free writing." Analyzing sentences for variety is a revising strategy.

42. _____ attempt to identify topics areas in which students may need extra motivational activities. *(Rigorous) (Skill 1.4)*

    A. Diagnostic Assessments

    B. Readiness Assessments

    C. Interest Assessments

    D. Evaluation Assessments

    Answer: C. Interest Assessments
    Interest assessments attempt to identify topics of high interest or areas in which students may need extra motivational activities.

43. **Exposition occurs within a story:** *(Rigorous) (Skill 10.6)*

    A. After the rising action

    B. After the denouement

    C. Before the rising action

    D. Before the setting

    Answer: C. Before the rising action
    Exposition is where characters and their situations are introduced. *Rising action* is the point at which conflict starts to occur and is often a turning point. *Denouement* is the final resolution of the plot.

44. **A running record is one way to evaluate:** *(Easy) (Skill 1.4)*

    A. Fluency

    B. Vocabulary

    C. phonics skills

    D. pragmatics

    Answer: A. Fluency
    A running record is a tool used to evaluate fluency in readers. It can help a teacher to gauge accuracy, automaticity, and reading rate in words per minute.

45. **The systematic exploration of a concept, event, term, piece of writing, element of media, or any other complex item is known as _____.** *(Average) (Skill 1.10)*

   A. synthesis

   B. evaluation

   C. analysis

   D. context

   Answer: C. Analysis
   People often think of analysis as the exploration of the parts that make up a whole. It is one of the three main types of critical thinking.

46. **An _____ is a long poem usually of book length reflecting values inherent in the generative society.** *(Average) (Skill 2.1)*

   A. epistle

   B. epic

   C. essay

   D. allegory

   Answer: B. Epic
   An epic is a long poem usually of book length reflecting values inherent in the generative society. Epic devices include an invocation to a Muse for inspiration, purpose for writing, universal setting, protagonist and antagonist who possess supernatural strength and acumen, and interventions of a god or gods.

47. An _____ is a letter that is not always originally intended for public distribution, but due to the fame of the sender and/or recipient, becomes public. *(Average) (Skill 5.12)*

    A. epistle

    B. epic

    C. essay

    D. allegory

    Answer: A. Epistle
    An epistle is a letter that is not always originally intended for public distribution, but due to the fame of the sender and/or recipient, becomes public.

48. Stories that are more or less universally shared within a culture to explain its history and traditions are known as: *(Average) (Skill 5.12)*

    A. legend

    B. novel

    C. myth

    D. fable

    Answer: C. Myth
    Stories that are more or less universally shared within a culture to explain its history and traditions are known as myths.

49. **A highly imaginative tale set in a fantastical realm dealing with the conflicts between heroes, villains and/or monsters is known as a:** *(Average) (Skill 5.12)*

    A. poem

    B. romance

    C. drama

    D. short story

    Answer: B. Romance
    A highly imaginative tale set in a fantastical realm dealing with the conflicts between heroes, villains and/or monsters is known as a romance.

50. **In these type stories, the hero is usually on a quest and is aided by other-worldly helpers. More often than not, the story focuses on good and evil and reward and punishment.** *(Average) (Skill 5.12)*

    A. Myths

    B. Tall tales

    C. Fairy Tales

    D. Fables

    Answer: C. Fairy Tales
    In fairy tales, the hero is usually on a quest and is aided by other-worldly helpers. Examples include *The Three Bears, Little Red Riding Hood, Snow White, Sleeping Beauty, Puss-in-Boots, Rapunzel,* and *Rumpelstiltskin.*

51. **Presented in a historically-accurate setting, these stories are known as:** *(Easy) (Skill 5.12)*

   A. Modern Fantasy

   B. Science Fiction

   C. Modern Realistic Fiction

   D. Historical Fiction

   Answer: D. Historical Fiction
   Historical fiction stories are presented in a historically accurate setting.

52. **Attributing human characteristics to an inanimate object, an abstract quality, or an animal is known as:** *(Easy) (Skill 4.14)*

   A. Simile

   B. Metaphor

   C. Personification

   D. Hyperbole

   Answer: C. Personification
   Attributing human characteristics to an inanimate object, an abstract quality, or an animal is known as personification.

53. **A deliberate exaggeration for effect or comedic effect is known as:** *(Easy) (Skill 4.14)*

   A. Simile

   B. Metaphor

   C. Personification

   D. Hyperbole

   Answer: D. Hyperbole
   A deliberate exaggeration for effect or comedic effect is known as hyperbole.

54. **Mr. Michaela's students are writing essays using the writing process. Which of the following is not a technique they will use to prewrite?** *(Skill 7.1)* *(Average)*

A. Clustering

B. Listing

C. Brainstorming

D. Proofreading

Answer: D. Proofreading should be reserved for the final draft.

55. **Miguel completes an organizer for a writing project. His teacher reviews his work and conferences with him. Miguel is ready to begin writing his ideas down in sentence and paragraph for. This next step after the prewriting stage of the writing process is known as:** *(Easy)* *(Skill 7.3)*

A. Drafting

B. Prewriting

C. Revising and Editing

D. Proofreading

Answer: A. Drafting
Students compose the first draft. They should follow their notes or writing plan from the prewriting stage.

56. **In this step of the writing process, students examine their work and make changes in wording, details, and ideas.** *(Easy)* *(Skill 7.3)*

A. Drafting

B. Prewriting

C. Revising and Editing

D. Proofreading

Answer: C. Revising and Editing
Revision is probably the most important step in the writing process. In this step, students examine their work and make changes in wording, details, and ideas.

57. During this final step known as _____, students may have their work displayed on a bulletin board, read aloud in class, or printed in a literary magazine or school anthology. *(Easy) (Skill 7.3)*

   A. Drafting

   B. Prewriting

   C. Publishing

   D. Proofreading

   Answer: C. Publishing
   In the final step of the writing process, publishing, students may have their work displayed on a bulletin board, read aloud in class, or printed in a literary magazine or school anthology.

58. _____ is discourse that is informative in nature. *(Easy) (Skill 5.2)*

   A. Description

   B. Narration

   C. Exposition

   D. Persuasion

   Answer: C. Exposition
   Exposition is discourse that is informative in nature. The writer doesn't care whether the reader follows the directions or not. The only purpose is to provide the information in case the reader does decide to use it.

59. **Read the following sentences.**

Gabe looks sleepy this morning. Why is he so tired? He had forgotten that he had a big report to write for his Social Studies class. The report is due today, and Gabe had wanted to give his best effort to the assignment. With his deadline approaching, he had burned the midnight oil.

Based upon these sentences, the idiom "burned the midnight oil" means: *(Average) (Skill 5.1)*

A. Rested too little

B. Worked too late at night

C. Wasted a lot of energy

D. Stressed out over his assignment

Answer: B. Worked too late at night
"Burned the midnight oil" implies someone worked overtime or to capacity, usually to get something accomplished that has a deadline.

60. **Mrs. Amalent meets with her students individually as they complete a book report project. She is careful to focus on specific aspects of their work in progress that is done well, and she makes suggestions for improvements. This type of evaluation provides feedback to help these students learn:** *(Average) (Skill 4.4)*

A. Formative

B. Summative

C. Both A and B

D. Neither A, nor B

Answer: A. Formative
Evaluation of student progress has two primary purposes: summative, to measure student progress or achievement, and formative, to provide feedback to students to help them learn.

61. **Which of the following strategies encourages print awareness in classrooms?** *(Easy) (Skill 2.1)*

    A. Word walls

    B. Using big books to read to students

    C. Using highlighters to locate upper- case letters

    D. All of the above

    Answer D: All of the above
    Classrooms rich in print provide many opportunities for students to see, use, and experience text in various forms. Word walls, big books, and highlighting certain textual features are all ways to expose students to various forms of text.

62. **_____ assessments are generally program- or teacher-focused.** *(Rigorous) (Skill 4.4)*

    A. Diagnostic Assessments

    B. Readiness Assessments

    C. Interest Assessments

    D. Evaluation Assessments

    Answer: D. Evaluation Assessments
    Evaluation assessments are generally program- or teacher-focused.

63. **_____ defined as focusing attention on one thing only.** *(Rigorous) (Skill 1.8)*

    A. Association

    B. Visualization

    C. Concentration

    D. Repetition

    Answer: C. Concentration
    Concentration can be defined as focusing attention on one thing only. When you read for a particular purpose, you will concentrate on what you read.

64. **Teaching students how to interpret _____ involves evaluating a text's headings, subheadings, bolded words, and side notes.** *(Easy) (Skill 5.1)*

    A. Graphic organizers

    B. Text structures

    C. Textual marking

    D. Summaries

    Answer B: text structures
    Studying text structures, including the table of contents, glossary, index, head- ings, etc., is an excellent way for students to increase comprehension of a text. Knowledge of these tools helps students to understand the organization and flow of their reading.

65. **Identify the sentence type:**

    Madison went to Paris during the winter vacation, but her best friend stayed home because she had made other plans with some friends.
    (Average) (Skill 6.6)

    A. simple

    B. compound

    C. complex

    D. compound-complex

    Answer: D. compound-complex
    A compound-complex sentence is a sentence that has two or more coordinate independent clauses and one or more dependent clauses.

66. **The teacher states, "We will work on the first page of vocabulary words. On the second page we will work on the structure and meaning of the words. We will go over these together and then you will write out the answers to the exercises on your own. I will be circulating to give help if needed." What is this an example of?** *(Rigorous)* *(Skill 4.14)*

    A. Evaluation of instructional activity

    B. Analysis of instructional activity

    C. Identification of expected outcomes

    D. Pacing of instructional activity

    Answer B: Analysis of instructional activity
    The successful teacher carefully plans all activities to foresee any difficulties in executing the plan. This also assures that the directions being given to students will be clear, avoiding any misunderstanding.

67. **Spelling instruction should include:**
    (Average) (Skill 2.2)

    A. Breaking down sentences

    B. Developing a sense of correct and incorrect spellings

    C. Identifying every word in a given text

    D. Spelling words the way that they sound

    Answer: B. Developing a sense of correct and incorrect spellings
    Developing a sense of correct and incorrect spellings is part of the developmental stages of spelling and is a phase that is typically entered later in elementary school. Breaking down sentences involves paragraph analysis, identifying every word in a given text is not necessary to construct meaning from that text, and spelling words the way that they sound is not an effective way to teach spelling.

68. **Children typically learn the majority of their words and phrases from:**
   (Easy) (Skill 3.9)

   A. School

   B. Reading

   C. Peers

   D. Other

   Answer B: Reading
   Reading builds vocabulary, but in young children oral language develops from their environment.

69. **In the _____ stage of writing, students write in scribbles and can assign meaning to the markings.** *(Rigorous) (Skill 6.1)*

   A. role-play writing

   B. experimental writing

   C. early writing

   D. conventional writing

   Answer A: role-play writing
   In the role-playing stage, the child writes in scribbles and assigns a message to the symbols. Even though an adult would not be able to read the writing, the child can read what is written, although it may not be the same each time the child reads it. In experimental writing, the student writes in the simplest form of recognizable writing. In the early writing stage, children start to use a small range of familiar text forms and sight words in their writing. Finally, in the conventional writing stage, students have a sense of audience and purpose for writing.

70. **Children are taught phonological awareness when they are taught all but which concept?** *(Average) (Skill 1.1)*

    A. The sounds made by the letters

    B. The correct spelling of words

    C. The sounds made by various combinations of letters

    D. The ability to recognize individual sounds in words

    Answer: B. The correct spelling of words
    Phonological awareness happens during the pre-K years or even earlier and involves connecting letters to sounds. Children begin to develop a sense of correct and incorrect spellings of words in a transitional spelling phase that is traditionally entered in elementary school.

71. **Answering questions, monitoring comprehension, and interacting with a text are common methods of:** *(Average) (Skill 4.4)*

    A. Whole-class instruction

    B. Comprehension instruction

    C. Research-based instruction

    D. Evidence-based instruction

    Answer: B. Comprehension instruction
    Comprehension instruction helps students learn strategies that they can use independently with any text. Answering questions, monitoring comprehension, and interacting with a text are a few strategies that teachers can teach to their students to help increase their comprehension. Research-based, evidence-based, and whole-class instruction relate to specific reading programs available.

72. **Which of the following is NOT characteristic of a folktale?**
    (Average) (Skill 5.14)

    A. Considered true among various societies

    B. A hero on a quest

    C. Good versus evil

    D. Adventures of animals

    Answer: A. Considered true among various societies
    There are few societies that would consider folktales to be true as folktale is another name for fairy tale, and elements such as heroes on a quest, good versus evil, and adventures of animals are popular, fictional, themes in fairy tales.

73. **A (n) _____ can be used to estimate a student's reading level and also to assess a student's ability to use word identification strategies.** *(Average) (Skill 4.4)*

    A. Anecdotal Record

    B. Rating Scale

    C. Informal Reading Inventory

    D. None of the above

    Answer: C. Informal Reading Inventory
    An informal reading inventory can be used to estimate a student's reading level and also to assess a student's ability to use word identification strategies. The IRI can assist a teacher in determining reading fluency as well as strengths and weaknesses in the progress of reading comprehension.

74. **Which of the following is important in understanding fiction?** *(Rigorous) (Skill 4.1)*

   I.   Realizing the artistry in telling a story to convey a point.
   II. Knowing fiction is imaginary.
   III. Seeing what is truth and what is perspective.
   IV. Acknowledging the difference between opinion and truth.

   A. I and II only

   B. II and IV only

   C. III and IV only

   D. IV only

   Answer: A. I and II only
   In order to understand a piece of fiction, it is important that readers realize that an author's choice in a work of fiction is for the sole purpose of conveying a viewpoint. It is also important to understand that fiction is imaginary. Seeing what is truth and what is perspective and acknowledging the difference between opinion and truth are important in understanding nonfiction.

MATHEMATICS

75. **Which of the following is a true statement regarding manipulatives in mathematics instruction?** *(Average) (Skill 26.4)*

   A. Manipulatives are materials that students can physically handle

   B. Manipulatives help students make concrete concepts abstract

   C. Manipulatives include fingers, tiles, paper folding, and ice cream sticks

   D. Manipulatives help students make abstract concepts concrete

   Answer: D. Manipulatives help students make abstract concepts concrete
   Manipulatives are materials that students can physically handle and move, such as fingers and tiles. Manipulatives allow students to understand mathematic concepts by allowing them to see concrete examples of abstract processes. Manipulatives are attractive to students because they appeal to their visual and tactile senses.

76. **All of the following are tools that can strengthen students' mathematical understanding EXCEPT:** *(Easy) (Skill 26.3)*

   A. Rulers, scales, and protractors

   B. Calculators, counters, and measuring containers

   C. Software and hardware

   D. Money and software

   Answer: C. Software and hardware
   Students' understanding of mathematical concepts is strengthened when they use tools to help make the abstract concepts become concrete realities. Teachers have a wide variety of tools available to help students learn mathematics. These include all of the above except for hardware. Hardware technically is not a tool but part of the infrastructure of the classroom.

77. **Which of the following is not a good example of helping students make connections between the real world and mathematics?** *(Average) (Skill 26.2)*

   A. Studying a presidential election from the perspective of the math involved

   B. Using weather concepts to teach math

   C. Having student helpers take attendance

   D. Reviewing major mathematical theorems on a regular basis

   Answer: D. Reviewing major mathematical theorems on a regular basis
   Theorems are abstract math concepts, and reviews, while valuable, are not an example of using everyday events to teach math. Teachers can increase student interest in math by relating mathematical concepts to familiar events in their lives and using real-world examples and data whenever possible. Instead of presenting only abstract concepts and examples, teachers should relate concepts to everyday situations to shift the emphasis from memorization and abstract application to understanding and applied problem solving. This will not only improve students' grasp of math ideas and keep them engaged, it will also help answer the perennial question, "Why do we have to learn math?"

78. **Which of the following is an example of the associative property?** *(Rigorous) (Skill 11.2)*

A. $a(b + c) = ab + bc$

B. $a + 0 = a$

C. $(a + b) + c = a + (b + c)$

D. $a + b = b + a$

Answer: C. $(a + b) + c = a + (b + c)$
The associative property is when the parentheses of a problem are switched.

79. **Jen, Tim and Anna are members of the same family. Tim is 5 years older than Jen. Anna is 6 years older than Tim. The sum of their three ages is 31 years. What is the age of each family member?** *(Easy)(Skill 13.7)*

A. 12,500

B. 15,000

C. 11,800

D. 10,500

Answer: C. 11,800
This problem can be solved using a table as shown below where Jen's age is guessed then Tim's and Anna's ages are calculated. The calculations are stopped when the condition in the problem "the sum of their three ages is 31 years" is reached.

Jen's age	Tim's age	Anna's age	The sum of all ages
1	1 + 5 = 6	6 + 6 = 12	1 + 6 + 12 = 19
2	2 + 5 = 7	7 + 6 = 13	2 + 7 + 13 = 22
3	3 + 5 = 8	8 + 6 = 14	3 + 8 + 14 = 25
4	4 + 5 = 9	9 + 6 = 15	4 + 9 + 15 = 28
5	5 + 5 = 10	10 + 6 = 16	5 + 10 + 16 = 31

The column on the right, where all ages are added, shows whether the main condition ("The sum of their three ages is 31 years") is satisfied or not. The last row of the table shows: Jen = 5, Tim = 10 and Anna = 16 to satisfy the condition in the problem.

80. **Mathematical operations are done in the following order:**
(Rigorous) (Skill 11.4)

A. Simplify inside grouping characters such as parentheses, brackets, square roots, fraction bars, etc.; multiply out expressions with exponents; do multiplication or division, from left to right; do addition or subtraction, from left to right

B. Do multiplication or division, from left to right; simplify inside grouping characters such as parentheses, brackets, square roots, fraction bars, etc.; multiply out expressions with exponents; do addition or subtraction, from left to right

C. Simplify inside grouping characters such as parentheses, brackets, square roots, fraction bars, etc.; do addition or subtraction, from left to right; multiply out expressions with exponents; do multiplication or division, from left to right

D. None of the above

Answer: A. Simplify inside grouping characters such as parentheses, brackets, square roots, fraction bars, etc.; multiply out expressions with exponents; do multiplication or division, from left to right; do addition or subtraction, from left to right
When facing a mathematical problem that requires all mathematical properties to be performed first, you do the math within the parentheses, brackets, square roots, or fraction bars. Then you multiply out expressions with exponents. Next, you do multiplication or division. Finally, you do addition or subtraction.

81. _____ **lines or planes form a 90-degree angle to each other. (Easy)(Skill 18.1)**

A. Parallel

B. Complimentary

C. Supplementary

D. Perpendicular

Answer: D. Perpendicular
Perpendicular lines or planes form a 90-degree angle to each other. This angle is known as a right angle.

82. **The least common multiple of a group of numbers is the _____ number that all of the given numbers will divide into. The LCM will always be the _____ of the given numbers or a multiple of the _____ number.** *(Rigorous)(Skill 12.1)*

    A. largest; largest; smallest

    B. smallest; smallest; largest

    C. largest; smallest; smallest

    D. smallest; largest; largest

    Answer: D. smallest; largest; largest
    The least common multiple of a group of numbers is the smallest number that all of the given numbers will divide into. The LCM will always be the largest of the given numbers or a multiple of the largest number.

83. **Numbers that can only be factored into 1 and the number itself:** *(Average)(Skill 12.1)*

    A. Prime numbers

    B. Composite numbers

    C. Whole numbers

    D. Round numbers

    Answer: A. Prime numbers
    Prime numbers are numbers that can only be factored into 1 and the number itself. When factoring into prime factors, all the factors must be numbers that cannot be factored again (without using 1).

84. **A number is divisible by 5 if:** *(Rigorous) (Skill 12.1)*

    A. it is an even number.

    B. It is divisible by 3.

    C. the number formed by its last two digits is evenly divisible by 4.

    D. the number ends in either a 5 or a 0.

    Answer: D. the number ends in either a 5 or a 0.
    A number is divisible by 5 if the number ends in either a 5 or a 0. The number 225 ends with a 5 so it is divisible by 5. The number 470 is also divisible by 5 because its last digit is 0.The number 2,358 is not divisible by 5 because its last digit is 8, not 5 or 0.

85. **These lines share a common point, and intersecting planes share a common set of points, or line:** *(Average) (Skill 18.1)*

    A. Parallel

    B. Perpendicular

    C. Intersecting

    D. Skew

    Answer: C. Intersecting
    Angles can be classified in a number of ways. Intersecting lines share a common point, and intersecting planes share a common set of points, or line.

86. **These angles have sides that form two pairs of opposite rays:** *(Rigorous)(Skill 18.1)*

    A. Alternate interior

    B. Alternate exterior

    C. Corresponding

    D. Vertical

    Answer: D. Vertical
    Angles can be classified in a number of ways. Vertical angles have sides that form two pairs of opposite rays.

87. **If a right triangle has legs with the measurements of 3 cm and 4 cm, what is the measure of the hypotenuse?** *(Average) (Skill 18.3)*

    A. 6 cm

    B. 1 cm

    C. 7 cm

    D. 5 cm

    Answer: D. 5 cm
    If you use the Pythagorean Theorem, you will get 5 cm for the hypotenuse leg.

88. **If the radius of a right circular cylinder is doubled, how does its volume change?** *(Rigorous) (Skill 19.2)*

    A. No change

    B. Also is doubled

    C. Four times the original

    D. Pi times the original

    Answer: C. Four times the original
    If the radius of a right circular cylinder is doubled, the volume is multiplied by four because in the formula, the radius is squared. Therefore, the new volume is 2 x 2, or four times the original.

89. **Find the area of a rectangle if you know that the base is 8 cm and the diagonal of the rectangle is 8.5 cm:** *(Rigorous) (Skill 19.3)*

A. 24 cm²

B. 30 cm²

C. 18.9 cm²

D. 24 cm

Answer: A. 24 cm²
The answer is A because the base of the rectangle is also one leg of the right triangle, and the diagonal is the hypotenuse of the triangle. To find the other leg of the triangle, you can use the Pythagorean Theorem. Once you get the other leg of the triangle that is also the height of the rectangle. To get the area, you multiply the base by the height. The reason the answer is A and not D is because area is measured in centimeters squared, not just centimeters.

90. **An item that sells for $375.00 is put on sale at $120.00. What is the percentage of decrease?** *(Average) (Skill 12.2)*

A. 25%

B. 28%

C. 68%

D. 34%

Answer: C. 68%
In this problem you must set up a cross-multiplication problem. You begin by placing $x/100$ to represent the variable you are solving for over 100%, and then you place 120/375 to represent the new price over the original price. Once you cross-multiply, you get 68, which is the percentage decrease.

91. **What is a translation?**
(Rigorous) (Skill 20.2)

   A. To turn a figure around a fixed point

   B. When the object has the same shape and same size, but figures face in different directions

   C. To "slide" an object a fixed distance in a given direction

   D. The transformation that "shrinks" or "makes it bigger"

   Answer: C. To "slide" an object a fixed distance in a given direction
   A translation is when you slide an object a fixed distance but do not change the size of the object.

92. **What measures could be used to report the distance traveled in walking around a track?** *(Easy) (Skill 17.2)*

   A. Degrees

   B. Square meters

   C. Kilometers

   D. Cubic feet

   Answer: C. Kilometers
   Degrees measure angles; square meters measure area; cubic feet measure volume; and kilometers measure length.

93. **Corporate salaries are listed for several employees. Which would be the best measure of central tendency?** *(Average) (Skill 21.4)*

$24,000	$24,000
$26,000	$28,000
$30,000	$120,000

A. Mean

B. Median

C. Mode

D. No difference

Answer: B. Median
The median provides the best measure of central tendency in this case, as the mode is the lowest number and the mean would be disproportionately skewed by the outlier, $120,000.

94. **Given a drawer with 5 black socks, 3 blue socks, and 2 red socks, what is the probability that you will draw two black socks in two draws in a dark room?** *(Rigorous) (Skill 22.5)*

A. 2/9

B. 1/4

C. 17/18

D. 1/18

Answer: A. 2/9
In this example of conditional probability, the probability of drawing a black sock on the first draw is 5/10. It is implied in the problem that there is no replacement, therefore the probability of obtaining a black sock in the second draw is 4/9. Multiply the two probabilities and reduce to lowest terms.

95. **Suppose you have a bag of marbles that contains 2 red marbles, 5 blue marbles, and 3 green marbles. If you replace the first marble chosen, what is the probability you will choose 2 green marbles in a row?** *(Average) (Skill 22.3)*

    A. 2/5

    B. 9/100

    C. 9/10

    D. 3/5

    Answer: B. 9/100
    When performing a problem in which you replace the item, you multiply the first probability fraction by the second probability fraction and replace the item when finding the second probability.

96. **In probability, the sample space represents:**
    (Average) (Skill 22.1)

    A. An outcome of an experiment

    B. A list of all possible outcomes of an experiment

    C. The number of times you must flip a coin

    D. The amount of room needed to conduct an experiment

    Answer: B. A list of all possible outcomes of an experiment
    The sample space is the list of all possible outcomes that you can have for an experiment.

97. **Deduction is:**
    (Average) (Skill 13.1)

    A. Logical reasoning

    B. The process of arriving at a conclusion based on other statements that are known to be true

    C. Both A and B

    D. Neither A nor B

    Answer: C. Both A and B
    Deductive reasoning moves from a generalization or set of examples (such as numbers) to a specific conclusion or solution.

98. **Find the inverse of the following statement: If I like dogs, then I do not like cats.**
    (Rigorous) (Skill 24.1)

    A. If I like dogs, then I do like cats.

    B. If I like cats, then I like dogs.

    C. If I like cats, then I do not like dogs.

    D. If I do not like dogs, then I like cats.

    Answer: D. If I do not like dogs, then I like cats.
    When you take the inverse of the statement, you negate both statements. By negating both statements you take the opposite of the original statement.

99. **Find the converse of the following statement: If I like math, then I do not like science.** *(Average) (Skill 24.2)*

    A. If I do not like science, then I like math.

    B. If I like math, then I do not like science.

    C. If I do not like math, then I do not like science.

    D. If I like math, then I do not like science.

Answer: A. If I do not like science, then I like math.
When finding the converse of a statement, you take the second part of the statement and reverse it with the first part of the statement. In other words, you reverse the statements.

100. **Which of the following is the basic language of mathematics?** *(Easy) (Skill 24.5)*

    A. Symbolic representation

    B. Number lines

    C. Arithmetic operations

    D. Deductive thinking

Answer: A. Symbolic representation
Symbolic representation is the basic language of mathematics. Converting data to symbols allows for easy manipulation and problem solving. Students should have the ability to recognize what the symbolic notation represents and convert information into symbolic form.

101. **The mass of a cookie is closest to:**
(Easy) (Skill 17.1)

A. 0.5 kg

B. 0.5 grams

C. 15 grams

D. 1.5 grams

Answer: C. 15 grams

102. **A car is rented in Quebec. The outside temperature shown on the dashboard reads 17°C. What is the temperature in degrees Fahrenheit? (Use the formula** $F = \frac{9}{5}C + 32$ **.)** *(Average) (Skill 17.3)*

A. 27.2°F

B. 41.4°F

C. 62.6°F

D. 88.2°F

Answer: C. 62.6°F

Use the order of operations. First multiply $\frac{9}{5}$ and 17. Then add 32 to the result.

$$F = (\frac{9}{5}\square$$
$$= 30.6 + 32$$
$$= 62.6$$

103. The two solutions of the quadratic equation $ax^2 + bx + c = 0$ are given by the formula $x = \dfrac{-b \pm \sqrt{b^2 - 4ac}}{2a}$. What are the solutions of the equation $x^2 - 18x + 32$?
(Rigorous) (Skill 12.4)

A. ⁻5 and 23

B. 2 and 16

C. $9 \pm \sqrt{113}$

D. $9 \pm 2\sqrt{113}$

Answer: B. 2 and 16

Substitute in the formula: $a = 1$, $b = {}^-18$, $c = 32$: $x = \dfrac{18 \pm \sqrt{18^2 - 4(32)}}{2}$. Then apply the standard order of operations: $x = \dfrac{18 + 14}{2}$ and $x = \dfrac{18 - 14}{2}$, or $x = 16$ and $x = 2$. Be sure to apply the standard order of operations after substituting in the formula.

104. Which of the following is not equivalent to 3 km? *(Average) (Skill 17.3)*

I. 3.0×10^3 m
II. 3.0×10^4 cm
III. 3.0×10^6 mm

A. I

B. II

C. III

D. None of the above

Answer: B. II
There are 1000, or 103 meters in each kilometer; 100, or 10^2 cm, in each meter; and 10 millimeters in each centimeter. Remember to add exponents when multiplying: for example, 3.0×10^3 m $= 3.0 \times 10^3 \times 10^2$ cm, or 3.0×10^5 cm.

105. A right angle is: *(Easy) (Skill 18.1)*

A. greater than 90 and less than 180 degrees

B. greater than 0 and less than 90 degrees

C. exactly 90 degrees

D. exactly 180 degrees

Answer: C. exactly 90 degrees
Angles are classified according to their size. Right angles are exactly 90 degrees.

106. A simple closed surface formed from planar polygonal regions is known as a: *(Easy)(Skill 19.4)*

A. vertex

B. polyhedron

C. edge

D. face

Answer: B. polyhedron
We refer to three-dimensional figures in geometry as solids. A solid is the union of all points on a simple closed surface and all points in its interior. A polyhedron is a simple closed surface formed from planar polygonal regions.

Use the data below to answer questions 107-110.
The following are the amounts of groups of seeds counted during preparation for a science experiment:

70	80	86
90	91	90
87	70	98
54	63	62
98	76	70

107. **Find the median of the given test scores:** *(Average)(Skill 12.1)*

   A. 84

   B. 79

   C. 80

   D. 83

   Answer: C. 80
   To determine the median, the numbers need to be placed in numerical order, like this:

   54 62 63 70 70 70 76 **80** 86 87 90 90 91 98 98

   The middle number determines the median. The median in this example is 84.

108. **Find the mean of the given test scores:**
   (Average)(Skill 12.1)

   A. 79

   B. 83

   C. 84

   D. None of the above

   Answer: A. 79
   The mean is the sum of all seed amounts divided by the number of seed amounts. In this case, the sum equals 1,185. There are 15 quantities. 1,185 divided by 15 equals 79. The mean (average) of the fifteen amounts is 79.

109. Find the mode of the given test scores: *(Average)(Skill 12.1)*

   A. 84

   B. 79

   C. 80

   D. 70

Answer: D. 70
The mode is the most frequent number. In this example, the mode is 70.

110. Find the range of the given test scores: *(Average)(Skill 12.1)*

   A. 46

   B. 44

   C. 64

   D. 34

Answer: B. 44
The range is found by subtracting the smallest number from the largest number. In this case:
$98 - 54 = 44$
The range is 44.

111. Which two fractions are equivalent? *(Easy)(Skill 12.5)*

    A. 5/2 and 2/5

    B. 4/3 and 8/6

    C. 1/4 and 2/4

    D. 1/4 and 2/4

Answer: B. 4/3 and 8/6
It is easier to compare fractions if they are written with the same denominator

5/2 and 2/5 with same denominator become 25/10 and 4/10
4/3 and 8/6 with same denominator become 8/6 and 8/6
Fractions 4/3 and 8/6 are equivalent because when written with a common denominator both denominators and numerators are equal.

112. 5 2/3 - 3 1/2 =
(Easy)(Skill 12.5)

    A. 2 2/3

    B. 2 1/6

    C. 2 ½

    D. 1 3/8

Answer: B. 2 1/6
Subtract whole numbers together and fractions together:
5 2/3 - 3 1/2 = (5 - 3) + (2/3 - 1/2)

Write fractions with the same denominator:
2 + (4/6 - 3/6) = 2 1/6

113. **2/5 × 3/7 =**
(Easy)(Skill 12.5)

A. 6/35

B. 7/35

C. 10/21

D. 14/15

Answer: A. 6/35
Multiply numerators and denominators:
2/5 × 3/7 = (2 × 3) / (5 × 7) = 6/35

114. **Lilian works 15 hours a week (Monday to Friday). Last week she worked 3 1/2 hours on Monday, 4 hours on Tuesday, 2 1/6 hours on Wednesday and 1 1/2 on Thursday. How many hours did she work on Friday?**
(Easy)(Skill 12.5)

A. 3 5/6

B. 4 ½

C. 3 1/6

D. 2 1/6

Answer: A. 3 5/6
The number of hours Lilian worked on Friday is unknown. Substitute n for hours.
The total (addition) for the 5 days is 15 hours. Add all the hours for 5 days:
3 1/2 + 4 + 2 1/6 + 1 1/2 + n = 15

Add whole numbers together and fractions together:
(3 + 4 + 2 + 1) + (1/2 + 1/6 + 1/2) + n = 15
10 + (1/2 + 1/2 + 1/6) + n = 15
10 + (1 + 1/6) + n = 15
11 + 1/6 + n = 15

For 11 + 1/6 + n = 15, to have the right hand side and the left hand side equal, n must be equal to 3 and 5/6.

Check:
11 + 1/6 + (3 + 5/6) = (11 + 3) + (1/6 + 5/6) = 14 + 6/6 = 14 + 1 = 15

115. **James read 2 books. He read the first one in one week with 25 pages everyday. He read the second book in 12 days with 23 pages everyday. What is the total number of pages that James read?**
(Easy)(Skill 12.5)

   A. 276 pages

   B. 451 pages

   C. 175 pages

   D. 476 pages

Answer: B. 451 pages
Pages read in the first book in one week (7 days) with 25 pages everyday:
$25 \times 7 = 175$ pages

Pages read in the second book in 12 days with 23 pages everyday:
$23 \times 12 = 276$ pages

Total number of pages read:
$175 + 276 = 451$ pages

116. **It takes John 25 minutes to walk to the car park and 45 to drive to work. At what time should he get out of the house in order to get to work at 9:00 a.m.?**
(Easy)(Skill 12.5)

   A. 7:45 a.m.

   B. 7:30 a.m.

   C. 7:50 a.m.

   D. 8:10 a.m.

Answer: C. 7:50 a.m.
The time it takes John to get to work: time to walk to car park + time to drive
$25 + 45 = 70$ minutes = 1 hour and 10 minutes

John needs to get out of the house 1 hour and 10 minutes before 9:00 am at
9:00 - 1:10 = 7:50 a.m.

History AND Social Science

117. The study of behavior of individual players in an economy, such as individuals, families and businesses is called:
(Easy) (Skill 31.5)

   A. Economics

   B. Microeconomics

   C. Macroeconomics

   D. Normative Economics

   Answer: B. Microeconomics
   Microeconomics refers to the part of economics concerned with single factors and the effects of individual decisions.

118. Ms. Gomez has a number of ESL students in her class. In order to meet their specific needs as second-language learners, which of the following would NOT be an appropriate approach? *(Easy) (Skill 30.7)*

   A. Pair students of different ability levels for English practice

   B. Focus most of her instruction on teaching English rather than content

   C. Provide accommodations during testing and with assignments

   D. Use visual aids to help students make word links with familiar objects

   Answer: B. Focus most of her instruction on teaching English rather than content
   In working with ESOL students, different approaches should be used to ensure that students (a) Get multiple opportunities to learn and practice English, and (b) Still learn content. Content should not be given short shrift or be "dumbed down" for ESOL students.

119. **Which one of the following is NOT a reason why Europeans came to the New World?** *(Rigorous) (Skill 29.9)*

    A. To find resources in order to increase wealth

    B. To establish trade

    C. To increase a ruler's power and importance

    D. To spread Christianity

    Answer: B. To establish trade
    The Europeans came to the New World for a number of reasons; they often came to find new natural resources to extract for manufacturing. The Portuguese, Spanish, and English were sent over to increase the monarch's power and to spread influences such as religion (Christianity) and culture. Therefore, the only reason given that Europeans didn't come to the New World was to establish trade.

120. **Which of the following were results of the Age of Exploration?** *(Easy) (Skill 29.6)*

    A. More complete and accurate maps and charts

    B. New and more accurate navigational instruments

    C. Proof that the Earth is round

    D. All of the above

    Answer: D. All of the above
    The importance of the Age of Exploration was not only the discovery and colonization of the New World, but also better maps and charts; new accurate navigational instruments; increased knowledge; great wealth; new and different foods and items not known in Europe; a new hemisphere as a refuge from poverty and persecution, and as a place to start a new and better life; and proof that Asia could be reached by sea and that the Earth was round; ships and sailors would not sail off the edge of a flat Earth and disappear forever into nothingness.

121. **The ancient civilization of the _____ invented the wheel.**
(Rigorous) (Skill 29.4)

A. Sumerians

B. Assyrians

C. Egyptians

D. Phoenicians

Answer: A. Sumerians
The ancient civilization of the Sumerians invented the wheel. They also developed irrigation through use of canals, dikes, and devices for raising water; devised the system of cuneiform writing; learned to divide time; and built large boats for trade.

122. **In order to put the Earth's spherical features on a flat map, they must be stretched in some way. This stretching is called _____.**
(Average) (Skill 30.2)

A. Distortion

B. Cartography

C. Projection

D. Illustrating

Answer: A. distortion
In order to put the Earth's features on a map they must be stretched in some way. This stretching is called distortion. Distortion does not mean that maps are wrong; it simply means that they are not perfect representations of the Earth or its parts.

123. The _____ tells you what information is found on the map. *(Easy) (Skill 30.2)*

A. Legend

B. Grid

C. Scale

D. Title

Answer: D. title
All maps should have a title, just like all books should. The title tells you what information is found on the map.

124. An important map property is _____, or correct shapes. *(Easy) (Skill 30.2)*

A. consistent scales

B. conformal

C. equal areas

D. relief

Answer: A. consistent scales
Many maps attempt to use the same scale on all parts of the map. Generally, this is easier when a map shows a relatively small part of the Earth's surface.

125. The quantity of a good or service that a producer is willing and able to sell at different prices during a given period of time: *(Average) (Skill 31.2)*

    A. demand

    B. supply

    C. market

    D. economy

Answer: B. supply
Price plays an important role in a market economy. Demand was defined above. Supply is based on production costs. The supply of a good or service is defined as the quantity of a good or service that a producer is willing and able to sell at different prices during a given period of time.

126. The _____ is the basis for the existence of economics. *(Rigorous) (Skill 31.2)*

    A. law of supply and demand

    B. value of the dollar

    C. scarcity of resources

    D. means of production

Answer: C. scarcity of resources
The scarcity of resources is the basis for the existence of economics. Economics is defined as the study of how scarce resources are allocated to satisfy unlimited wants.

127. Which political group pushed the Reconstruction measures through Congress after Lincoln's death? *(Rigorous) (Skill 29.12)*

A. The Radical Republicans

B. The Radical Democrats

C. The Whigs

D. The Independents

Answer: A. The Radical Republicans
In 1866, the Radical Republicans won control of Congress and passed the Reconstruction Acts, which placed the governments of the southern states under the control of the federal military. With this backing, the Republicans began to implement their policies such as granting all black men the vote and denying the vote to former Confederate soldiers. Congress had passed the Thirteenth, Fourteenth, and Fifteenth Amendments, granting citizenship and civil rights to blacks. Ratification of these amendments was a condition of readmission into the Union by the rebel states.

128. As a result of the Missouri Compromise:
(Average) (Skill 29.15)

A. Slavery was not allowed in the Louisiana Purchase

B. The Louisiana Purchase was nullified

C. Louisiana separated from the Union

D. The Embargo Act was repealed

Answer: A. Slavery was not allowed in the Louisiana Purchase
The Missouri Compromise was the agreement that eventually allowed Missouri to enter the Union. It did not nullify the Louisiana Purchase or the Embargo Act or separate Louisiana from the Union. As a result of the Missouri Compromise, slavery was specifically banned north of the boundary 36° 30'.

129. **Which country was a cold war foe of the United States?**
(Easy) (Skill 29.13)

A. Soviet Union

B. Brazil

C. Canada

D. Argentina

Answer: A. Soviet Union
The Soviet Union was a cold war superpower and foe of the United States in its determination to fight the spread of Communism.

130. **A newspaper article has the following title:**

"Hawaii is expensive, challenging place to run small business"

Which of the following ideas are likely to be found in this article:
(Rigorous) (Skill 8.1)

A. Hawaii is the place where the sport of surfing originated, and famous international surfing championships are held there every year.

B. Hawaii is in the middle of the Pacific Ocean, far away from the U.S. mainland and other large land-masses, so everything that can't be produced locally in-state has to be shipped or flown there over great distances.

C. Pure Hawaiian Kona coffee is some of the most prized and expensive coffee in the world.

D. None of the above

Answer: B. Hawaii is in the middle of the Pacific Ocean, far away from the U.S. mainland and other large land-masses, so everything that can't be produced locally in-state has to be shipped or flown there over great distances.

131. What is the most significant environmental change in Texas over the last century? (Rigorous) (Skill 30.5)

A. The number of square miles devoted to living space

B. Continued exploration for oil and gas

C. Development along the Gulf Coast

D. Changes in agricultural practices

Answer: A. The number of square miles devoted to living space
The most drastic change to the environment wrought by people has been the sheer number of square miles devoted to living space. Texas still maintains vast areas of agricultural and ranch land, but that number is shrinking by the year, as more and more people claim and put stakes down on land designed to be lived on exclusively. The farmers of the past lived on their land but also lived off it. Their houses were part of their farms and their jobs were working the land. Nowadays, skyscrapers dot the skylines of large cities along with high-rise apartment buildings, which serve the sole function of providing living areas for the people who work in the large cities.

132. The end to hunting, gathering, and fishing of prehistoric people was due to: (Average) (Skill 30.4)

A. Domestication of animals

B. Building crude huts and houses

C. Development of agriculture

D. Organized government in villages

Answer: C. Development of agriculture
Although the domestication of animals, the building of huts and houses, and the first organized governments were all important steps made by early civilizations, it was the development of agriculture that ended the once-dominant practices of hunting, gathering, and fishing among prehistoric people. The development of agriculture provided a more efficient use of time and, for the first time, a surplus of food. This greatly improved the quality of life and contributed to early population growth.

133. **Which of the following is most useful in showing differences in variables at a specific point in time?** *(Average) (Skill 34.11)*

   A. Histogram

   B. Scatter plots

   C. Pie chart

   D. Bar graph

   Answer: D. Bar graph
   Bar graphs are simple and basic, showing a difference in variables at a specific point in time. Histograms are good for summarizing large sets of data in intervals. Pie charts show proportions, and scatter plots demonstrate correlations, or relationships between variables.

134. **The New Deal was designed to get America back on its feet during:** *(Average) (Skill 29.5)*

   A. World War I

   B. The Pandemic Flu

   C. The Great Depression

   D. The Spanish American War

   Answer: C. The Great Depression
   The New Deal was designed to help America during The Great Depression, the economic crisis and period of low business activity in the U.S. and other countries, roughly beginning with the stock-market crash in October of 1929.

135. During the 1920s, the United States almost completely stopped all immigration. One of the reasons was: *(Rigorous) (Skill 31.3)*

A. Plentiful, cheap unskilled labor was no longer needed by industrialists

B. War debts from World War I made it difficult to render financial assistance

C. European nations were reluctant to allow people to leave since there was a need to rebuild populations and economic stability

D. The United States did not become a member of the League of Nations

Answer: A. Plentiful, cheap unskilled labor was no longer needed by industrialists
The United States almost completely stopped all immigration during the 1920s because their once much-needed cheap, unskilled labor jobs, made available by the once-booming industrial economy, were no longer needed. This had much to do with the increased use of machines to do the work once done by cheap, unskilled laborers.

136. In the 1800s, the era of industrialization and growth was characterized by: *(Average) (Skill 31.2)*

A. Small firms

B. Public ownership

C. Worker-owned enterprises

D. Monopolies and trusts

Answer: D. Monopolies and trusts
The era of industrialization and business expansion was characterized by big businesses and monopolies that merged into trusts. There were few small firms and there was no public ownership or worker-owned enterprises.

137. **Which one of the following would NOT be considered a result of World War II?** *(Rigorous) (Skill 31.4)*

A. Economic depressions and slow resumption of trade and financial aid

B. Western Europe was no longer the center of world power

C. The beginnings of new power struggles, not only in Europe but in Asia as well

D. Territorial and boundary changes for many nations, especially in Europe

Answer: A. Economic depressions and slow resumption of trade and financial aid
Following World War II, the economy was vibrant and flourished from the stimulus of war and the world's increased dependence on U.S. industries. Therefore, World War II didn't result in economic depressions and slow resumption of trade and financial aid. Western Europe was no longer the center of world power. New power struggles arose in Europe and Asia, and many European nations experienced changing territories and boundaries.

138. **The New Deal was:** *(Average) (Skill 31.6)*

A. A trade deal with England

B. A series of programs to provide relief during the Great Depression

C. A new exchange rate regime

D. A plan for tax relief

Answer: B. A series of programs to provide relief during the Great Depression
The New Deal consisted of a myriad of different programs aimed at providing relief during the Great Depression. Many of the programs were public works programs building bridges, roads, and other infrastructure.

139. **Which of the following is an example of a direct democracy?**
(Average) (Skill 32.2)

    A. Elected representatives

    B. Greek city-states

    C. The Constitution

    D. The Confederate states

Answer: B. Greek city-states
The Greek city-states are an example of a direct democracy, as their leaders were elected directly by the citizens, and the citizens themselves were given voice in government.

140. **Many governments in Europe today have which of the following type of government?**
(Average) (Skill 32.6)

    A. Absolute monarchies

    B. Constitutional governments

    C. Constitutional monarchies

    D. Another form of government

Answer: C. Constitutional monarchies
Over the centuries absolute monarchies were modified, and constitutional monarchies emerged. This form of government recognizes a monarch as leader but invests most of the legal authority in a legislative body such as a Parliament.

141. **Which of these is NOT a true statement about the Roman civilization?**
     (Rigorous) (Skill 29.16)

     A. Its period of Pax Romana provided long periods of peace during which travel and trade increased, enabling the spread of culture, goods, and ideas over the known world

     B. It borrowed the concept of democracy from the Greeks and developed it into a complex representative government

     C. It flourished in the arts with realistic approach to art and a dramatic use of architecture

     D. It developed agricultural innovations such as crop rotation and terrace farming

     Answer: D. It developed agricultural innovations such as crop rotation and terrace farming
     China developed crop rotation and terrace farming.

142. **The identification of individuals or groups as they are influenced by their own group or culture is called:** *(Average) (Skill 29.3)*

     A. Cross-cultural exchanges

     B. Cultural diffusion

     C. Cultural identity

     D. Cosmopolitanism

     Answer: C. Cultural identity
     Cross-cultural exchanges involved the discovery of shared values and needs as well as an appreciation of differences. Cultural diffusion is the movement of cultural ideas or materials between populations independent of the movement of those populations. Cosmopolitanism blurs cultural differences in the creation of a shared new culture.

143. Which of the following is not a right declared by the U.S. Constitution? *(Average) (Skill 32.3)*

A. The right to speak out in public

B. The right to use cruel and unusual punishment

C. The right to a speedy trial

D. The right not to be forced to testify against yourself

Answer: B. The right to use cruel and unusual punishment
A person who lives in a democratic society legally has a comprehensive list of rights guaranteed to him or her by the government. In the United States, this is the Constitution and its Amendments. Among these very important rights are:

- the right to speak out in public;
- the right to pursue any religion;
- the right for a group of people to gather in public for any reason that doesn't fall under a national security cloud;
- the right not to have soldiers stationed in your home;
- the right not to be forced to testify against yourself in a court of law;
- the right to a speedy and public trial by a jury of your peers;
- the right not to be the victim of cruel and unusual punishment; and
- the right to avoid unreasonable search and seizure of your person, your house, and your vehicle.

144. The cold weather froze orange crops in Florida and the price of orange juice increased. This is an example of what economic concept? *(Rigorous) (Skill 31.9)*

A. Output market

B. Input market

C. Supply and demand

D. Entrepreneurship

Answer: C. Supply and demand
Output markets refer to the market in which goods and services are sold. The *input market* is the market in which factors of production, or resources, are bought and sold.

145. John C. Fremont, Zebulon Pike, and Kit Carson are all well-known:
(Rigorous) (Skill 29.2)

A. Ministers

B. Doctors

C. Writers

D. Explorers

Answer: D. Explorers
Each of these gentlemen were explorers during the twentieth century and contributed to society during that time period.

146. Which if the following tribes did not inhabit the region that is now Texas?
(Average) (Skill 29.2)

A. Iroquois

B. Cherokee

C. Wichita

D. Apache

Answer: A. Iroquois
This tribe of Native Americans settled in Northern Pennsylvania.

147. **An input into the production process:** *(Rigorous) (Skill 31.7)*

A. Capital

B. Market

C. Need

D. Resource

Answer: D. resource
A resource is an input into the production process. When resources are limited in supply, they are scarce. There are not enough of them to produce all of the goods and services that society wants. Resources are called "factors of production" and there are four factors of production: labor, capital, land, and entrepreneurship.

148. **An individual who has the ability to combine the land, labor, and capital to produce a good or service:**
(Average) (Skill 31.7)

A. market analyst

B. stockbroker

C. entrepreneur

D. CEO

Answer: C. entrepreneur
An entrepreneur is an individual who has the ability to combine the land, labor, and capital to produce a good or service. The entrepreneur is the one who bears the risks of failure and loss and the one who will gain from the profits if the product is successful.

149. The _____ River begins in Minnesota and flows to the Gulf of Mexico draining 31 states. *(Average) (Skill 30.1)*

    A. Amazon

    B. Nile

    C. Mississippi

    D. Maumee

    Answer: C. Mississippi
    The Mississippi River spans 2,320 miles and flows to the Gulf of Mexico draining 31 states.

150. The United States and Canada share: *(Average) (Skill 30.1)*

    A. Manitoba

    B. Idaho

    C. Mississippi River

    D. The Great Lakes

    Answer: D. The Great Lakes
    The Great Lakes are a group of five large freshwater bodies in central North America. They include: Lake Superior, Lake Michigan, Lake Huron, Lake Erie, and Lake Ontario.

151. Although many religions are represented in both countries, the main religion in the United States and Canada is: *(Easy) (Skill 33.1)*

    A. Christianity

    B. Islam

    C. Free Market

    D. Buddhism

    Answer: A. Christianity
    Christianity is thought to be the main religion in the United States and Canada.

152. A term that economists use to describe and measure personal and collective wellbeing is known as: *(Easy) (Skill 33.1)*

    A. Quality of Life

    B. Term of Endearment

    C. Personal Objective

    D. Collective Action

Answer: A. Quality of Life
The quality of life is the standard of health, comfort, and happiness experienced by an individual or group.

153. A connection among people by blood, marriage or adoption is called: *(Easy) (Skill 33.2)*

    A. Clan

    B. Kinship

    C. Society

    D. Culture

Answer: B. Kinship
Kinship refers to individuals related by blood. Kinship is also referred to as blood ties or common ancestry.

154. Which of the Following is NOT an example of capitalism? *(Average) (Skill 31.4)*

    A. free market and supply and demand

    B. competition

    C. government control of production and property

    D. unequal distribution of wealth

Answer: C. government control of production and property
Capitalism refers to an economic and political system in which a country's trade and industry are controlled by private owners for profit, rather than by the state.

155. A person who believes in the Social Darwinist theory of survival of the fittest would agree that: *(Rigorous) (Skill 31.7)*

A. poor people should get help from the government

B. rich nations should give aid to poor nations

C. individuals should succeed through their own efforts

D. government should tax the rich to help the poor

Answer: C. individuals should succeed through their own efforts
Now largely discredited, this theory stated that individuals, groups, and peoples are subject to the same Darwinian laws of natural selection as plants and animals.

156. Made a fortune in steel; founded U.S. Steel; philanthropist who advocated giving away wealth: *(Rigorous) (Skill 31.13)*

A. J.P Morgan

B. Andrew Carnegie

C. Henry Ford

D. Cornelius Vanderbilt

Answer: B. Andrew Carnegie
Andrew Carnegie was a Scottish-American industrialist who led the enormous expansion of the American steel industry in the late 19th century. He was also one of the most important philanthropists of his era.

157. **The Federal Reserve System directly influences the United States economy by causing changes in:** *(Rigorous) (Skill 31.11)*

    A. the amount of income taxes collected

    B. the size of the federal budget

    C. the supply of money in circulation and credit rates

    D. wages and prices

    Answer: C. the supply of money in circulation and credit rates
    The Federal Reserve System, often referred to as the Federal Reserve simply "the Fed," is the central bank of the United States. It was created by the Congress to provide the nation with a safer, more flexible, and more stable monetary and financial system.

158. **During the Kennedy Administration a nuclear test ban treaty followed this event that brought the world closer to nuclear war than any other event since World War II:** *(Rigorous) (Skill 29.19)*

    A. Bay of Pigs invasion

    B. building of the Berlin Wall

    C. Vietnam War

    D. Cuban Missile Crisis

    Answer: D. Cuban Missile Crisis
    The Cuban Missile Crisis was a confrontation between the United States and the Soviet Union in 1962 over the presence of missile sites in Cuba; one of the "hottest" periods of the cold war.

SCIENCE

159. **Laboratory activities contribute to student performance in all of the following domains EXCEPT:** *(Average) (Skill 38.1)*

A. Process skills such as observing and measuring

B. Memorization skills

C. Analytical skills

D. Communication skills

Answer: B. Memorization skills
Laboratory activities develop a wide variety of investigative, organizational, creative, and communicative skills. The laboratory provides an optimal setting for motivating students while they experience what science is. Such learning opportunities are not focused on memorization but on critical thinking and doing. Laboratory activities enhance student performance in the following domains:

Process skills: observing, measuring, and manipulating physical objects
Analytical skills: reasoning, deduction, and critical thinking
Communication skills: organizing information and writing
Conceptualization of scientific phenomena

160. _____ **are single-celled prokaryotic life forms.** *(Average) (Skill 46.2)*

A. Bacteria

B. Archaea

C. Viruses

D. Fungi

Answer: B. Archaea
Archaea are also known as archaebacteria because they are single-celled prokaryotic life forms. In older taxonomical systems, they were classified along with bacteria, but new genetic evidence shows that they are more closely related to eukaryotes. Archaea are noted for their ability to live in harsh conditions that are unsuitable for other organisms; they are often found in environments with extreme temperature, pH, and salinity.

161. In Photosynthesis, _____ is a waste product.
(Average) (Skill 46.2)

A. Oxygen

B. Sunlight

C. Carbon Dioxide

D. ATP

Answer: A. Oxygen
Photosynthesis is the process by which plants make carbohydrates from the energy of the Sun, carbon dioxide, and water. Oxygen is a waste product. Photosynthesis occurs in the chloroplast where the pigment chlorophyll traps energy from the Sun.

162. What impact did television have on politics and society in the 1950's and 1960's?
(Average) (Skill 29.5)

A. created a larger gap between the rich and poor

B. rock and roll emerged to the forefront

C. eroded regional cultural differences and gave a larger spotlight to candidates

D. workers became less efficient as they spent more time watching television

Answer: C. eroded regional cultural differences and gave a larger spotlight to candidates
In the 1950s and 60s, television news produced perhaps some of its finest performances. The televised debates between Kennedy and Nixon were credited with giving JFK a slim election victory.

163. **The largest group in the plant kingdom:**
   (Average) (Skill 46.1)

   A. Trophists

   B. Chloroplasts

   C. Fungi

   D. Angiosperms

   Answer: D. Angiosperms
   Angiosperms are the largest group in the plant kingdom. They are the flowering plants that produce seeds for reproduction. They first appeared about seventy million years ago when the dinosaurs were disappearing.

164. **The term given to the response of plants to grow toward or away from a stimulus in the environment:**
   (Average) (Skill 46.1)

   A. Tropism

   B. Competition

   C. Cellular Respiration

   D. Photosynthesis

   Answer: A. Tropism
   Tropism is the term given to the response of plants to grow toward or away from a stimulus in the environment. In phototropism, light sends the hormone auxin to the portion of the plant receiving the most shade so that it starts to grow toward the light.

165. **Spaces between neurons:**
(Average) (Skill 46.3)

A. Synapses

B. Axons

C. Dendrites

D. myelin sheaths

Answer: A. synapses
In the Nervous System, the neuron is the basic unit. It consists of an axon, which carries impulses away from the cell body, the dendrite, which carries impulses toward the cell body and the cell body, which contains the nucleus. Synapses are spaces between neurons. Chemicals called neurotransmitters are found close to the synapse. The myelin sheath, composed of Schwann cells, covers the neurons and provides insulation.

166. **Students in Mrs. Smith's class are learning about various types of rocks. She has set up stations for them to observe various samples. Three of them are: sandstone, amber, and limestone. These are samples of:** *(Average) (Skill 52.1)*

A. Sedimentary rocks

B. Metamorphic rocks

C. Igneous rocks

D. None of the above

Answer: A. Sedimentary rocks
Sedimentary rocks are types of rock that are formed by the deposition of material at the Earth's surface and within bodies of water. Three examples are: sandstone, amber, and limestone.

167. **The function of the _____ is to carry oxygenated blood and nutrients to all cells of the body and return carbon dioxide waste to be expelled from the lungs.** *(Average) (Skill 46.3)*

    A. Respiratory System

    B. Digestive System

    C. Circulatory System

    D. Nervous System

    Answer: C. Circulatory System
    The function of the circulatory system is to carry oxygenated blood and nutrients to all cells of the body and return carbon dioxide waste to be expelled from the lungs. Animals evolved from an open system to a closed system with vessels leading to and from the heart.

168. **These lead blood away from the heart:** *(Easy) (Skill 46.3)*

    A. Veins

    B. Arterioles

    C. Capillaries

    D. Arteries

    Answer: D. Arteries
    Arteries lead blood away from the heart. All arteries carry oxygenated blood except the pulmonary artery.

169. Sound waves are produced by:
(Easy) (Skill 45.3)

A. Pitch

B. Noise

C. Vibrations

D. Sonar

Answer: C. Vibrations
Sound waves are produced by a vibrating body. The vibrating object moves forward and compresses the air in front of it; it then reverses direction so pressure on the air decreases and the air molecules expand. The vibrating air molecules move back and forth, parallel to the direction of motion of the wave as they pass the energy from adjacent air molecules closer to the source to air molecules farther away from the source.

170. The Doppler Effect is associated most closely with which property of waves?
(Average) (Skill 45.5)

A. Amplitude

B. Wavelength

C. Frequency

D. Intensity

Answer: C. Frequency
The Doppler Effect accounts for an apparent increase in frequency when a wave source moves toward a wave receiver or apparent decrease in frequency when a wave source moves away from a wave receiver. (Note that the receiver could also be moving toward or away from the source.) As the wave fronts are released, motion toward the receiver mimics more frequent wave fronts, while motion away from the receiver mimics less frequent wave fronts. Meanwhile, the amplitude, wavelength, and intensity of the wave are not as relevant to this process (although moving closer to a wave source makes it seem more intense).

171. **The energy of electromagnetic waves is:**
(Rigorous) (Skill 45.1)

A. Radiant energy

B. Acoustical energy

C. Thermal energy

D. Chemical energy

Answer: A. Radiant energy
Radiant energy is the energy of electromagnetic waves. Light, visible and otherwise, is an example of radiant energy. Acoustical energy, or sound energy, is the movement of energy through an object in waves. Energy that forces an object to vibrate creates sound. Thermal energy is the total internal energy of objects created by the vibration and movement of atoms and molecules. Heat is the transfer of thermal energy. Chemical energy is the energy stored in the chemical bonds of molecules. For example, the energy derived from gasoline is chemical energy. Other forms of energy include electrical, mechanical, and nuclear energy.

172. **Photosynthesis is the process by which plants make carbohydrates using:**
(Average) (Skill 45.2)

A. The Sun, carbon dioxide, and oxygen

B. The Sun, oxygen, and water

C. Oxygen, water, and carbon dioxide

D. The Sun, carbon dioxide, and water

Answer: D. The Sun, carbon dioxide, and water
Photosynthesis requires the energy of the Sun, carbon dioxide, and water. Oxygen is a waste product of photosynthesis.

173. Which of the following is not an example of a physical change?
(Easy) (Skill 42.1)

A. burning

B. cutting

C. freezing

D. bending

Answer: A. burning
A physical change in a substance doesn't change what the substance is. Burning is an example of this.

174. What cell organelle contains the cell's stored food?
(Rigorous) (Skill 46.2)

A. Vacuoles

B. Golgi apparatus

C. Ribosomes

D. Lysosomes

Answer: A. Vacuoles
In a cell, the subparts are called organelles. Of these, the vacuoles hold stored food (and water and pigments). The Golgi apparatus sorts molecules from other parts of the cell; the ribosomes are sites of protein synthesis; and the lysosomes contain digestive enzymes.

175. Enzymes speed up reactions by:
(Rigorous) (Skill 46.6)

A. Utilizing ATP

B. Lowering pH, allowing reaction speed to increase

C. Increasing volume of substrate

D. Lowering energy of activation

Answer: D. lowering energy of activation
Because enzymes are catalysts, they work the same way: They cause the formation of activated chemical complexes, which require a lower activation energy. Therefore, the answer is D. ATP is an energy source for cells, and pH or volume changes may or may not affect reaction rate, so these choices can be eliminated.

176. Blood cells are known as:
(Rigorous) (Skill 46.3)

A. Plasma

B. Erythrocytes

C. Leukocytes

D. Platelets

Answer: B. Erythrocytes
Also called red blood cells; Erythrocytes contain hemoglobin, which carries oxygen molecules.

177. _____ make up _____, which make up tissues.
(Rigorous) (Skill 46.2)

A. Cells; DNA

B. Cells; Organelles

C. Organisms; Organelles

D. Organelles; Cells

Answer: D. Organelles; Cells
Organelles make up cells, which make up tissues. Tissues make up organs, and groups of organs make up organ systems. Organ systems work together to provide life for the organism.

178. What is the most accurate description of the water cycle?
(Rigorous) (Skill 45.2)

A. Rain comes from clouds, filling the ocean. The water then evaporates and becomes clouds again.

B. Water circulates from rivers into groundwater and back, while water vapor circulates in the atmosphere.

C. Water is conserved except for chemical or nuclear reactions, and any drop of water could circulate through clouds, rain, groundwater, and surface water.

D. Weather systems cause chemical reactions to break water into its atoms.

Answer: C. Water is conserved except for chemical or nuclear reactions, and any drop of water could circulate through clouds, rain, groundwater, and surface water.
All natural chemical cycles, including the water cycle, depend on the principle of conservation of mass. Any drop of water may circulate through the hydrologic system, ending up in a cloud, as rain, or as surface or groundwater. Although choices A and B describe parts of the water cycle, the most comprehensive answer is C.

179. **Which of the following astronomical entities is not part of the galaxy the Sun is located in?** *(Easy) (Skill 40.5)*

A. Nebulae

B. Quasars

C. Pulsars

D. Neutron stars

Answer: B. Quasars
Nebulae are visible in the night sky and are glowing clouds of dust, hydrogen, and plasma. Neutron stars are the remnants of super novae, and pulsars are neutron stars that emit radio waves on a periodic basis. A quasar is a distant galaxy that emits large amounts of visible light and radio waves.

180. **_____ maintain a fluid environment for _____ exchange in mammals.** *(Average) (Skill 46.4)*

A. Lungs; gas

B. Blood vessels; blood

C. Carbon dioxide molecules; air

D. None of the above

Answer: A. Lungs; gas
Lungs maintain a fluid environment for gas exchange in terrestrial animals, while gills allow aquatic animals to exchange gases in a fluid medium by removing dissolved oxygen from the water.

181. **Internal energy that is created by the vibration and movement of atoms and molecules is classified as: _____. *(Rigorous) (Skill 45.6)***

    A. Mechanical energy

    B. Acoustical energy

    C. Radiant energy

    D. Thermal energy

    Answer: D. Thermal energy
    Thermal energy is the total internal energy of objects created by the vibration and movement of atoms and molecules. Heat is the transfer of thermal energy. Acoustical energy, or sound energy, is the movement of energy through an object in waves, while radiant energy is the energy of electromagnetic waves. Electrical energy is the movement of electrical charges in an electromagnetic field.

182. **A teacher explains to the class that energy is neither created nor destroyed. Therefore, this means that _____. *(Average) (Skill 41.1)***

    A. matter never changes form

    B. matter must change form

    C. matter changes form only if it is a liquid

    D. none of the above

    Answer: B. Matter must change form
    The law of conservation of energy states that energy is neither created nor destroyed. Since energy is neither created nor destroyed, we know that it must change form. For example, an animal may die, but its body will either be consumed by other animals or it will decay into the ecosystem. Either way, it enters another form and the matter still exists in some form or another.

183. **Resistance of motion of surfaces that touch each other is considered:** _____
    (Average) (Skill 44.1)

    A. Friction

    B. Inertia

    C. Gravity

    D. Force

    Answer: A. Friction
    Surfaces that touch each other have a certain resistance to motion. This resistance is friction.

184. **This type of ecosystem is located close to the poles, both north and south of the poles.**
    (Average) (Skill 52.5)

    A. Tundra

    B. Savanna

    C. Taiga

    D. Temperate Deciduous Forest

    Answer: C. Taiga
    Taiga is located north and south of the equator, close to the poles, while the tundra is located even further north and south of the taiga.

185. A _____ would be a good choice when graphing the percent of time students spend on various after-school activities. *(Average) (Skill 37.2)*

A. Line graph

B. Pie chart

C. Histogram

D. Bar graph

Answer B: Pie chart
Graphing utilizes numbers to demonstrate patterns. The patterns offer a visual representation, making it easier to draw conclusions. The type of graphic representation used to display observations depends on the data that is collected. Line graphs are used to compare different sets of related data or to predict data that has not yet be measured. A bar graph or histogram is used to compare different items and make comparisons based on this data. A pie chart is useful when organizing data as part of a whole.

186. **This view of the ancient Greeks which affects scientific thinking states that moral and political obligations of an individual are dependent upon an agreement between people to form society.** *(Rigorous) (Skill 36.3)*

A. Scientific Political Ethics Principal

B. Utilitarianism

C. Kantianism

D. Social Contract Theory

Answer D: Social Contract Theory
Social contract theory is a view of the ancient Greeks that states that a person's moral and/or political obligations are dependent upon a contract or agreement between people to form society.

187. Destructive land-use practices can induce _____ when not properly planned. *(Easy)* *(Skill 39.6)*

A. global warming

B. avalanches

C. hurricanes

D. volcanic eruptions

Answer B: avalanches
Destructive land-use practices such as mining have induced landslides and avalanches when not properly planned and monitored. Other destructive practices from human activities include global warming and waste contamination, but these are unrelated to land-use practices. Hurricanes are nature-induced and not caused by humans.

188. These types of volcanoes have been built from lava flows, as well as cinders and ash: *(Rigorous) (Skill 40.2)*

A. Cinder cone volcanoes

B. Shield volcanoes

C. Warped volcanoes

D. Composite volcanoes

Answer D: Composite volcanoes
Composite volcanoes are described as being built by both lava flows and layers of ash and cinders. The other three types of volcanoes have different characteristics than that of composite volcanoes.

189. _____ cells are found in protists, fungi, plants, and animals.
     (Rigorous) (Skill 46.2)

   A. Prokaryotic

   B. Eukaryotic

   C. Chromosomal

   D. DNA

   Answer: B. Eukaryotic
   Eukaryotic cells are found in protists, fungi, plants, and animals. They contain many organelles, which are membrane-bound areas for specific cell functions.

190. **These assist in blood clotting:**
     (Easy) (Skill 46.3)

   A. Plasma

   B. Erythrocytes

   C. Leukocytes

   D. Platelets

   Answer: D. Platelets
   Platelets assist in blood clotting, and are made in the bone marrow.

191. **The brain of the cell:**
     (Easy) (Skill 46.2)

   A. Nucleus

   B. Ribosomes

   C. Golgi Apparatus

   D. Mitochondria

   Answer: A. Nucleus
   The nucleus is the brain of the cell. It contains Chromosomes, Chromatin, Nucleoli, and a Nuclear Membrane.

192. _____ is the division of somatic cells.
    (Easy) (Skill 46.2)

    A. Mitosis

    B. Meiosis

    C. Reproduction

    D. Respiration

    Answer: A. Mitosis
    Mitosis is the division of two somatic cells. Two cells result from each division.

193. **This geological process can change granite (igneous rock) into gneiss (metamorphic rock)?**
    (Easy) (Skill 52.1)

    A. Heat and pressure

    B. Cooling

    C. Compacting and cementing

    D. Melting

    Answer: A. Heat and pressure
    Heat and pressure have the combined ability to change granite into gneiss.

194. _____ theorized that all individual organisms, even those of the same species, are different, and those individuals that happen to possess traits favorable for survival would produce more offspring.
(Rigorous) (Skill 48.2)

A. Louis Pasteur

B. Antony van Leeuwenhoek

C. Jean Baptiste Lamarck

D. Charles Darwin

Answer: D. Charles Darwin
Darwin theorized that all individual organisms, even those of the same species, are different, and those individuals that happen to possess traits favorable for survival would produce more offspring. Thus, in the next generation, the number of individuals with the favorable trait increases, and the process continues.

195. _____ refers to the chance deviation in the frequency of alleles (traits) resulting from the randomness of zygote formation and selection.
(Average) (Skill 48.2)

A. Genetic Drift

B. Consolidation

C. Recombination

D. Isolation

Answer: A. Genetic Drift
Genetic drift refers to the chance deviation in the frequency of alleles (traits) resulting from the randomness of zygote formation and selection. Because only a small percentage of all possible zygotes become mature adults, parents do not necessarily pass all of their alleles on to their offspring. Genetic drift is particularly important in small populations because chance deviations in allelic frequency can quickly alter the genotypic makeup of the population. In extreme cases, certain alleles may completely disappear from the gene pool.

196. The theory of seafloor spreading explains:
(Rigorous) (Skill 38.1)

A. The shapes of the continents

B. How continents collide

C. How continents move apart

D. How continents sink to become part of the ocean floor

Answer: C. How continents move apart
In the theory of seafloor spreading, the movement of the ocean floor causes continents to spread apart from one another. This occurs because crust plates split apart, and new material is added to the plate edges. This process pulls the continents apart, or it may create new separations and is believed to have caused the formation of the Atlantic Ocean.

197. Weather occurs in which layer of the atmosphere?
(Average) (Skill 38.3)

A. Troposphere

B. Stratosphere

C. Mesosphere

D. Thermosphere

Answer: A. Troposphere
The atmosphere is divided into four main layers based on temperature.
The troposphere is the layer closest to the Earth's surface and all weather phenomena occur here, as it is the layer with the most water vapor and dust. Air temperature decreases with increasing altitude. The average thickness is 7 miles (11 km). The Stratosphere is a layer that contains very little water so clouds in this layer are very rare. The ozone layer is located in the upper portions of the stratosphere. Air temperature is fairly constant but does increase somewhat with height due to the absorption of solar energy and ultraviolet rays from the ozone layer. Air temperature decreases with height again in the mesosphere, which is the coldest layer, with temperatures in the range of -100°C at the top. The thermosphere extends upward into space. Oxygen molecules in this layer absorb energy from the Sun, causing temperatures to increase with height.

198. Which of the following types of rock are made from magma?
(Average) (Skill 39.1)

A. Fossils

B. Sedimentary

C. Metamorphic

D. Igneous

Answer: D. Igneous
Metamorphic rocks are formed by high temperatures and great pressures. Fluid sediments are transformed into solid sedimentary rocks. Only igneous rocks are formed from magma.

199. _____ occurs when one species benefits from the other without causing it harm.
(Average) (Skill 48.4)

A. Competition

B. Commensalism

C. Mutualism

D. Parasitism

Answer: B. Commensalism
Symbiosis is when two species live close together. One example is commensalism, which occurs when one species benefits from the other without causing it harm.

200. Which of the following is the best definition of *meteorite*?
(Easy) (Skill 41.3)

A. A meteorite is a mineral composed of mica and feldspar

B. A meteorite is material from outer space that has struck the Earth's surface

C. A meteorite is an element that has properties of both metals and nonmetals

D. A meteorite is a very small unit of length measurement

Answer: B. A meteorite is material from outer space that has struck the Earth's surface

Meteoroids are pieces of matter in space, composed of particles of rock and metal. If a meteoroid travels through the Earth's atmosphere, friction causes burning and a "shooting star" or meteor. If the meteor strikes the Earth's surface, it is known as a meteorite. Note that although the suffix -*ite* often means a mineral, choice A is incorrect. Choice C refers to a metalloid rather than a meteorite, and choice D is simply a misleading pun on *meter*.

CPSIA information can be obtained
at www.ICGtesting.com
Printed in the USA
BVOW04s2012311017

499155BV00016B/703/P

9 781607 876205